T0305193

Gateways to Globalisation

Gateways to Globalisation

Asia's International Trading and Finance Centres

Edited by

François Gipouloux

Research Director, Centre National de la Recherche Scientifique (CNRS), France

Edward Elgar

Cheltenham, UK • Northampton, MA, USA

© François Gipouloux 2011

All rights reserved. No part of this publication may be reproduced, stored in a retrieval system or transmitted in any form or by any means, electronic, mechanical or photocopying, recording, or otherwise without the prior permission of the publisher.

Published by
Edward Elgar Publishing Limited
The Lypiatts
15 Lansdown Road
Cheltenham
Glos GL50 2JA
UK

Edward Elgar Publishing, Inc.
William Pratt House
9 Dewey Court
Northampton
Massachusetts 01060
USA

A catalogue record for this book
is available from the British Library

Library of Congress Control Number: 2011929464

ISBN 978 0 85793 424 6

Typeset by Servis Filmsetting Ltd, Stockport, Cheshire
Printed and bound by MPG Books Group, UK

Contents

Maps

Figures

Tables

Contributors

Loïs Bastide is completing a PhD in Sociology at the École Normale Supérieure in Lyon (France). His skills in the Indonesian language have allowed him to conduct extensive ethnographic fieldworks in Indonesia, Malaysia and Singapore, as part of his research on semi-skilled and unskilled Indonesian migrant workers in neighbouring countries. He has been teaching the sociology of work and labour relations, and social theory at the University of Poitiers. His publications include: 'Ethnographie de l'ailleurs et ailleurs ethnographiques: postcolonialité, subjectivation et construction des espaces de l'enquête en Asie du sud-est', in L. Roulleau-Berger (ed.) *Sociologies et cosmopolitisme méthodologique*, Toulouse: Presses Universitaires du Mirail (forthcoming).

Patrizia Carioti (PhD) is Associate Professor and Chair of the *History of East Asia* and of the *History and Civilisation of the Far East* at 'L'Orientale', University of Naples. Her field of studies covers the international context of the Far East, and focuses on 16th–18th-century Chinese and Japanese maritime history, their historical interactions and their relations with the Europeans. She has spent more than 10 years abroad, researching in Japan (University of Tokyo), China (Xiamen University), Taiwan (Academia Sinica) and The Netherlands (Leiden University). Among her publications are: *Cina e Giappone sui mari, nei secoli XVI e XVII* (China and Japan at Sea, in the XVI and XVII Centuries), Napoli: Edizioni Scientifiche Italiane, 2006; *Zheng Chenggong (Serie Minor)*, Napoli: Istitute Universitario Orientale, 1995; has also been translated into Chinese: Bai Di [Patrizia Carioti], *Yuandong guoji wutaishang de fengyun renwu Zheng Chenggong*, Guangxi 1997; (co-author with Lucia Caterina) *La via della porcellana. La VOC e la Cina* (The Porcelain Route: The VOC and China), Genova: Il Portolano, 2010; (co-editor with Franco Mazzei) *Oriente, Occidente e dintorni*, Napoli: Il Torcoliere, 5 vols, 2010.

Peter W. Daniels is Professor of Geography, University of Birmingham. His publications include (with J.R. Bryson and B. Warf) *Service Worlds: People, Organisations, Technologies*, London and New York: Routledge, 2004; and (with J.R. Bryson) *The Handbook of Service Industries*, Cheltenham, UK and Northampton, MA, USA: Edward Elgar, 2007; as well as journal papers on the rise of advanced services in the economies of the United Kingdom, Europe, North America and the Asia-Pacific and their role in globalisation and international trade.

Du Debin (PhD) is a Professor of East China Normal University (ECNU), Shanghai, China. He is the Director of the Institute of China Innovation and heads the Department of Urban and Regional Economics at ECNU. His research focuses primarily on urban and regional development, especially on the Research and Development (R&D) of the multinational corporations and urban innovation in China. He is one of the pioneering scholars in the field of R&D globalisation in China and has published extensively in Chinese as well as in English journals. He was a Research Fellow of the United Nations Centre for Regional Development in 2001 and a Senior Fulbright Visiting Scholar at University of California, Berkeley, 2003–2004.

Alice Ekman is Senior Consultant in Chinese Affairs and Associate Lecturer at Sciences Po, Paris. Prior to working in France, she was Research Officer at the French Embassy in Beijing. She holds a Master's degree from the London School of Economics and Political Science (China focus), a BA in Politics, Philosophy and Economics from the University of Kent and Institut d'Etudes Politiques de Lille, and is now completing a PhD on Chinese practice of diplomacy at Sciences Po, within the Center for International Studies and Research. Her skills in Mandarin and her acute understanding of East Asia have allowed her to conduct extensive fieldwork in the region. She regularly contributes to international research projects on contemporary Chinese economy and society.

François Gipouloux, Director of Research at the Centre National de la Recherche Scientifique (CNRS), is the co-ordinator of the European Union-funded research programme 'Sustainable Urbanisation in China: Historical and Comparative Perspectives, Mega-trends towards 2050'. His research covers the dynamics of urbanisation in China, and the comparative analysis of economic institutions and business practices in Europe and Asia over a prolonged period (13th–19th century). His recent publications include: *The Asian Mediterranean: Port Cities and Trading Networks in China, Japan and Southeast Asia, 13th–21st Century*, Cheltenham, UK and Northampton, MA, USA: Edward Elgar, 2011; *La Chine au XXIe siècle: une nouvelle superpuissance économique?*, Paris: Armand Colin, 2005.

Hisasue Ryoichi is a Research Fellow at the Institute of Developing Economies, Japan External Trade Organization (IDE-JETRO), and a former Research Associate at the National Graduate Institute for Policy

Studies (Tokyo, Japan). He obtained a PhD in area studies from the Graduate School of Arts and Sciences, the University of Tokyo. As a specialist of Asian economic history, his research focuses on native commercial network, financial institution, economic framework and system, and gateway cities. He has published several books and papers widely in the field of economic, banking and entrepreneurial history, and is the author of 'The Rise and Fall of the Bank of Canton', *Ajia Keizai Vol. XLIX, No.3*, Institute of Developing Economics (IDE), 2008; and 'The Foundation of the China and Southern Bank', *Ajia Keizai Vol.LI, No.7*, Institute of Developing Economics (IDE), 2010.

Hu Ying is currently office manager of the China-ASEAN Free Trade Area Business Portal Operational Center (see http://www.asean-cn.org). She obtained her PhD in Economics at the École des Hautes Etudes en Sciences Sociales in 2009. Her dissertation and subsequent research has focused on Foreign Direct Investment and regional development in China.

Christine Hung teaches at Le Havre University, France. She obtained a PhD and did postdoctoral research at the École des Hautes Etudes en Sciences Sociales in Paris and was a Visiting Scholar at Tsinghua University. For 10 years she has been a collaborator on international projects of multinational enterprises, particularly international investments, international negotiations and technology transfer. Her research field focuses on investment risks encountered by Western firms in the Chinese market.

Meng Jianjun is a Research Fellow at the Center for Industrial Development and Environmental Governance in the School of Public Policy and Management, Tsinghua University (Beijing, China). He obtained his PhD from Tokyo Institute of Technology in 1994. A specialist of development economics, his research focuses on industrial and regional development in China, the China urbanisation process, and the Sino-Japan environmental network. His publications include: 'Population Migration and Economic Development in China' (Social Protection and Employment Policy), European Union working paper, Cardiff, 2003; 'Formation and Future of China's Three Major Industrial Zones: Is China a Developed Country?', Japan Center for Economic Research, Tokyo, March 2009.

Pierre Miège is Associate Professor of Sociology at the School of Social Development and Public Policy (SSDPP) at Beijing Normal University. After completing a PhD on the Chinese Work Unit and its dismantlement, his research has focused on the reconfiguration of social services (especially health services) in urban and rural China since the late 1990s. Since 2004, he has taken part in several research projects on the social determinants of the HIV/AIDS epidemic, and the localisation of research and development centres in Chinese cities.

Christopher J. Smith is Professor and Chair in the Department of Geography and Planning at the University at Albany (SUNY), and Director of the University's Globalization Studies programme. His research interests focus on the impacts of global forces in the world's largest urban regions, covering cities both in the 'core' and on the 'periphery' of the global economy, and the socio/spatial consequences of 'megaproject' construction in China's cities.

Sung Yun-Wing (PhD in Economics, University of Minnesota) is currently Chair and Professor of the Economics Department, Director of the Shanghai-Hong Kong Development Institute and Associate Director of the Hong Kong Institute of Asia-Pacific Studies in the Chinese University of Hong Kong. His research interest covers international trade and economic development in China, Hong Kong and Taiwan.

James J. Wang is Associate Professor and Head of the Department of Geography, University of Hong Kong. Born in Beijing, he received his BEco from the People's University of China, MPhil from Hong Kong University and PhD from the University of Toronto. His research specialities lie in nodal transport development such as port, airport and railway stations. He is a Council Member of the Hong Kong Society for Transport Studies, and Fellow of the Chartered Institute of Logistics and Transport. He has published widely in many internationally refereed journals and is an Editorial Board Member of the *Journal of Transport Geography and Transportmetrica*. He participated in port-city planning projects and strategic studies for more than 25 Chinese and other Asian port cities.

Xu Xun is currently a PhD student of economics at University of Hawaii at Manoa and a Research Assistant at the East-West Center. He received his BA from Beijing Foreign Studies University. His main research interests are macroeconomics and the Chinese economy. His dissertation focuses on China's economic reforms.

Yuan Zhigang (PhD in Economics, École des Hautes Etudes en Sciences Sociales, Paris) is Professor and Dean of the School of Economics, Fudan University. He is a pioneering scholar on the macroeconomic issues in China. His research interests focus on disequilibrium theory, employment theory, economics of social security and pensions, China's household consumption, the financial reforms and the real estate industry. He has many influential publications in these fields and also participates actively in policy-making processes in China. His recent books include: *Unifying* *the Rural Urban Labor Market and the National Competitiveness*, Fudan University Press, 2010; (with Wan Guanghua) *Competition between the Developing Nations: China and India*, Fudan University Press, 2009; and *Global Financial Crisis and the Chinese Economy*, Shanghai People's Press, 2009. Among his recent journal papers are: (with Shao Ting) 'Historical Role, Function and Reform in the Orientation of China's State-owned Enterprises', *Academic Monthly*, 2010; (with Xianyan Fan and Yinyin Qiu) 'The Study of the Effects of Wealth on Consumption of Residents in Shanghai', *Fudan Journal of Humanities and Social Sciences* (Social Sciences Edition), 2009.

Zhang Li (PhD, University of Washington) is Professor of the School of Social Development and Public Policy and Director of English-taught Master's Program in Chinese Society, Fudan University. He is the author of *China's Limited Urbanization: Under Socialism and Beyond*, Nova Science Publishers, Inc., New York, 2004; co-author of *The Western Pearl River Delta: Growth and Opportunities for Cooperative Development with Hong Kong*, The Hong Kong Institute of Asia-Pacific Studies, 2005; *Hong Kong and the Western Pearl River Delta: Cooperative Development from a Cross-boundary Perspective*, The Hong Kong Institute of Asia-Pacific Studies, 2004; and over 50 articles published in internationally refereed journals and books.

Simon X.B. Zhao (PhD) is Director of the International Center for China Development Studies in the University of Hong Kong. He has worked with Academia Sinica and the State Planning Commission, China. He is a prominent scholar worldwide on global and Chinese financial centers of development, frequently providing consultation services to both national and municipal governments in China. In total, he has published about 100 academic papers, of which 60 were in international refereed journals and 30 in ISI (SSCI) Citation Journals.

Preface

This volume is the result of a three-year research project, *La Méditerranée asiatique et ses plates-formes commerciales* (*International Trading Hubs in East and Southeast Asia*) 2006–2009, funded by the Agence Nationale de la Recherche (France).[1]

The research has involved extensive data collection, field studies and interviews in China, Japan, Singapore and Hong Kong. Our team included historians, economists, sociologists, anthropologists and sinologists who have repeatedly exchanged findings in order to grasp the regional character of trade and finance beyond national borders and traditional academic frameworks, bringing each perspective (historic, geographical and structural) into play.

We hope that this collective effort offers, in addition to its regional framework, up-to-date information that strengthens an original trans-disciplinary analysis of a region and its economic characteristics, which will be of interest to readers within academia and well beyond.

A strong geographical perspective has been adopted for the analysis, which defines trading and financial hubs as global cities which frequently have more in common and closer linkages with each other than with their corresponding hinterlands. These global cities illustrate the extent to which world trends deeply penetrate the national territorial interior and processes that were presumed to be controlled by the State.

The study documents the fact that today major urban centres (Tōkyō, Ōsaka, Singapore, Hong Kong, Shanghai) situated on the periphery of the maritime corridor of East Asia form a system characterised by the intensity of their economic linkages and integration into the world economy. We have seen that since the mid-1980s, these major Asian cities have become the worldwide-oriented centres for production, trade and research.

The research has also shown that the concentration of control capabilities goes along with the dispersion of manufacturing capabilities (at the regional, national and global levels). As a result Hong Kong, as well as Singapore, or the Tōkyō-Yokohama conurbation, for instance, implements a new logic of agglomeration and takes part in a new geography

---

[1] Project no. ANR-05-BLAN-037.

of centrality and marginality. By grasping the dynamics of economic flows, the emergence of gravity centres and the evolution of hierarchies, 'International Trade and Finance Hubs in East and Southeast Asia' shows the existence of a system of cities characterised by a functional division of the work and responsibilities within a polycentric region.

The network of configuration of East Asian trade and financial hubs finally leads to the questioning of new attributes of sovereignty. Hong Kong shows that sovereignty no longer rests exclusively upon the territory, but on the function. In that sense, it also depends on the capacity to model economic spaces, to create and to impose technical, financial and legal norms.

These past three years of field studies and four workshops have helped to produce accurate analysis of the different East and Southeast Asia trading and financial cities and to document the degree and character of their interdependence. Specifically, field studies and documentary research have generated empirical knowledge and elaborated a conceptual framework on the following issues:

1 the power of attraction of the East Asian maritime corridor;
2 a typology of great trading centres;
3 the transnational production system – a growing characteristic of intra-Asiatic trade;
4 the articulation between global and local levels in trading and financial centres;
5 current economic competition within the region.

I would like to thank the numerous contributors to our programme which has resulted in this book. They include Professor Hamashita Takeshi, Professor Lin Cheng and Professor Sonoda Shigeto. Deng Jianping, Guo Chenzi, Sheng Xin, Tan Minmin and Wu Liping have provided tireless research assistance. I am also grateful to Loïs Bastide, Alice Ekman and Pierre Miège who have offered many precious suggestions and made valuable improvements to my introductory essay. Finally I am indebted to Peter Daniels and Mia Turner for the editing of several chapters, to Hanna Ai, Sébastien Goulard and Hu Ying for the preparation of the index and to Sébastien Goulard for one of the cover photographs.

François Gipouloux, Peking, 3 March 2011

1. From entrepôts to service integrators: Asian metropolises in a changing flows and nodes configuration

François Gipouloux

INTRODUCTION: A GLOBAL ECONOMY OF CITIES

During the last three decades, Asian megalopolises have spearheaded economic, technological and social change. Tōkyō, Hong Kong, Singapore, Shanghai and arguably many others, have accelerated East Asia's comeback at the centre of the world economic arena. Far from being an integrated space, the region can be seen in various ways: as an heterogeneous assemblage of nation-states; or a huge manufacturing zone, mainly anchored in the coastal areas of China, in which subcontracting activities are generating an increasing flow of exports towards North American, European and Asian markets. A mere dozen urban centres are servicing this manufacturing belt, and form strategic nodes for international finance, containerised transport, export-oriented manufacturing industries, and international information networks. In those different centres, the intensity of per capita international activity is largely superior to that within the nation-state they belong to.

Theses cities are located on the rim of a maritime corridor stretching from Vladivostok to Singapore which derives its economic vitality from the flows of goods, capital, technology and migrations that criss-cross it. Highly polarised, this economic area includes fragments of China (coastal areas), part of the Korean peninsula, Japan and Southeast Asian countries' territories into its transnational dynamics.

Shanghai, Hong Kong and Singapore are also and above all new nodes in the network of international economic relations. Yet, this situation is not as new as it seems. For centuries a system of cities, linked by commercial exchanges, has existed in Asia. The 19th century and the predominance (or rise) of colonial powers has only extended the ramifications of this urban network.

In the late 20th century, Asian megalopolises in the context of globalisation tend to become again what they were before the 17th century: major actors of international trade and centres for new elaboration of technical norms. As medieval Italy *repubbliche marinare*, they manage to weave among themselves encompassing links, creating multifarious networks. Nowadays, cities are not only the main creators of wealth, they are also the focus of concentration for research and development (R&D), techno-logical innovation and institutional creativity. Standing at the crossroads of four intertwinned flows: goods, capital, information and migrations of highly qualified personnel, East Asian cities compete with each other to attract capital, technologies and talents.

What is the role of Asian cities in the new configuration of the worldwide metropolitan archipelago? To what extent cities physiognomies are reshaped by their vocation to capture flows? How does such a situation renew our vision of the relations between cities and states, and cities and territories?

PAST SCHOLARSHIP, NEW FIELDS OF STUDY

World city studies were started by Peter Hall in the mid-1960s, with a first systematic analysis of their various attributes (such as politics, trade, finance, culture and education).[1] Elaborating furthermore on a world city hypothesis, John Friedmann then linked the cities' structural change to the level of integration intothe world economy.[2] Friedmann also empha-sised the role of mega-cities as concentrators of international capital that exhibit strong income polarisation. Global capital anchors in certain cities used as 'basic points' (to follow its terminology) a specific articulation of production and markets.

Since Friedmann's seminal article, a wide body of literature in economic geography, urban economics, sociology and regional studies has enriched – and sometimes criticised – his interpretative framework and brought about new perspectives.[3] While the concept of world or global cities became a widely accepted paradigm, the analytical scheme has been considerably renewed by John Friedmann himself, and later Saskia Sassen[4] and Manuel Castells.[5] What have been the main paradigm shifts in that field?

---

[1]   Hall (1966).
[2]   Friedmann (1986). See also Friedmann (1995), Friedmann and Wolff (1982), Friedmann (1998).
[3]   Rimmer (1998). See Cassis (2007), Daniels and Harrington (2007) , McGee (1967); Taylor (1999), Korff (1987).
[4]   Sassen (1991).
[5]   Castells (1989).

Sassen considered that only three cities – London, New York and Tōkyō –deserved the rank of global cities in the early 1990s. She insisted upon the strategic role for major cities, created both by the spatial dispersal and new forms of global integration. Global cities are in her view (1) highly concentrated command points in the organisation of the world economy; (2) key locations for finance and specialised service firms; (3) the sites for production and innovation, and finally (4) markets for the products and innovation produced.[6]

Another theoretical breakthrough has been brought about by Castells and his conception of an informational economy, operating through 'a space of flows'. Unlike in Sassen's analysis, world cities are not characterised as centres of command or points in a static configuration, but as a process by which 'centres of production and consumption of advanced services and their ancillary local societies are connected in a global network'.[7] The preeminence of cities is therefore derived from their ability to capture flows and redirect them, more than from the mere attributes they possess.

The richness and diversity of the literature on the world cities cannot conceal however its heavy dependency on empirical studies conducted on a handful of global cities located within large countries: London, New York, more rarely Tōkyō.[8] Very few studies have been conducted in order to fully investigate the great variety of the processes through which global cities are emerging in Asia. In fact, the eurocentrism inherent to the main components of the global city concept has been underlined by several critics.[9] In this volume, this point is strongly emphasised by several contributions (Daniels, Ekman, Zhao).

More specifically, the paradigm of the global city does not fully take into consideration the post-industrial city as it appears in Asia – in Hong Kong and Singapore in particular.[10] Nor is it completely satisfactory to understand the peculiar pattern of China's urbanisation: hybrid metropolises, both Chinese and Soviet-style, with large portions of rural space included within a city's administrative borders, an atrophy of services and hypertrophy of the manufacturing sector.

There is so far very little cross fertilisation between the various conceptual frameworks on world/global city and a very rich empirical body of research undertaken by Chinese geographers, urban planners, economists and sociologists.[11] Undoubtedly, the re-entry of China into the world

6   Sassen (1991), p. 4.
7   Castells (1996), p. 380.
8   Fujita (1991).
9   King (1995), Robinson (2002).
10 Shahid and Nabeshima (2006).
11 See the special issue of *The China Review* (2010).

economy has transformed the situation. Moreover, this conceptual framework is going to be altered under the combined effect of the financial crises
of 2008–2009 and China's massive urbanisation and domestic market
take-off.

To what extent have East Asian metropolises fitted in to the changing
global city landscape? What gaps remain to be bridged to get a better
comprehension of this phenomenon? A new agenda needs to fully integrate the historical, geographical, socio-economic and political peculi-
arities which have determined the pathways in the formation of global
cities in East Asia. Even only partially, our research attempts to address
this new field and tries to bring fresh answers by mobilising original
approaches.

As trading routes are changing, new commercial and financial flows
appear which are moving more rapidly and which are at the same time
more vulnerable. Displacement of traditional centres of gravity, fluid
hierarchy of hubs and platforms, evolving migration patterns: all these
elements are creating a new geography of economic power in East Asia,
which the chapters by Sung, Wang and Bastide will explore in detail. These
changes deeply impact the configuration of trading and financial centres.
The complex spatial hierarchy of Asian cities is not set once and forever, as
several chapters in this volume will show. It evolves with time and is fluid.
But what are the main drivers of these shifts in urban hierarchies? How are
the newcomers challenging the previous global cities configuration?

1   Analysing the historical trajectory of a city has shed some light on
    its present functions and physiognomy. Hisasue's chapter shows for
    instance how the relatively disaffection of Edo for financial matters
    has hampered the emergence of Tōkyō as a global financial player in
    the 20th century. The entrepôt can provide another good illustration
    of this point. It seemed promising to link the vision on the world city
    network to history and to show continuity between the entrepôts of
    the past and those of late 20th-century globalisation. Obviously, the
    geographical setting is no longer a prevalent issue. These cities often
    share a common location but belong to different systems. This het-
    erogeneity of political, economic and legal frameworks makes room
    for intermediation, as has been amply demonstrated by, for example,
    Shanghai as a point of articulation between the coastal treaty port
    economies and inland China in the 19th and early 20th centuries, or
    later Hong Kong's intermediary role with mainland China, or the
    position of Singapore in the Malay world.

2   This leads us to the second idea developed here and illustrated in
    various ways in this volume (see for example chapters by Sung and

Wang). Although the entrepôt's character has evolved over time, its main functions have not been altered. The entrepôt has been transformed instead into a service integrator, with a distinctive ability to combine high value-added services for transnational operations, from shipping to legal advice, and from auditing to advertising.

3   The hierarchy of these gateways is not static but fluid. Newcomers need to carve out niches, as the chapters on Hong Kong, Singapore and Shanghai will demonstrate. The urban network that underpins East Asia's economic dynamism conceals a subtle hirerachy which is not firmly set but rather varies according to economic fortunes, political ideals, and geopolitical tensions. The way relatively autonomous, cosmopolitan, internationalised cities are commanding economic flows raises the question of the configuration of polities, sovereignty, international relations, and last but not least, the issues of threat and security. As the security of traditional nation-states is ensured by national defense forces, the highly volatile environment and the lack of strategic depth of these platforms raises the question of their vulnerability and the best way to protect them.

The methodology used for our research has been a combination of the most accurate statistical data collection along with field studies and extensive interviews in the following cities: Beijing, Hong Kong, Shanghai, Singapore and Tōkyō. Several socio-economic indicators have been retained to measure the intensity of these interdependences:

- the concentration of strategic functions: the headquarters of multinational corporations, banks, and financial institutions;
- the attraction of foreign direct investment (FDI) in high value-added sectors (high-tech industries, financial services, logistics);
- the predominance of services in GDP and employment;
- the formation of a hub for maritime and air transport; and
- the concentration of research and development activities.

We aim at generating valuable insights into the criteria determining the process of the creation of world cities in East Asia, and to contribute to a better knowledge of their specific attributes. Our investigations also have limitations in their scope due to the format of the research programme on which this volume is based, and to the four seminars held in Beijing and Paris, which have strongly structured the final results of our research. While part of a giant urban archipelago stretching from Bangkok to Singapore in Southeast Asia, and from Beijing to Tōkyō in Northeast Asia, large metropolises such as Bangkok, Taipei or Seoul do not figure in our analysis of East Asian trading and financial centres, although these cities play a prominent role at the regional level. Bangkok acts as a catalyst for the Greater Mekong Area; Taipei, especially since the recent Economic Cooperation Framework Agreement (ECFA, June 2010), has ambitions to become a new gateway for China, while Seoul already has a well-established status hub for air transportation in northeast Asia, aggressively competing with Hong Kong and Tōkyō. More studies are needed to outline a systematic typology of East Asian megalopolises.

Similarily, other areas are left unexplored in this volume and require further research: for example, metropolitan planning, the urban rural divide, urban public policies, urban governance, social and lifestyle issues. Some of those questions will be covered by an ongoing research project on urbanisation in China. This volume reflects a collective work organised around workshops. Once again, the objective was not to study all the East Asian metropolises but to deepen the analysis of the ones which have been identified as playing a major role today.

THE WEIGHT OF HISTORY

The scope covered by the historical part of this volume (Part I) is the link between past and present, especially as far as the ancient specialisation in finance or the entrepôt function is concerned. The first issue is well-illustrated by Hisasue's chapter. Focusing on its origins and the process of its development and failures, it examines the role of Tōkyō as a financial centre since the 17th century. As the second largest economy before it was surpassed by China in 2010, Japan sought to make Tōkyō into an international financial centre. This endeavour has been nurtured by an ambitious programme of deregulation.

Although Tōkyō has been developed as a domestic financial centre since the Edo period, Hisasue's critical appraisal describes its failure to evolve into an open platform devoted to cross-border financial activity. Surprisingly, this under-achievement can be traced back to the passive role played by Edo during the Tokugawa period (1603–1868) when the main economic and financial centre at that time was not Edo, but Ōsaka, where the taxes in kind were cashed in the rice exchange houses. It is only after the Meiji restoration in 1868 that a modern currency and banking system, along with a stock exchange and a central bank, were established in Japan, and gave Tōkyō a more visible role in finance.

The second chapter touches upon another issue, the role of Nagasaki as an entrepôt in the 17th century, at the periphery of a recently unified Japan. Since the 16th century, a continuum of trade routes has linked

Europe with the Indian and Asian worlds. Entrepôts were established at the strategic intersections of those routes: Malacca and Aceh, before the rise of the Portuguese at the beginning of the 16th century; the Ryūkyū archipelago, an offshore entrepôt for trade between China and Japan, in the 15th–16th century and Hoi An, in central Vietnam, as well as Taiwan in the 17th century.[12] Brunei, before partly falling under control of the Sarawak White Rajahs in the 19th century was a bustling entrepôt in the 16th and 17th centuries whose economic influence reached the southern Philippines and today's Malaysian provinces of Sabah and Sarawak as well as China. Aceh at the end of the 16th century was one of the most important urban agglomerations of the Indonesian archipelago and was more populated than Hormuz.[13]

The entrepôt is a prominent place in international trading networks.[14] It has usually been an import-export centre, and more recently a re-exporting centre, where warehousing was highly developed. The entrepôt is also a place where raw materials (such as rice, spices, timber and sandalwood) brought in from the hinterland were exchanged against manufactured products coming from abroad. The role of the entrepôt's hinterland is crucial in providing raw materials and provisions and supplies of water. Equally critical is the role of port officials in collecting tolls and duties and in some case adjudicating disputes.

To reduce risk and uncertainty, the entrepôt provided foreign merchants with interpretors, and legal safeguards. On the other hand, especially in the case of China and Japan, the host country found it convenient to have controlled trading stations where foreign traders could be separated from protracted contacts with the local populace.

Entrepôts have generally been located at the edge of distinct polities or at the boundaries dividing rival economic areas. It is necessary to note their cosmopolitan, multicultural and pluri-religious features, as well as the striking non-interference of urban institutions, since the entrepôt prosperity depends on the cooperation of two social groups: the local powers and merchants. In this context, Nagasaki appears in the 17th century as an entrepôt of a special type.

Carioti's chapter on Nagasaki in the 17th century shows how potent and relatively independent great lords (*daimyō*) of Kyūshū were, as they had reoriented their fortune towards maritime trade. To reach this objective, they needed the help of Chinese merchants living in Nagasaki. There, the Chinese were not only traders, but also interpreters, mediators and even

---

[12]   See Wills, Jr (2002).
[13]   Dos Santos Alves (1990), p. 102.
[14]   Wills, Jr (2002). See also Blussé (2000); Haneda (2009).

secret informers, especially at the time of the Shogunate military expeditions to Korea (1592–1598). The foreign community's role was all the more important since the Japanese retreated from overseas trade due to the fierce competition coming from Chinese as well as European traders. Carioti insists on the growing role played by the Zheng Chenggong's (Koxinga) family as a commercial overseas empire, extending from Japan to the Philippines and Indonesia. The strength of this trading and military network has even been reinforced by the so-called seclusion policy of Japan (*sakoku*).

She also insists on a common characteristic we will find in many entrepôts: the importance of informal channels where private transactions and smuggling went on unchecked and therefore were not registered.

The role of Nagasaki in the Zheng Chenggong network was also prominent in military strategy since he was the main opponent to Manchu's rule in southern China. This interplay of economic interest and military stakes was hinged on Nagasaki, as the Japanese military government *bakufu* had granted a *de facto* monopoly to Zheng's commercial fleet. Nagasaki was thus at the core of a complex web of trade issues, diplomatic intrigues and geopolitical challenges involving a great many players: the Japanese administration, Chinese opponents to the Qing Dynasty and Dutch traders.

THE CITY AS A SERVICE INTEGRATOR

In the late 20th century, the increase in the scale and complexity of international transactions profoundly altered the structure of the entrepôt preeminence by redirecting traditional services (transport, warehousing, trading intermediation) towards a set of sophisticated functions and transforming the quality of the legal environment. These changes are at the core of the second part of this volume: the relationship between high value-added services and metropolitan dynamism.

Globalisation transformed the nature of the entrepôt, making it a sophisticated platform for providing high-end services. Its basic functions, however, remained unaltered. The articulation of container traffic and air transport, financial functions and coordination of international sub-contracting, makes a network of cities appear at the forefront, more than the national states. Investments are today realised in *nodes* (multifunctional ports and airports) more than in *links* (roads and canals). Value does not derive from the control of commercial routes, but instead from the command on a value-added generation, and on research and innovation.

Another trend will determine the evolution of cities in the hierarchy of world centres. Corporate control mechanisms are vital in a globalised economy. How do regional headquarters in East Asia choose their location? What are the criteria to select one platform rather than another? Through carefully conducted field research, Hung's chapter delineates the correlation between the performance of multinational firms and the meticulous choice of their regional headquarters (RHQ). Far from being a transitory organisational structure, RHQs have become a strategic feature of the success of multinational operations. Hung then shows how the choice between Hong Kong, Shanghai or Beijing as the main location of RHQ has a long-lasting impact on the Asian strategy of a firm. It also sheds light on how the determinants of location – market size, cost reduction considerations and the degree of overall commercial efficiency – offer differentiated choices to creatively manage the tension between globalisation and localisation.

Headquarter economies will reshape the landscape and hierarchy of Chinese major cities. Indeed, big cities are magnets for investment because of the advantages in education, high-techology, research facilities, information and finance. They attract degree holders seeking to start a white-collar career. There is also fierce competition in big cities, but it is often perceived as different from the over-reliance on *guanxi* (personal connections) versus the capabilities in second-tier cities in China.

Surprisingly, the number of RHQs was lower in Shanghai than in Beijing at the end of 2007. Since the headquarter economy deeply impacts on the service expansion (especially in finance, accounting and consulting), their role as a catalyst for regional development should be stressed by the central authorities, observes Hung. The added-value of the regional headquarters is the key in the global integration of multinational firms and their regionalisation process.

Fiscal policies also have crucial consequences on the competitiveness of an urban centre. A global city has to provide a reliable and attractive fiscal environment. Hu examines how fiscal privileges granted to foreign enterprises since the early 1980s have been considered as a critical tool to attract foreign direct investment in China. Great Chinese metropolises have all adopted differentiated tax policies which have skewed competition between cities and worsened fiscal discrepancies between them.

More specifically, Hu studies the preferential tax treatment in several large Chinese cities: Beijing, Shanghai, Shenzhen, Tianjin and Hong Kong. The most common incentive used to attract investment from multinational corporations has been the exemption or reduction of the enterprise income tax, and the exemption and reduction on custom duties. To attract advanced technology enterprises, each city created a wide range of tax incentives. Beijing favoured the R&D expenses incurred by the high technology enterprises. Shanghai, by contrast, favoured tax policies aiming at reducing the implementation costs of technological improvements. In contrast to other mainland Chinese cities, Hong Kong has no tax discrimination, in order to comply with WTO regulations and international usage, and prefers using indirect methods facilitating a reduction in investment cost, such as tax credit for investment and expenses deduction.

Generally speaking, preferential tax treatment in China depends upon the activity, the location and the length of the Sino-foreign contractual arrangements, and the authorities favour direct preferential tax treatment to allow tax reduction or exemption.

Many problems arise from such a policy, as Hu points out, including imprecision in the objective of the preferential treatment, and blurred priorities. Moreover, since the power of management related to fiscal privileges remains in the hands of the central government and does not come from local authorities, confusion and disorder occur in the management of preferential tax treatment. Paradoxically, the proliferation of tax and administrative charges levied on foreign enterprises hampers the eagerness of municipal authorities to attract foreign direct investment. They have no other means to overstep their power by setting up various tax privileges and get only mixed results since the confusion increases and foreign investors lose confidence.

The Role of High Value-added Services

Most of the cities under consideration in this volume have already become major actors of international trade, finance and innovation. The ability to provide a wide range of advanced producer services has been a crucial factor in the emergence of global cities. The service sector does not only promote production efficiency but it also boosts technical progress and innovation. At the crossroads of these intertwinned flows, goods, capital, information (both data and elaborated knowledge), migrations, hubs (especially of highly qualified personnel) such as Hong Kong and Singapore tend to become what we could term *service integrators*, offering sophisticated integration solutions for either the logistics chain or the financial services.

Offshore trade is becoming a determinant activity and exports of service are playing an increasingly important role. As a matter of fact, service frees itself from production constraints. Exports of goods and services are organised towards other countries, far away from one's own base. Hong Kong is thus organising the exports from inland provinces in China without having the goods transiting through its port. After outsourcing, more and more elaborated forms of offshore trade are emerging.

From this point of view, Sung's contribution offers a thorough comparison between Hong Kong and Shanghai. The originality of his approach is not only to compare Hong Kong and Shanghai's performance as service centres, but to put the question of their respective competitiveness into the larger framework of their hinterlands: the Pearl River Delta and the Yangzi River Delta. The indisputable advantage of Shanghai is that it benefits from a larger hinterland than Hong Kong. Moreover, its economic specialization is different. It also exhibits, at least in recent years, higher economic growth.

Since the industrial network supporting both cities is quite different, it appears that it also corresponds to two periods in China's economic development. It also highlights the differences in the quality of institutions. Although Shanghai exhibits faster growth, the two hubs are also competing in the field of institutions. As far as this latter issue is concerned, Hong Kong keeps the edge, with the rule of law, the quality of its trained personnel and the truly internationalised nature of its elite.

As far as the performance of the financial centre is concerned, Sung's conclusions converge with that of Zhao, Zhang and Smith, and with that of Xu and Meng. Shanghai needs to upgrade the quality of its economic institutions. The city has no autonomy in the realm of institutional change, and its ability to adjust to international financial requirements, especially in the legal field, remains severely hampered by the lengthy process of economic reforms in China.

The pragmatism of Beijing's authorities and their determination to transform the Renminbi into an international currency, seem to allow, however, a ' dual centre model' that will make full use of the comparative advantages of both Hong Kong and Shanghai.

The Emergence of Logistics Hubs on China's Maritime Seaboard

Among highly sophisticated services, logistics has become a central function for international trade. Within East Asia's maritime corridor, the opening of new calls, the rotation of mother vessels and the determination of maritime routes are decided by great exchange flows outside the area. Transit time has to be as short as possible because the operation costs of supercarriers are high. Major maritime companies are generally choosing direct calls in Singapore, Hong Kong, Shanghai, and then rely on feeder vessels.

Two phenomena have reshaped this landscape: the economies-of-scale in cargo transportation and the emergence of limited global actors in maritime shipping. The determination of call is a function of cargo demand,

and the mother vessel serves the nearest port where freight is generated. More harbour calls are now decided by markets. There is thus the 'Japan service', the 'China service' and the 'Taiwan service'.

The logistics chain concept has deeply renewed the transport industry. It has resulted in the emerging of the transport of cargo (by air, sea or land) and freight management, which was usually operated by the forwarding agent. Shipping companies go well beyond the concept of port-to-port transportation and are offering high value-added services: maritime transport, transshipment, consolidation, customs clearance, inspection and insurance and land transportation. The management of such an extended logistics chain requires highly reliable information systems, integrating the demand forecasting, production planning, orders and inventories management as well as transport.

In the case of Singapore, the logistics sector has evolved to become an industry of its own, capturing the latent value-added brought by merchandise flows. This has been implemented through services maximising the fluidity of merchandise circulation. The Singaporian strategy has sucessfully attracted and fixed foreign direct investments, guaranteeing the rapid redistribution of import and export flows on global markets. These significant scale economies have been realised by merging in a single space the value and supply chains.

The anchoring of flows on platforms like Shanghai, Hong Kong or Singapore depends on the ability of those metropolitan areas to combine highly efficient infrastructures with sophisticated services. Although the former are fixed, the latter are extremely volatile. They can unravel and swiftly re-aggregate on other sites, as has been the case for financial professionals leaving Hong Kong in the mid-1990s and coming back after the return of the colony to mainland China.

For Hong Kong, the logistics industry is the vector for the evolution towards a *cyber port*, capable of becoming a virtual centre for the whole region. It is still a physical space, determined by the quality of its infrastructures, but increasingly, it has become a de-territorialised space, where the concentration of competences, of knowledge and of creativity has reached a critical mass. In that sense, the future of Hong Kong could be prefigured by the evolution of London or New York. These metropolises are no longer great ports yet they command considerable flows of goods whose loading and offloading is undertaken elsewhere.

The future of the freight industry is at stake in the logistics management. From that point of view, Hong Kong benefits from many conditions to remain a major logistics hub: efficient infrastructure and proximity to the powerful manufacturing engine of the Pearl River Delta. However, its competitive edge goes beyond those attributes.

As it is able to set up complex commercial ventures or projects linked with mainland China by articulating high-end services (such as banking, insurance accounting, auditing and legal expertise), Hong Kong operates as a service integrator. Its competences are not limited to freight management and transportation. They include the management of the initial public offerings of large Chinese corporations, the financing and engineering of large infrastructural projects in China or the implementation of large-scale advertising operations.

Hong Kong is therefore evolving from an economy whose dynamism came from international transport (mainly from mainland China and the rest of the world) towards the status of a communication hub. This shift reflects an adaptation to increasingly intangible exchanges, in which information technologies are going to impact significant productivity gains.

Wang's chapter focuses on the way Hong Kong has upgraded its gateway function in the last three decades. More precisely, it analyses factors underpinning Hong Kong's port throughputs and airport connectivity. He strongly reasserts the role of gateways in the emergence of the global city and reminds us that if London and New York are nowadays prominent financial centres, it is also because they were once salient gateway cities.

Drawing upon the theoretical framework of the gateway cities elaborated by Burghardt – a city in command of the connections between a tributary area and the outside world – Wang addresses two central questions left unanswered by the world city theory and the centrality/intermediacy conceptual framework: how is a world-city status affected by the growth of nearby urban centres partly taking over its functions? How will it react to this change? Using Hong Kong as an illustration, Wang analyses the process of regionalisation of the Hong Kong port and the creation of new container terminals in Shenzhen and Guangzhou. Will Hong Kong be marginalised and become a regional place?

Wang's conclusion is two-fold: with China's entry into the world economy, North American and European markets have become more important for Hong Kong, which today is not the sole gateway for Chinese exports. In addition, air transport is playing a growing role in Hong Kong's re-exports. This new situation allows Hong Kong to capture a much higher value than in its maritime shipping industry. Finally, since the multiplication of the Free Trade Agreements in Asia will undoubtedly lower or abolish most tariff barriers, Hong Kong's positioning as an intermediary will prove indispensable in reducing non-tariff barriers with production centres proliferating in mainland China.

Dealing with Singapore's evolution from a trading post to a global city, Bastide's contribution provides a comprehensive survey of the successive shifts in Singapore's competitive advantage. For more than a century, its geographic setting has constituted its main advantage in trade. Located at the tip of the Malay Archipelago, Singapore has fully utilised its location at the crossroads of strategic trade routes between Europe, India and China. While distance became a less critical factor in transportation, Singapore has reorganised its assets around an emerging 'archipelago economy' shaped by the multinational firms' global sourcing and offshoring strategies.

Singapore has moved up the value chain to consolidate its position within the new geography of economic power. Starting as an entrepôt, it became an oil trading centre capable of evolving into a buoyant commodity exchange and derivative market.

Bastide argues that Singapore has firmly anchored its development strategy with foreign capital, and this choice has inevitably characterised the city-state development since its inception. His main argument is that Singapore succeeded in keeping continuous pace with the swiftly shifting needs of global capital, and in offering a rapidly adjusting sophisticated environment. This evolution has prompted Singapore to reduce its historical dependency upon geographical factors, and to move up the value chain within the network of multinational corporations. A new phase in this process is now opened as some Singapore enterprises, often backed by the government, are venturing abroad and reducing their heavy dependency on foreign direct investment.

Another salient feature of the East Asian metropolises is the uneven growth of their service sector. When we try to identify cities with the highest growth of service industries in the last two decades, Hong Kong leads without doubt. In contrast, the service industry's backwardness is striking in China. Generally speaking, the underdevelopment of the service sector is partly a heritage of the command economy, in which only the material production was taken into consideration. Even in coastal areas, GDP and employment structure remain towered over by the manufacturing sector.[15]

How to assess in the metropolises under consideration the growing importance of services and the shift in manufacturing activities? While the economy is oriented towards knowledge accumulation rather than the mere production of goods, the development of advanced producer services in global cities makes possible the diffusion of new management methods. Those innovations are often transmitted by consultants. Service is, however, a wooly domain. It goes from catering and distribution to the lawyer or the auditor, and includes engineering or insurance companies as

---

[15]   See Lu Dadao et al. (2007).

well. It is worth noting that the distinction between industry and services is uneasy because maintenance operations, design and marketing are still located within the enterprise while its production has migrated. This is particularly obvious in the case of Hong Kong firms.

This trend goes along with a de-materialisation of the economy. Moreover, such an alteration of the productive activity blurs the borders between manufacturing within the enterprise and between one enterprise and its subcontractors. In the textile, automobile and garment industries, a growing share of design, research and development is embedded in the production process. Besides, not only entire sequences of the manufacturing process are outsourced, but also crucial parts of knowledge are incorporated in the final product which is assigned to independent services companies.

Offshore Production and its Implications

The case of Hong Kong clearly shows the extent to which economic activity of a city can deeply penetrate into a territory abiding by different rules. Unlike Singapore, which has created a metropolitan region in the growth triangle with Johore and Riau, extending across the borders of Malaysia and Indonesia, no bilateral negotiation defines the process of regional development between the provincial Guangdong government and the Hong Kong Special Administrative Region. A proxy of this evolution is the development of offshore trade. A growing quantity of products manufactured outside Hong Kong – although by SAR companies – is directly shipped to overseas customers. In 2009, offshore trade represented HK$196.6 billion, nearly 30 per cent of the value of total exports of services by Hong Kong.[16]

This evolution has reshaped the service industry in Hong Kong and stimulated the demand for trade supporting activities, outside the SAR. The contribution of trade and cargo handling activities is declining in Hong Kong's GDP while its contribution to GNP increases. The reason for that is quite simple: a number of service companies – container terminal handling operators, transport companies, quality control departments or even test laboratories – have invested heavily in Guangdong province.

For many years Chinese cities have been estranged by such a transformation. In 2009 the service sector in China accounted for 42 per cent of the country's GDP and 34 per cent of total employment. This relatively low proportion – lower than in other middle income countries

[16] Hong Kong Census and Statistics department, Press release, 11 February 2011.

(55 per cent and 54 per cent, respectively) – stems from the heritage of the Soviet-style command economy, as mentioned earlier. But it is also linked to the peculiar model of development followed by China in the last 30 years, with a strong focus on manufacturing and manufactured exports.

This relative backwardness of services in China affects the dynamism of exports. Shanghai is a case in point. There, the capacity to collect the hinterland production still remains under-developed. Let us only take the re-export proportion as a proxy. Shanghai exports can be broken down into exports of domestic products and re-exports of products manufactured in the rest of China. Sung Yung-win convincingly shows that during the period preceding reforms the proportion of Shanghai re-exports within total Chinese exports remained high (13.6 per cent in 1979). But this proportion was rather the consequence of central planning which imposed the choice of Shanghai to Chinese exporters than the intrinsic capacities of the city in managing external trade. This ratio has declined considerably during the reform era to reach a mere 2.3 per cent in 1992, a very low proportion for a metropolis of this importance.

Moreover, Shanghai exports were, as early as 1985, overtaken by those of Guangdong province. Built-up under a high bureaucratic scrutiny and import-substitution policies, Shanghai industries were no longer competitive in the global market. Inter-provincial barriers, and the poor efficiency of Shanghai's import-export corporations, dominated by an administrative logic, rather than market impetus, hinder the emergence of Shanghai as an international trading hub.

Research and Developement as Strategic Tools

Other intangible assets are crucial elements in attracting multinational companies: the availability of qualified engineers and domestic research facilities. While China devoted 1.3 per cent of its GDP to R&D in 2005 (against 2.7 per cent in the US), most of the expenses in that sector were assumed by foreign companies. Less than a quarter of large and medium size enterprises in 2005 had their own research centre, and nearly 90 per cent of high technology exports were realised by foreign-funded enterprises.[17] One striking feature in the case of China is the lack of fluidity in the transition from laboratory to production workshop.

Du and Miege's chapter focuses on the factors underpinning the localisation of foreign R&D centres in Beijing and Shanghai. In a context where patent application by Chinese enterprises is still lagging behind foreign

---

[17]   *Le Monde*, 12 November 2010.

and leading domestic companies in high tech sectors, foreign technology has been of strategic importance in upgrading both the quality and value of Chinese exports. The setting-up of foreign R&D centres by foreign companies is crucial in this catching-up process.

Drawing on extensive interviews in both cities, Du and Miege add a significant element to our comprehension of a metropolis' attractiveness. Zhongguancun, the technological park in Beijing is famous among more than a hundred other special technology zones all over China. More than 15 multinational firms have settled their manufacturing facilities and/or R&D centres there. More generally, the formation of clusters for foreign direct investment indirectly induces the formation of clusters in R&D activities.

Shanghai's strategy, with its Zhangjiang high-tech park, has been different from the one in Beijing and has been targeting local manufacturing industries. Different motivations underly the localisation decision of R&D centres by foreign firms in China. The choice of Beijing is often linked to the need for a foreign company to remain close to government agencies in order to be informed, and in some cases, to anticipate changes in the regulatory framework and in the establishment of industrial standards. A second reason is the proximity to Chinese industrial partners. The final reason is market access. Shanghai and Beijing are both sizeable markets, but Shanghai often outpaces Beijing because its potential market extends well beyond the city proper and includes the neighbouring provinces of Zhejiang, Jiangsu, Anhui and Hubei, with their highly diversified consumer basins.

Surprisingly, Du and Miege's interviews reveal a fact that does not appear in most international surveys on cities competitiveness: a relative insensitivity of MNE establishing R&D centres to the volume of the skilled labour force, the quality of infrastructure or even a favourable tax regime, but a strong concern for the lack of creativity among young Chinese graduates, their English proficiency and their relatively low mobility.

R&D centres in China are mainly 'Development-oriented', that is adapting products to the Chinese market, rather than creating new products for worldwide consumers. Among the main problems explaining the conspicuous weakness of research activities are the lack of clear ownership rights and a dearth of private venture capital.

Finally, the two cities have highly differentiated images: while Beijing is perceived as a high-tech centre for software development and a platform for media and cultural industries, Shanghai appears as a major manufacturing centre. The two different paths of development followed in the last decades have also induced different strategies in localising R&D centres.

THE NEW GEOGRAPHY OF ECONOMIC POWER

Part III of this volume deals with the complementarity and rivalry between Asian trade and financial centres. It focuses on two distinct issues, the criterion of competitiveness for great Asian urban centres and the hierarchy of international finance centres.

Cities and regions offering comparable attributes are competing to attract regional headquarters in a given location, or becoming the locus of manufacturing activities, research centres or even military bases. What then becomes determinant are *potentialities*: the population densities and level of revenues, the quality of training for human resources, the level of taxation and its main determinant (local or central government) as well as positioning against other sites.

Therefore, the economic expansion of a city could be compared to a circle whose radius is set by capital market access, access to information, transportation system, international connections and resources in highly qualified human capital. This constitutes the comparative advantage of a given city, determines its position in a network of cities and the economic space it is able to control.

A trading and financial centre is at the same time a gateway, a hub and a nodal point. It is at first a physical space, determined by the quality of its infrastructures; but more and more, it concerns a virtual or de-territorialiased space, which can be qualified as hyper-space or meta-space. A space where the concentration of expertise, knowledge, creativity and imagination reaches a critical mass. How to draw the map of these networks and nodes?

One possible way to address this issue is to investigate the degree of complementarity and rivalry among great Asian metropolises, and to look at their evolving hierarchies. As mentioned earlier, there is no stable state in the configuration of flows and networks which shape the East Asia maritime corridor. This complex game is very open due to the multiplicity of levels of interaction and to the proliferation of actors: enterprises, cities, local and central governments.

Daniels' chapter examines the impact of the global crisis of 2007–2009 to explore the main challenges facing emerging centres in East and Southeast Asia in their competition with the global financial centres of Western Europe and North America, whose vulnerability has been evidenced by the crisis. Highly developed value-added financial services are crucial to allow Asian centres to fully integrate the financial architecture of the global economy. Since the imbalance continues between manufactured products flowing towards Europe and North American markets, and service expertise flowing into Asia, upgrading the status of Asian financial centres should go through enhancing the local regional added value of services, rather than seeking a head-on competition with leading global financial centres such as London and New York. Despite the large and liquid capital markets offered by mainland Chinese investors, reforms in the fiscal regime of Shanghai and Beijing have not yet met the expectations of the international financial community.

In the short and medium term, Daniels foresees a focus on an interregional agenda that will raise the local/regional added value of the services provided for regional markets and allow a better use of the large capital reserves. This agenda, however, will have to take into account the challenge that arises from cities in contiguous regions: Mumbai versus Singapore, and Shanghai and Beijing versus Hong Kong.

Do we observe a new generation of world cities, with Asian characteristics, in contrast with the old generation of global cities such as New York, London and Tōkyō? From a different angle, Ekman's chapter reviews the emergence of Asian cities on the stage of global hubs. She shows how the rise of China is, among other factors – the globalisation of the economy and a massive urbanisation – at the origin of the increasing weight of East Asian centres in the global economy, while the financial crisis of 2007–2009 has amplified it.

The club of global trade and financial centres is shifting eastwards, as part of a long-term trend. To reach this position, Ekman argues that they will have to develop a niche strategy for global cities rather than blindly copy existing features of global cities. She also suggests that a vast majority of East Asian trade and financial centres have been skillfully promoting communication, technology, culture and sports at the global level in order to gain international recognition, but that their identity and specific role within the global economy have still to be reinforced.

The Emergence of International Financial Centres (IFC) in Asia

The establishement of a city into an international financial centre is a salient feature of this rise to world-city status. Institutions are at the core of the emergence of an IFC. Several related chapters converge on this point. Three kinds of financial centres have been defined, according to the intermediation services offered:

- the traditional centre which performs as a net creditor vis-à-vis the rest of the world through its banking and stock exchanges;
- the dedicated domestic centre, offering financial services to domestic institutions, but not exporting capital;

- the international financial centre which is actually an offshore banking centre in which non-resident financial institutions are the main actors.

At the end of the 19th century, large banks and exchange houses appeared in Tōkyō while a dense web of regional banks mushroomed at the local level, founded by former feudal lords, wealthy families and guild members. Tōkyō then gradually became Japan's largest domestic financial centre, while Ōsaka's preeminence faded away. Since Japan's economy needed connections with the international financial system, this critical linkage was provided by the Yokohama Specie Bank.

In the case of Tōkyō, Hisasue shows how the Japanese government was keen to keep foreign influence away from the domestic economy by confining areas of contacts with foreign banks to Yokohama and Kōbe, and not Tōkyō or Ōsaka. Yokohama was never intended to become anything but a window on the international finance system. With the expansion of Japan's colonial empire in the first half of the 20th century, the yen was increasingly accepted as a major currency in northeast Asia, while arbitrage between the gold backed Japanese currency and the silver backed Chinese currency was brisk in Dalian, Shanghai and Yokohama.

Although a wide array of deregulatory measures was adopted from the mid-1980s, Tōkyō's ambition to become an international financial centre fell short of expectations. The growth of the stock market was a consequence of a bubble, and there were only 25 foreign companies listed on the stock exchange in 2007. Foreign investment and commercial banks established in Japan used Tōkyō to cover their Japan-related business. The conclusion is straightforward: despite the huge size of its domestic financial market, Tōkyō is not equipped to struggle with places like Hong Kong or Singapore to reach the level of a first-class open platform for cross-border financial activites.

Yuan's chapter echoes that of Sung, in that it focuses on a peculiar ambition of Shanghai: to become the new Hong Kong of China. However, Yuan's analysis distinguishes itself from the above-mentioned contributors on several points. Yuan claims that Shanghai's contribution to China's economy places the city in position of becoming a major hub for foreign trade. It also grapples with a highly sensitive issue: the need for China to achieve the full convertibility of the Renminbi as a pre-condition for Shanghai to become a fully-fledged international financial centre. But there is more. The shortage of laws and supporting measures in line with international practice in the financial sector: the standards of financial regulation, the rules governing financial innovation, risk control, foreign exchange trading and market access. The main issue here is the fact that government regulation is dominated by administrative intervention leaving little room for supervision in accordance with the law. Besides, Yuan argues that China's interest rate and exchange rate are far from being determined by market forces. The lack of flexibility in the exchange rate system and a non-market oriented interest rate mechanism are major hindrances to Shanghai becoming an international financial centre.

Although some limited improvements have been implemented in the recent years, with for instance the increase of Qualified Foreign Investors in 2007, much remains to be accomplished in the relaxation of constraints on capital account management and the free convertibility of the Renminbi.

Finally, Shanghai's future status as an IFC is hampered by a conspicuous shortage of financial professionals, fewer than 200,000, while there are 770,000 in New York and 350,000 in Hong Kong. According to Yuan this is clearly related to the discouraging effect of high personal income tax in China.

In the case of Shanghai, however, it has been observed that the margin of manoeuvre with regard to the central government has been narrow, and the city's autonomy is limited in this respect. Nothing in the financial sector can be undertaken without the consent of the Banking Regulatory Commission, established in Beijing. Moreover, the nerve centres of all professional associations are located in Beijing.

How are the roles between Hong Kong, Shanghai and Beijing distributed in international finance? Instead of an open rivalry, we are rather witnessing functional distributions of roles in international finance: Beijing keeps the upper hand on the elaboration of regulations; Shanghai is servicing the domestic market; Hong Kong is managing sophisticated financial products. While Shanghai's ambition is to become an international financial centre, it is difficult to envision it in the short term. It took about 30 years for Hong Kong and Singapore to reach this position. This process is considerably delayed by the lack of full convertibility of the Renminbi, and by the under-developement of capital markets in China. It is also necessary to take into account the role of Beijing which defines, elaborates and applies the financial regulations.

The competitiveness of financial centres, as far as institutions are concerned, is at the core of Zhao, Zhang and Smith's chapter. Several factors in fact influence the creation of a new configuration of major financial poles in China: the growing internationalisation of the Chinese economy, and the relaxation of some of the rules regarding banking and insurance trades after China's entry to the WTO. They insist on the decisive role of information in the establishment of these centres. The way information is generated, transmitted and interpreted is indeed crucial to the viability of financial institutions.

Taking into consideration the hierachical nature of the Chinese power structure and the context of the post-WTO entry period, Zhao, Zhang and Smith analyse the impact of information on the spatial restructuring of China's financial centres. They have measured the ranking of the financial centres using the criteria of the public listings of Chinese enterprises on stock markets.

From a different perspective, their chapter converges with those of Hung and Du and Miege, concluding that the spatial concentration of corporate regional headquarters in specific Chinese centres form strategic control points, corresponding to the upper tier of the financial centre system. They anticipate that China's financial centres will be dominated by a three-tier hierarchy: Hong Kong will remain an international fundraising platform for mainland enterprises, Beijing will become the strategic financial centre through its policy-making and regulatory roles, and Shanghai will be the leading domestic capital formation centre for mainland enterprises since the Chinese currency, the Renminbi, is not yet fully convertible.

Contrary to the commonly accepted view, the possibility of Shanghai out-performing Beijing is downgraded by its relative weakness as an information heartland, since the country is still dominated by state-led economic development. Despite far-reaching improvements in communication and information technology accomplished by Shanghai, it is unlikely that it will upset in the short run the function of Beijing as a key site for evaluating local information under the state-led developmental model.

Meng and Xu's contribution shifts the focus to the relationship between China's financial system and the country's economic performance. In line with Zhao, Zhang and Smith, and to some extent with Sung and Daniels, they contend that neither Shanghai nor Beijing currently qualifies as a global financial centre. The two main reasons for reaching this stern conclusion are the lack of structural reforms in China's financial system, in particular the absence of a complete liberalisation of the capital account, and the limited participation of both cities in the global financial business. Focusing their analysis on the functions both Shanghai and Beijing have performed in China's economic growth, they do not separate great China metropolises from their hinterland, bringing our attention to the fact that Shanghai's GDP share in the Yangzi River Delta area gradually decreases after 2000 while Beijing is assuming an increasing role in the Bohai Economic Region.

A critical part of their argument is that Beijing and Shanghai have been inefficient as national financial centres in supporting China's economic growth. The structural change in China's economy during the 30 first years of reforms has been inseparable from a robust growth of the private and foreign-funded sectors, while the share of state-owned enterprises has steadily shrunk. They claim, with detailed statistical evidence, that funds from the banking industry and the financial market are not equally distributed across all sectors. While state-owned enterprises and share-holding companies capture the lion's share (75 per cent of domestic loans in 2003), the individual and private sector received only 7.5 per cent of domestic bank loans and obtained about 90 per cent of their funds for fixed asset investment through self-fundraising at rates often three times superior to those of the banks.

Finally, Xu and Meng offer a slightly divergent view from Zhao since they foresee Shanghai as the best candidate to become an IFC, but remind us that it will hinge on China's capacity to promote both substantial economic development and sound financial reform.

CONCLUSION: THE NEW INTERNATIONALISATION OF EAST ASIA'S METROPOLISES

There are now many gateways in Asia, fiercely competing to capture value-added and expertise. The great shipping trades are now determining the location of container terminals, while for many decades the flows were directed by the location of the ports.

Despite their differences, the models of economic organisation exhibited by the Asian metropolises under consideration share several common features:

1   Cities control a territory, which is not necessarily contiguous, or even fragments of a national space. The emergence of highly internationalised urban places on China's maritime seaboard induces centrifugal movements. They accentuate the cleavage between a trading and cosmopolitan emerging power and the autarchic remains of a country where state enterprises command a strong share in key sectors like energy, transport and communication. There is no stable state in the configuration of flows and hubs in the maritime corridor of East Asia. Territories are submitted to a complex and very open game combining the interactions of a multiplicity of actors: enterprises, cities, central governments.

2   Under the new configuration of international economic relations, the control over nodes through which wealth is concentrated and transits is more important than the occupation of territories. Similarly, the projection of economic influence goes well beyond administrative borders, as examplified by the role of Hong Kong in China.

3   The quality of the legal environment also constitutes a fundamental
     factor in the attractiveness of Asian metropolises. The elaboration
     of commercial law is characterised in China by the preponderant
     place occupied by arbitration, but also by the deliberated retention
     of unclear areas so that local authorities can benefit in dealings with
     foreign companies in a wide margin of negotiations. Will the legal
     arrangements induced by globalisation lead to the triumph of the *lex
     mercatoria* or to the emergence of a private legal system similar to
     the *law merchant* during the Middle Ages? The remarkable develop-
     ment of arbitrage in Hong Kong illustrates the magnitude taken by a
     fundamental governance mechanism, whose authority does not rely
     on government only: arbitration carried out there allows a significant
     number of mainland Chinese companies to benefit from the guarantee
     of the rule of law, and from the advantages of the British legal system.
     The invisible influence of law extends well beyond the place where it is
     elaborated and exerted.

4   The regional Free Trade Agreements mushrooming in East Asia
     also have a decisive impact on metropolisation. In particular, the
     proliferation of regional free trade agreements (Asean Free Trade
     Area (AFTA), Closer Economic Partnership Arrangement (CEPA),[18]
     Economic Cooperation Framework Agreement (ECFA)[19]) tend to
     reinforce the role of great metropolises: the Hong Kong–Shenzhen–
     Pearl River Delta–Guangzhou area now forms an urban continuum
     that could be termed greater Hong Kong. The involvement of
     Taiwanese banks in the lower Yangzi cities will even reinforce their
     links with Shanghai. Even if the project has recently been denied by
     Beijing, it is revealing that Guangzhou planned in late 2010 to merge
     the nine cities[20] of the Pearl River Delta into a super-sized megalopo-
     lis, with a total population of 42 million. At stake is the integration
     of infrastructures, industries, urban/rural activities, environmental
     protection and public services.

5   China's massive urbanisation strategies over the next decades will
     have a strong impact on the re-alignment of the East Asian urban
     archipelago. Urbanisation has cumulative effects. Human resources,
     especially in boundary-free jobs (information technology, accounting)
     go where capital goes, that is big cities. Finance and talents are chan-
     neled to big cities as their population continue to swell.

[18]   Concluded between Hong Kong and mainland China.
[19]   Concluded between Taiwan and mainland China.
[20]   Guangzhou, Foshan, Zhaoqing, Shenzhen, Dongguan, Huizhou, Zhuhai, Zhongshan
and Jiangmen.

The potential consequences of the huge urbanisation trend in China on the current configuration of network cities in East Asia it still unknown. It remains to be seen if it will have a disruptive effect with huge demand for services, high quality personnel, capital, or if it will on the contrary reinforce the strength of already existing centres. More generally, changes that are occuring in our mental representation of riches are not, as before, linked to territory. Globalisation has deeply altered this notion. Space and its frontiers have been disturbed by this new configuration of the economy. As soon as capital, knowledge and expertise become mobile, localisation, that is the territorial roots of economic activities, complies with other rules.

PART I

The legacy of history

2. Tokyo's changing role as a financial center since the seventeenth century

Hisasue Ryoichi

INTRODUCTION

This chapter aims to elucidate the role of 'Tokyo' as a financial center with respect to the economic history of modern Japan. First of all, before we consider the past, I must make clear that the image of Tokyo as an 'international financial center' is fictitious.[1] This misunderstanding has been created by the image of a huge Japanese economic presence in the global economy since the late 20th century.

Tokyo has played the role of the main domestic financial center since the late 19th century, and the needs of Japanese cross-border finance has been mainly provided and settled in other financial centers such as London or New York. Since the 1980s, as the second largest economic power in the world, the Japanese government has attempted to nurture Tokyo as an international financial center. Deregulation was started and it has been accelerated since the end of the 1990s, however, cross-border financial activity is still not active even now.

The major reason for Tokyo's weak position as international financial center is caused by its origin and nature. An international financial center must be an 'open platform' which anyone can access and use. However, Tokyo has been developed as a domestic financial center since the Edo Period, and has never been an 'open platform' for the cross-border financial activity. Therefore, administrators and domestic financial institutions lack the ability to understand the fundamental rules or governances of international financial center. This chapter describes the origins, developmental process and failures of Tokyo as an international financial center.

---

[1] 'International financial center' which leads cross-border financial activity, has to possess the following features: be based on a hard currency which has liquidity and convertibility; have a concentration of financial and capital markets (short and long term capital, equities, foreign exchange, futures and other derivatives, etc.); mature relevant legal frameworks and taxation; financial, political and social stability; advanced social infrastructure and low cost; abundant experts and professionals.

STRUCTURAL CHANGE IN DOMESTIC FINANCE: FROM EDO (1603–1867) TO MEIJI (1868–1912)

As mentioned above, Tokyo plays the role of domestic financial center in Japan. This has its origins in the Edo period (1603–1867), as Edo (currently known as 'Tokyo') was the de facto administrative capital of Japan. Edo was founded in the 11th century by a local powerful clan and Edo castle (the present imperial palace) was built in 1456 by Dokan Ota, a warlord of eastern Japan. In 1590, Ieyasu Tokugawa, later the first Tokugawa Shogun (great general), moved into Edo and started his administration there in 1600. From that point on, Edo's population rapidly increased and reached more than 1 million by the early 18th century. Then the prosperity of Edo guided the gradual formation of financial institutions, because merchants in Edo needed settlement services with Osaka.

During the Edo period, Osaka was the main economic center of Japan. The fundamental economic structure of the Tokugawa government was organized on the rice standard, a taxation system based on the rice productivity of an area. Under this system, all tax income from farmers was paid in actual rice. Consequently, the Tokugawa government and Han (local governments of a feudal clan) established official rice warehouses to cash their rice-based tax income in Osaka. From the middle of the 16th century, Osaka developed into a huge commercial hub in Japan, and consequently, major north or south bound trading ships called at Osaka from all over the country. As a result of this economic infrastructure, the rice exchange system came into being and boosted the commodity and financial business in Osaka. The Tokugawa government and Han had to repatriate the funds or necessary commodities to Edo or their local territory,[2] and then exchange houses came into existence, especially in Osaka and Edo.

Edo did not however usurp the role of main financial center, because the Tokugawa government adhered to the policy of separating the roles of the two cities. Obviously, this policy was an arbitrary decision that the Tokugawa government used to try to keep merchants' influence away from its administrative power. Therefore, the major financial purveyors to the Tokugawa government (termed the 'Ten Majors', 'Jyunin-Ryogae', 十人両替) were mainly Osaka merchants. They diversified their businesses from rice trading into finance, and were appointed to the position of the 'Ten Majors' by the Osaka City Magistrate. With this authorization, the

---

[2]   Feudal lords in the Edo period were required to spend every other year in residence in Edo. Because of this system, each Han had mansions (*de facto* embassies) in Edo which were enormously expensive to maintain.

Map 2.1   Domestic, financial and commercial networks between Osaka and Edo in the Edo period

'Ten Majors' established a guild ('Kabu-Nakama', 株仲間)[3] and handled government related remittances, lending, money market quotations and so on. Edo became a major economic center in eastern Japan, but until the Meiji period it had only a passive role secondary to Osaka.

After the Meiji restoration in 1868, Edo was renamed 'Tokyo' and become the only capital city of Japan. Under the new government and new economic framework, Japan modernized its domestic financial system. The new government introduced a modern currency system (the 'New Currency Ordinance' of 1871), a modern banking system (the 'National Banking Ordinance' of 1872), land tax reform (1873), a stock exchange (the Tokyo Stock Exchange and the Osaka Stock Exchange were established in 1878) and a central bank (the Bank of Japan was established in 1882 and monopolized the issue of banknotes).

[3]   'Kabu-Nakama' was an exclusive commercial and industrial guild with the authorization of Tokugawa government or feudal clans. The guild paid license fees and forfeited the right to monopolize the market. Through this guild, Tokugawa government and feudal clans controlled and stabilized the domestic economy.

Source: Hiroshige Utagawa '*Meishu Edo Hyakkei-Bunmei-Kaika; Bakumatsu Suruga Chou*', circa 1856–1858.

Figure 2.1   Echigoya House in Nihonbashi, Edo

These reforms encouraged the formation of modern banks in Tokyo because the close relationship with central government was an important factor to running a large-scale financial business under the nation-state system. 'Daiichi Kokuritsu Bank' (第一国立銀行、The First National Bank) and 'Mitsui Bank' (三井銀行) were typical examples. Mitsui diversified their business under the name of 'Echigoya' (Echigoya (越後屋) was the biggest dealer in kimono fabric in Edo) from the Edo period and they had already opened a financial division ('Echigoya-Mitsui Exchange House', 越後屋三井両替店) in 1683. This exchange house handled official funds from the Tokugawa government and the new Meiji government, and issued the first yen currency note in 1871. In 1872, Mitsui established the 'Mitsui-Ono Joint Banking Corporation' as a joint business with the 'Ono Organization', a major diversified business group from the Edo period. However, in 1873, the government intervened and reorganized this bank as 'Daiichi Kokuritsu Bank' under the National Banking Ordinance of 1872. Mitsui renamed its exchange business division as 'Mitsui Exchange Bank' in 1874 and reorganized it as 'Mitsui Bank' in 1876. Both 'Daiichi Kokuritsu Bank' and 'Mitsui Bank' were strongly linked with the government and the new economic order of modern Japan. They encouraged the formation and growth of modern industrial businesses. For example, Mitsui established spinning, mining, machinery, brewery and other companies.

Source: Showa-shi Kettei-ban: Showa-Zenshi, Meiji 18 nen [Showa History: Pre-Showa History – Civilization and Enlightenment: From the End of Tokugawa Era to 18th Year of the Meiji], Mainichi Newspapers Company, 1984.

Figure 2.2   Daiichi Kokuritsu Bank

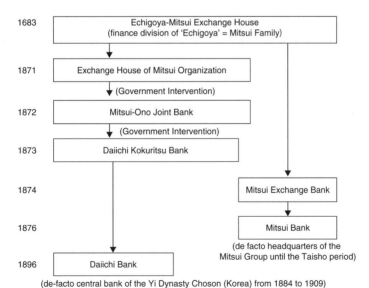

Figure 2.3   From exchange house to modern bank: the case of Echigoya-Mitsui

At the same time, many regional and local banks mushroomed throughout Japan after the government authorized to issue non-convertible bank notes in 1876.[4] From 1873 to 1879,153 banks were established based on the 'National Banking Ordinance' of 1872. The founders or investors were local elites (former feudal lords and their vassals) and wealthy families such as landlords or guild members. Even old establishments of the Edo period tried to adapt themselves to new economic and social circumstances of the Meiji period. These banks took deposits from actors in the local and regional economies and accumulated wealth in the 'Han (feudal clan) – regional economic area' in the Edo period, and in turn lent this to local and regional industries such as silk manufacturing, cotton spinning, paper manufacturing, mining and so on. In this sense, on the local and regional level, modernization and industrial development in Meiji Japan was inherited from the economic development in the Edo period.

However, soon large banks with major capital and governmental connections were established in Tokyo and Tokyo gradually became the biggest domestic financial center in Japan. Osaka, the biggest commercial and financial center in the Edo period, eventually lost its position of preeminence. Osaka's business model was commercially-based, and particularly linked with the rice trade resulting from the land tax system. However, the land tax reforms of 1873 severely undermined the economic function of Osaka, and major Osaka merchant capitalists, such as most of the members of the 'Ten Majors', could not maintain their power in the new business environment. For example, Kounoike (鴻池), a well-established financier since 1656 and one of the 'Ten Majors', established a modern-style banking business as 'Daijyusan Kokuritsu Bank' (第十三国立銀行、The Thirteenth National Bank, later renamed 'Kounoike Bank') in 1877. However, their business did not develop well because of the lack of political connections with the central government in Tokyo. The only exceptional case is the 'Sumitomo Bank' (住友銀行、currently 'Sumitomo-Mitsui Banking Corporation', 三井住友銀行). This bank was established as a private limited company in Osaka in 1895 and reorganized as public limited company in 1912. It had the strong business and political background of the Sumitomo group (copper mining and a wide range of industrial businesses). In 1919, the bank was the third largest bank in Japan after Daiichi Bank and Mitsui Bank.

Generally speaking, Osaka kept its position as an economic center for

4 Banknote issue by the private capital banks ceased after the establishment of the Bank of Japan in 1882.

the western part of Japan but its earlier glorious days as a financial center were beyond recovery.

JAPANESE FINANCIAL LINKAGE WITH THE GLOBAL FINANCIAL SYSTEM: FROM THE LATE 19TH CENTURY TO THE FIRST HALF OF THE 20TH CENTURY

While Tokyo gradually became a domestic financial center from the late 19th century, its functions were far from cross-border finance, because the needs of cross-border finance were mainly provided and settled in other global financial centers such as London or New York. For this linkage with the global financial system, the 'Yokohama Specie Bank' was established in 1879. It was a semi-governmental exchange bank with capital of 1 million yen from the government and 2 million yen from private sources. Because of Japan's rapid economic growth and increasing linkage with the global economy, it needed an exchange bank that specialized in international trade settlement and foreign exchange. The interesting point of this newly established bank was that it was called 'Yokohama' rather than 'Tokyo'.

Map 2.2   Tokyo, Yokohama, Osaka and Kobe

Yokohama opened as a port for foreign trade in 1859, and then this de facto foreign settlement rapidly grew to become the major external trading hub in Japan. Therefore many foreign banks also opened branches in Yokohama. In 1863, three British banks, 'Central Bank of Western India', 'Chartered Mercantile Bank of India, London, and China', and 'Commercial Bank of India', opened branches or agent offices in Yokohama. Then the 'Oriental Banking Corporation' (British, 1864), 'Bank of Hindustan, China and Japan' (British, 1864), 'Comptoir National d'Escompte de Paris' (French, 1867), Hong Kong and Shanghai Banking Corporation (British, 1869), Chartered Bank of India, Australia and China (British, 1880) opened branches or agent offices in Yokohama, not Tokyo.[5] Such a separation of economic roles between close but distinct cities is also seen in the example of Osaka and Kobe, and it was a result of the arbitrary decision that the Japanese government made to try to keep foreign influence away from the domestic economy.

However, Yokohama was never an international financial center as the global financial hub at the time was London or (mainly after World War I) New York, and the yen was not a key currency with high liquidity and convertibility. In this sense, the financial function of Yokohama was only a window to link with the global financial system, and on this basis, the Yokohama Specie Bank built a strong overseas branch network including London, New York, Bombay and Shanghai.[6]

From the early 20th century, the Japanese economy expanded rapidly into Asia (from Manchuria to Southeast Asia), and Japanese banks collaborated to form a new regional settlement system, which was mainly based in the areas of the silver standard such as China. It was a sub-system of the global financial system, and the regional financial center gradually formed in Shanghai. In line with this trend, not only the Yokohama Specie Bank but also the 'Bank of Taiwan' (the colonial bank in Japanese-governed Taiwan, established in 1899) and the 'Bank of Chosen' (the colonial bank in Japanese-governed Korea, established in 1911) expanded their cross-border financial activities as a reflection of Japanese economic expansion into Asia. Both were semi-governmental colonial banks which aimed to provide funds for colonial development, however, they gradually expanded their business to include cross-border finance.[7]

---

[5] However the 'Central Bank of Western India', 'Commercial Bank of India' and 'Bank of Hindustan, China and Japan' were bankrupted and closed their Yokohama branches in 1866 because of the Overland-Garney Crisis. 'Conservatoire National d'Escompte de Paris' withdrew from the Asian market in 1892.

[6] At the end of Meiji Period, the Yokohama Specie bank had 30 branches including 25 overseas branches.

[7] Business expansion by Japanese banks caused a conflict of interests with British banking networks such as HSBC, Chartered Bank and Mercantile Bank, especially from the south of Shanghai to the north of Dutch East India.

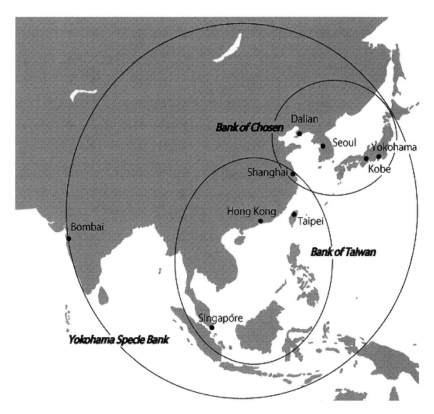

Map 2.3   Japanese financial linkages with Asia in the early 20th century

At the same time, the yen was increasingly used and accepted as a major currency in Northeast Asia, and the yen (gold-backed currency) – Chinese currency (silver-backed currency) speculation or arbitrage between Dalian, Shanghai and Yokohama by 'Dalian merchants' (Chinese specu-lators) was active in the 1920s. However, Japanese cross-border finances in Asia at this time only had a regional impact within the subsystem of the global financial system, and the financial role of Tokyo was virtually non-existent as final balances were settled in London or New York as before. Later in the 1930s, Japan formed an economic block called the 'Yen-area' in Northeast Asia during the great depression. It had an impact on the regional economy however the financial role of Tokyo or Yokohama still remained limited.

THE LIMITS OF FINANCIAL SECTOR IN POST-WAR JAPAN

The Japanese economy was utterly destroyed by World War II, and the government's priority was to re-establish key industries in post-war Japan. Therefore, the Japanese financial sector was strictly controlled by the administrator under the system called the 'convoy-system'. The Japanese government established three long-term credit banks ('The Industrial Bank of Japan' (established in 1902 but converted to long-term credit bank in 1952), the 'Long-Term Credit Bank of Japan' (1952), and 'The Nippon Real Estate Bank' (later 'The Nippon Credit Bank') in 1957), and other nongovernmental banks ('city bank', 'regional bank', 'mutual saving bank' and 'credit association') mainly provided short-term credit. Under this closed and tight financial policy, domestic capital accumulated and circulated, and such capital inflow helped Tokyo to recover its position as a domestic financial center. Since the 1960s, long-term credit, call-money markets and the stock exchange have been further developed. These tight administrative policies took away the ability of independent strategy and creative mindset from financial institutions, and made them dependent on the government.

In the 1980s, the Japanese economy established a firm position in the global economy, and aspects of the closed financial policy were gradually deregulated, such as the amendment of the foreign exchange control act (1980); the lifting of the regulation of foreign bonds denominated in yen (1985); the opening of stock exchange membership to foreign capital (1985); the start of Japanese government bond (JGB) futures (1985); approval of the Tokyo offshore financial market (1986); the start of stock index futures and options (1988 and 1989); the establishment of the Tokyo Financial Futures Exchange (1989) and so on. The area of financial services which exhibited the most growth in Tokyo in the 1980s was the foreign exchange market. Not only economic growth and deregulation, but also a strong and highly volatile yen rate after the 'Plaza Accord' in 1985, allowed the Tokyo market to establish its position as one of the three major foreign exchange markets in the world.

However, even though the Tokyo market expanded on the quantity basis in the 1980s, it was supported by inflated liquidity and a high trade surplus, and most financial activities were domestically based. Moreover, from a balanced viewpoint, it was doubtful that Tokyo became an international financial center as a result of the deregulations of the 1980s. If 'international financial center' is defined as being a market for cross-border finances, clearly Tokyo was not a true international financial center at that time. For example, the growth of the stock market was simply a bubble caused by excessive domestic liquidity, and there were no active listings or fund raising on the Tokyo stock market by foreign companies. The Tokyo Stock Exchange established a foreign companies section in 1973,[8] and the highest number of foreign companies listed was 127 in 1991.[9] However, almost all foreign companies had a mother market and Tokyo was just a destination for alternative listings. Only 25 foreign companies were listed on the TSE in August 2007. Another example is the banking sector, which kept the position of top groups in the global banking industries on the asset basis. Eleven Japanese banks were ranked in the Fortune's top 50 global bank in 1980, and 22 banks were ranked in the same list in 1990. However, it was simply a result of the inflated assets and value of the Japanese yen.

In the 1990s, the limits and nature of the Tokyo market were exposed with the collapse of the Japanese financial system.

IN GLOBAL COMPETITION: FROM THE 1990s TO PRESENT

The Japanese stock market index hit its historic high of 38915 points (Nikkei 225 basis) in 1989 and then began the long-term downward trend (see Figure 2.4); land prices also started to fall drastically after 1991. The collapse of the bubble economy brought asset price deflation, and the shrinking real economy accelerated stock deflation. Such downturn cycles caused a structural recession with a deflationary spiral. The Japanese financial system faced serious difficulties, and financial institutions, such as major banks, stockbrokers and insurance companies were in trouble or became bankrupt from the mid to late 1990s.

Therefore, the Japanese government carried out reforms of the financial sector and the then Prime Minister Hashimoto said that the government would develop Tokyo as an international financial center comparable with London and New York by 2001. In line with this 'Big Bang' policy starting from 1996, the Japanese government liberalized financial related laws such as foreign exchange controls and securities exchange regulations. Thanks to these reforms, financial services were drastically improved, and the Japanese are able to access a range of financial products and global financial markets on the retail sectors.

However, in the recession, which Japan had not experienced since the 1920s, financial trading in Tokyo was also reduced. As the following figures

---

[8] There has been no distinct category between domestic companies and foreign companies since February 2005.
[9] See http://www.tse.or.jp/english/listing/foreign/frhistorye.pdf (accessed May 2011).

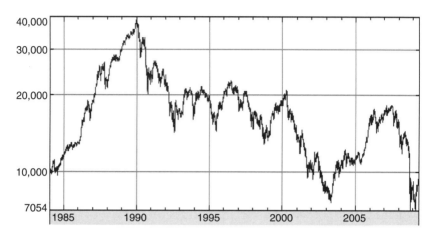

Figure 2.4   Nikkei 225 Index: 1984–2008

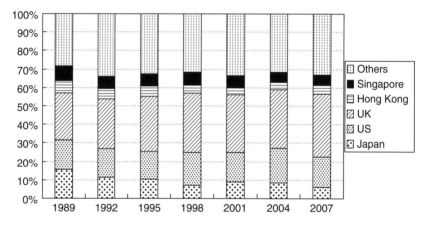

Source: Bank for International Settlements (2001), p. 18; Bank for International
Settlements (2007c), p. 13.

Figure 2.5   Market share of global foreign exchange 1989–2007

(2.5–2.9) show, Tokyo's market share of foreign exchange, bond issues, off-shore finance and external lending remained stagnant. There are clear signs that the Tokyo financial market was deteriorating from the 1990s.

Relatively speaking, Tokyo's position in the global financial market is still inconsequential. As the above figures show, cross-border financial trading in the Tokyo market is still not active in the early 21st century and a number of factors underlie the reason for this:

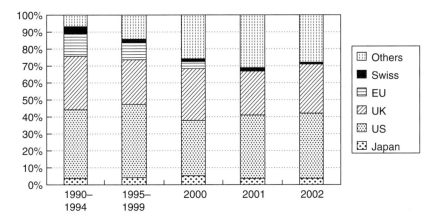

Source: *Wagakuni Kinyu/Shihon Shijyo no Kokusaika no tame no Kenkyukai Zacho Torimatome* (2003), p. 2.

Figure 2.6 *Market share of global bond issues 1990–2002*

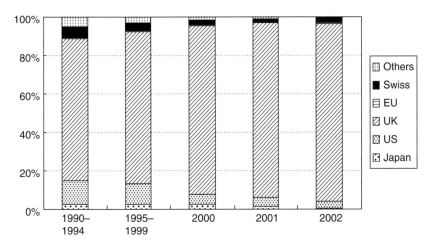

Source: *Wagakuni Kinyu/Shihon Shijyo no Kokusaika no tame no Kenkyukai Zacho Torimatome* (2003), p. 4.

Figure 2.7 *Market share of global bond issues by non-resident basis 1990–2002*

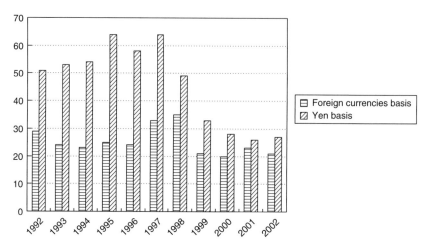

Gateways to globalisation

Note: In trillion JPY.

Source: *Wagakuni Kinyu/Shihon Shijyo no Kokusaika no tame no Kenkyukai Zacho Torimatome* (2003), p. 20.

Figure 2.8   Quantity of Tokyo offshore market 1992–2002

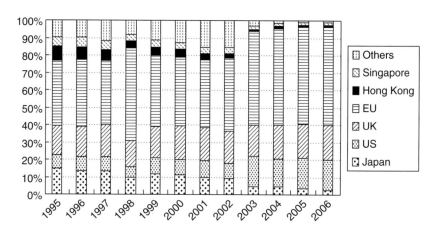

Source: Bank for International Settlements (2007a).

Figure 2.9   Market share of global external loans 1995–2002

1 a sluggish and unstable financial environment since the 1990s, especially the crash of the financial system caused by the huge non-performing loan problem in the late 1990s;

2 English, the *lingua franca* in global business and financial circles, is not in common use in Japan;

3 the lack of the attitude necessary to create innovative business models or skills for cross-border finance, not only in the financial institutions but also in the supportive professional industries and services such as legal, accounting and consulting among others. Japanese financial institutions especially have followed the policy of administrator after the post-war era. They abide by the principle of 'peace-at-any-price' in everything;

4 administrators do not understand the basic concept of an international financial center as 'open platform'. Therefore they are not able to establish the necessary governance principles such as clarity of the rule, adherence of the principle and respect of private sectors. Japan still has complicated and unclear law enforcement practices such as administrative directives or tactical pressure.

Obviously, Tokyo is not an 'open platform' for global finance that anyone can access and use. If there are other markets which are efficient and convenient, why do the global financial institutions and their customers have to use the Tokyo financial market? As a reflection of this, more than 70 percent of the foreign financial institutions (including investment and commercial banks) with branches in Tokyo said they only cover Japan-related business.[10]

With the global wealth shift into Asia in the early 21st century, Tokyo seems likely to lose out to the competition from other financial centers in Asia such as Hong Kong and Singapore. Tokyo has a huge market size and liquidity backed by domestic funds. However, Hong Kong and Singapore have the necessary and efficient conditions, such as professional services, skilled work force and a clear and fair regulative framework. The most important factor is that many transactions are carried out in English, not in local or native languages.

The 'Study Group working on the internationalization of the Japanese financial and capital markets' in 2004 (subsidized by the Ministry of Finance) suggested the importance of strategic alliances with Asian markets and said that this may become key for the future of the Tokyo market. In fact, rapid growth of Asia from the 1990s, especially the

[10] Kokusai Kinyu Jyohyo Center (2007), *Evaluation and Strategy for the Tokyo Financial and Capital Market by Foreign Financial Institutions*, p. 17.

Table 2.1 Financial markets in Tokyo, Hong Kong and Singapore: 1996 and 2006

	1996			2006		
	Tokyo	Hong Kong	Singapore	Tokyo	Hong Kong	Singapore
Foreign Financial Institutions	n.a.	178	140	95	122	111
Volume of the Foreign Exchange Market	161	90	105	199	102	125
Total Value of the Stock Market	3011	449	215	4614	1715	384
Global Asset Balance of the Banking Sector	1361	728	507	2036	710	699
Global Debt Balance of the Banking Sector	911	732	507	1049	612	699

Note: In US$ billions.

Source: Kokusai Kinyu Jyohyo Center (2007), p. 6.

economic growth in China, has created huge financial and capital needs in the region. For example, the following table shows clearly that Chinese state-owned and private-owned enterprises listed on the Hong Kong stock market have arranged a huge quantity of funds. However, Tokyo will never take over the role of Hong Kong. Historically, Hong Kong has played a role as a regional financial center for the overseas Chinese networks in place since the late 19th century and now it has become an international financial center which provides a place for matching Chinese enterprises and global risk money. More important thing is that Hong Kong is a part of People's Republic of China under the 'one country two systems' after 1997.

However, the 'GFCI Report' in 2007 pointed out the following: 'Hong Kong seems the most likely Asian city to emerge – assisted by a strong regulatory system and a well-skilled financial services workforce. But the future of Asia is still the subject of conjecture.' This is largely because financial centers in Asia exist not only in Tokyo and Hong Kong but also in Sydney, Singapore and Shanghai.

Specifically, Shanghai used to be an international financial center in

*Table 2.2   Equity funds raised by China-related companies on the Hong
Kong Stock Exchange 1993–2006*

	1993	1994	1995	1996	1997	1998	1999
H share	8,141.52	9,879.81	2,991.35	7,871.66	33,084.23	3,552.52	4,263.69
Red Chip	15,079.23	13,226.54	6,673.61	19,009.11	80,984.81	17,374.85	55,581.59
Total	23,220.75	23,106.35	9,664.96	26,880.77	114,069.04	20,927.37	59,845.28

	2000	2001	2002	2003	2004	2005	2006
H share	52,394.87	6,832.08	18,046.20	48,266.54	60,399.66	159,126.32	306,186.47
Red Chip	293,658.67	19,081.27	52,722.23	4,893.23	26,457.28	22,429.83	50,774.81
Total	346,053.54	25,913.35	70,768.43	53,159.77	86,856.94	181,556.15	356,961.28

Note: In HK$ millions.

Source: Hong Kong Stock Exchange (2007).

Asia and is now China's biggest domestic financial center,[11] and has clear intentions to revive its role as a global financial hub. Therefore the Chinese government formally announced to promote Shanghai as an international financial center in March 2009. At least for now, because of the non-liberalized renminbi, the poor legal framework and controls on freedom of the press, Shanghai has played no more than the role of domestic financial center. Closely resembling Tokyo in the 1980s, it is not easy to build an 'open platform' for the cross-border finance, however, no one can deny the future potential of the Shanghai market.

Under this structural change and cross-border competition in Asia, the Tokyo market has not been able to attract global financial activity until now. More than 44 percent of the foreign financial institutions in Tokyo recognize that financial market reforms in Japan could be quite effective but are simply not enough when compared with Hong Kong or Singapore.[12]

On December 21, 2007, the Financial Service Authority (FSA) published the 'Plan for Strengthening the Competitiveness of Japan's Financial and Capital Markets'. The FSA press release announced the following:

[11]   However, Shanghai's past is not to be compared with the present, because the basic precondition is totally different. International settlement is no longer protected by extraterritorial rights in Shanghai.
[12]   Kokusai Kinyu Jyoho Center (2007), *Evaluation and Strategy for the Tokyo Financial and Capital Market by Foreign Financial Institutions*, p. 7.

Map 2.4   Financial centers in Asia

> Strengthening the competitiveness of the country's financial and capital
> markets has become a pressing policy issue. Attractive financial and capital
> markets are expected to provide good investment opportunities for the finan-
> cial assets held by Japanese households that amounts more than 1,500 trillion
> yen [about US$14 trillion], and to supply domestic and foreign companies with
> the adequate amount of capital for growth. It is also expected that, with such
> markets, Japan's financial services industry will be able to generate high value
> added, thereby contributing to sustainable economic growth.[13]

The Plan incorporates specific measures to strengthen the competitiveness
in the following four policy areas:[14]

1.   Creation of vibrant markets in which investors can have confidence.
     A market infrastructure needs to be put in to place that enhances

---

[13]   See http://www.fsa.go.jp/en/news/2007/20071221.html (accessed May 2011).
[14]   *Ibid.*

diversity in financial services and raises customer benefits, while ensuring market fairness and transparency. The measures to be taken to achieve this objective include introducing a bill to the Diet (Japan's Parliament) that will enable diversification of exchange-traded investment funds and the establishment of markets in which professionals are engaged in vigorous transactions.

2. A business environment that invigorates the financial services industry and promotes competition. The FSA intends to put in place a competitive environment that can meet the needs of the times, which provides diverse and high-quality services. Various measures will be taken to this end, including the introduction of a bill to the Diet that will revamp the firewall regulation among banking, securities, and insurance groups, as well as broaden the scope of businesses in which banking and insurance groups are permitted to engage.

3. Improving the regulatory environment (better regulation). The FSA aims to enhance the effectiveness, efficiency and transparency of financial regulations by improving its supervisory method. This will include intensive dialogue with the industry with a view to sharing the principles for financial regulations, as well as close monitoring of market developments and an effective supervisory response.

4. Improving the broader environment surrounding the markets. The measures include developing internationally competitive individuals specializing in finance, law and accounting among others, and improving the urban infrastructure suitable for an international financial center.

The reaction from the financial industry was generally favorable, however, a high-quality international financial market with capital, information and human resources flow cannot be built in a day. There is no telling whether these market reforms launched by the Japanese government will succeed or not.

CONCLUSION

Tokyo established its role as a domestic financial center in eastern Japan in the Edo Period. After the Meiji restoration in 1868, under the new nation-state and new economic framework, Tokyo gradually became the largest domestic financial center in Japan. However, the needs of cross-border finance were mainly provided and settled in London or New York, and the international financial role of Tokyo remained minimal.

After World War II, the government's priority was to re-establish the

Japanese economy, and Tokyo once again played the role of domestic financial center from the 1960s onwards. In the 1980s, the Japanese economy established a firm position in the global economy, and the tight financial policy was gradually deregulated. The Tokyo financial market deteriorated during the depression of the 1990s, and the Japanese government carried out reforms of the financial sector called the 'Big Bang' policy.

However, it is doubtful that Tokyo ever became an international financial center because an international financial center is defined as being a market for cross-border finance, which clearly Tokyo was not. Tokyo's ranking position in the global financial market is still low, because it is based on domestically-related financial activities. Moreover, with the rapid rise of the Asian economy since the late 20th century, the Tokyo market is facing global competition with neighboring cities such as Hong Kong, Singapore and Shanghai.

As a reflection of difficult situation, Tokyo was ranked ninth as a financial center after London, New York, Hong Kong, Singapore and other cities (see appendix) in 2007, but was drastically reduced to 15th in 2008.

The GFCI Report (2007) pointed out: 'Current thinking is that Shanghai and Tokyo are unlikely to be global centers', and '[Tokyo] does not fare well in terms of regulation and business environment, but the size of the Japanese economy means Tokyo has good liquidity. It fares poorly on people but has good infrastructure and market access.'

In its attempt to become a true international financial center, Tokyo seems challenged on many fronts. However, Tokyo has been developed as a domestic financial center since the Edo Period, and has never been an 'open platform' for the cross-border financial activity. Therefore, administrator and domestic financial institutions lack the ability to understand the fundamental rules, governances and business models of international financial center. Political and business will and ability to overcome these challenges remains to be seen.

APPENDIX

Table 2A.1   Top 10 financial centers by GFCI Report

Center	Rank	GFCI Rating*	Overall Assessment
London	1	765	Most key success areas are excellent – London is in the top quartile in over 80% of its instrumental factors. Especially strong on people, market access and regulation. The main negative comments concern corporate tax rates, transport infrastructure and operational costs.
New York	2	760	Most areas are very strong – New York is also in the top quartile in over 80% of its instrumental factors. People and market access are particular strengths. Our respondents cited regulation (particularly Sarbanes-Oxley) as the main negative factor.
Hong Kong	3	684	Hong Kong is a thriving regional centre. It performs well in all of the key competitiveness areas, especially in regulation. Headline costs are high but this does not detract from overall competitiveness. Hong Kong is a real contender to become a genuinely global financial centre.
Singapore	4	660	Most areas are very good and banking regulation is often cited as being excellent. It performs well in four of the key competitiveness areas but falls to 9th place on general competitiveness factors alone. Definitely the second Asian centre just behind Hong Kong.
Zurich	5	656	A very strong niche centre. Private banking and asset management provide a focus. Zurich performs well in three of the key competitiveness areas but loses out slightly in people factors and in general competitiveness.
Frankfurt	6	647	Despite a strong banking focus, suffers from inflexible labor laws and skilled staff shortages. Market access, infrastructure and business environment are strong but Frankfurt falls outside the top ten GFCI rankings for people and general competitiveness.
Sydney	7	639	A strong national centre with good regulation, offering a particularly good quality of life. Sydney is strong in four of the key competitiveness areas but falls outside the top ten for people – many financial professionals leave for larger English-speaking centers.

Gateways to globalisation

Table 2A.1   (continued)

Center	Rank	GFCI Rating*	Overall Assessment
Chicago	8	636	Number two center in the US. Hampered by the same regulatory regime as New York. It scores highly for people but is let down by its infrastructure and market access rankings. Unlikely to overtake New York, it remains a powerful regional and specialist center.
Tokyo	9	632	Does not fare well in terms of regulation and business environment, but the size of the Japanese economy means Tokyo has good liquidity. It fares poorly on people but has good infrastructure and market access.
Geneva	10	628	A strong niche centre similar to Zurich. Private banking and asset management continue to thrive. Geneva is strong in business environment and general competitiveness but let down by infrastructure.

Note: The theoretical maximum GFCI rating is 1,000.

Source: City of London (2007).

3. 17th-century Nagasaki: entrepôt for the Zheng, the VOC and the Tokugawa *Bakufu*

Patrizia Carioti

THE HISTORICAL SETTING

With the arrival of the first Portuguese in Japan in 1543, the Chinese intermediary role was clearly delineated: the Portuguese were accompanied to the Japanese coast of Tanegashima by Chinese sea-traders, or more precisely, by Chinese pirates.[1] Soon after, Wang Zhi, the well known Chinese pirate established in Japan, brought the Portuguese to Hirado, where he had one of his bases, thanks to the protection of the *daimyō* Matsuura Takanobu, deeply involved in overseas trades.[2] Yet, in those days, when Japan was in a period of civil war, the *daimyōs* of Kyūshū, still free from any control by central authorities, were all eager to establish trade relations with Portugal. And as we know, the *daimyō* Ōmura Sumitada succeeded in bringing the Portuguese to his domain, offering them Mogi, Yokoseura, Fukuda, and Nagasaki.[3] In 1571, the port of Nagasaki was open up to the Portuguese and, at the same time, to the Chinese too: the Chinese trades and commodities were essential to Japan.[4] Also the maritime activities carried out by the Japanese merchants were vivacious and important: many *Nihon machi*, the Japanese Overseas communities, were rising in South East Asia, joining the Overseas Chinese communities.[5]

Yet, toward the end of the 16th century, Toyotomi Hideyoshi rose to power and affirmed his rule on a reunified country. Therefore, the control of Japanese private maritime activities became increasingly strict. As a consequence, the *daimyōs* of the Kyūshū coasts were forced to recuperate

[1]   See Jin Guoping (1996), pp. 85–135; Carioti (2003), pp. 24–39.
[2]   Hiradohan (1973), pp. 386–396, 397–403, 403–412; Toyama Mikio (1987), pp. 109–120; Carioti (forthcoming).
[3]   Yamamoto Kitsuna (1983), pp. 30–50; Carioti (2006a), pp. 88–92.
[4]   Yamawaki Teijirō (1983 [1964]).
[5]   Iwao Seiichi (1960).

their lost profits by financing the Chinese sea-traders, and hiring Chinese fleets and merchants.[6] Nevertheless, the Japanese authorities were not blind. Moreover, Hideyoshi was planning the invasion of Korea, as part of his design on China. In concomitance with Hideyoshi's requisition of Nagasaki (*chokkatsuchi*) in 1588, there was the first attempt to concentrate the Chinese presence of Kyūshū in the area of Nagasaki, in order to bring the Chinese settlers under stricter control and use them as interpreters and as an 'intelligence service' during the expeditions to Korea (1592–1598). As we can see, the importance of the Overseas Chinese in Japan was not only related to their private commercial functions, in the service of the Lords of Kyūshū: it was also directly connected to their role as mediators and interpreters, as well as secret informers. Hideyoshi's aim was the reunification of Japan, and thus preparing the way to the Tokugawa shogunate. In this contest, the Overseas Chinese had the Japanese emerging central authorities as their direct interlocutor.[7]

At the dawn of the 17th century, with the arrival of the Dutch and English East India Companies, the Tokugawa *bakufu* was by then formally established (1600; in 1603 Tokugawa Ieyasu became *shōgun*): the international role of the Overseas Chinese in Kyūshū was becoming essential.[8] It was not by chance, in fact, that the Tokugawa *bakufu* founded the *Tōtsūji kaishō* ('The Office of Chinese Interpreters') in Nagasaki.[9] Very often, the Chinese acted as interpreters between the Europeans and the Japanese authorities and that gave them significant political power. In Hirado and Nagasaki, the Chinese traders were commercial mediators in the service both of the Europeans and of the Japanese *daimyō*.[10]

Therefore, the attitude of the Tokugawa *bakufu* toward the Overseas Chinese was of careful concern: the Japanese authorities did not wish to stop the flux of import-export carried on by Chinese traders in Japan; on

[6] Carioti (2000), pp. 31–45.
[7] Concerning the overseas Chinese in Japan, see Luo Huangchao (1994).
[8] Historiographical Institiute (1955–1968), vol. 7, 1959. With regard to the Office of Chinese Interpreters, see Carioti (2010), pp. 62–75.
[9] Through that office, the Japanese authorities could exercise a deeper control over the Chinese settlers. Japan pursued a very careful and balanced policy: Hirado, with its important Chinese community, housed the Dutch and the English; Nagasaki continued to deal with the Iberians. During the first decades of the 17th century, both ports had the most relevant commercial function in Japan as international sea-trade stopping places. Kimibiya (1897); Historiographical Institiute (1955–1968) vol. 7, 1959. See also Sadamune (1959), pp. 51–66; Matsumoto (1952), pp. 111–117; Nakamura (1952), pp. I–XX; Chang (1972), pp. 3–19.
[10] They were also granted the official licences of *shuinsen* by the Tokugawa *shōgun*. Mention must be made of Li Dan or 'Captain China', head of the Chinese community of Hirao, and his group, who actually 'monopolized' the shogunal licences awarded to the Chinese merchants. See Iwao Seiichi (1958a), pp. 27–83; Iwao Seiichi (1936), pp. 63–119; Blussé (1990), pp. 245–264; Blussé (1981), pp. 87–105; Carioti (2006b), pp. 1–32.

the contrary, they intended to protect and develop the commercial relations with China. Yet, the incomes from international trades, until then in the hands of the coastal *daimyō*, had to be channelled into the national budget.[11]

It is during the first decades of 17th century that we see a sort of 'centralization' of both the Japanese and Chinese maritime activities. In the case of Japan, this centralization was guided and 'imposed' by the central authorities; in the case of China, it was a sort of 'spontaneous' reunification of several groups of pirates, smugglers and adventures-merchants under the flag of Li Dan first and of Zheng Zhilong – and the Zheng family in general – from 1625 onwards. And it is worth noting that the capital invested into the Chinese maritime activities by the Japanese *daimyō* and by the European delegates – especially Dutch and English – was a decisive element in the rising of a 'centralized' organization under the Zheng family command.[12] Therefore, if the Chinese sea-traders were greatly favoured by their reunification, the same cannot be said for the Japanese maritime activities. The strict control exercised by the Tokugawa *bakufu* on the Japanese overseas activities was counter-productive: the Overseas Japanese slowly retreated from the international setting of South and Far East Asia seas. The competition with the Chinese traders as well as that with the Europeans was too hard.

From 1633, according to the so-called *sakokurei* ('Closed Country' decrees), the Japanese merchants were prohibited from going abroad and the Overseas Japanese were requested to return to Japan: it was the end of the *shuinsen* system. In 1635, the *bakufu* limited the arrival of the Chinese fleets to the sole port of Nagasaki. That was a significant decision, in order to concentrate the Chinese settlers of Kyūshū mainly in Nagasaki. Another restriction was concerned with Japanese merchants being allowed to buy Chinese commodities: only the merchants from Sakai, Kyōto, Ōsaka, Nagasaki and Tōkyō, provided with official licences (*gokashō shōnin*) were allowed to buy Chinese merchandise, according to the fixed price established by the authorities following the *itowappu* system (*pancado*).

In 1639, Portugal was expelled too, and two years later, in 1641, the Dutch United Company was forced to move from Hirado to Deshima (Nagasaki): with the third *shōgun*, Tokugawa Iemitsu, Japan had entered the so-called *sakoku*. In Nagasaki, there were only two foreign settlements: the Chinese community and the Dutch.

---

[11] On the *shuinsen* system, see: Iwao Seiichi (1958b); Iwao Seiichi (1960).
[12] See Carioti (1996), pp. 29–67.

'COLD WAR' IN NAGASAKI

Notwithstanding this, Japan became linked to the two conflicting powers, though for different reasons. Through the Chinese community of Nagasaki, the archipelago depended commercially on the Zheng family, which by the 1640s had firmly established total supremacy over Chinese maritime trade.[13] The wide overseas activity carried out by the powerful Zheng organization is essential element for a proper comprehension of the historical events that took shape and developed in 17th-century Far East Asia. The economic, political and military influence exerted by the Zheng family, in particular during the years of Zheng Chenggong, extended throughout South and Far Eastern Asia – from Japan, to the Philippines, to Indonesia. In particular, Japan, which for centuries had been China's primary partner in maritime commerce and trade, was directly affected by the economic strategies employed by the Zhengs. These strategies became even more effective when Japan enacted the so-called *sakoku* policy, which strictly restrained international trade soley to the port of Nagasaki. On the other hand, the VOC turned out to be an indispensable protective shield against expanding European conquests and an increasingly important trading partner. Forced into neutrality, Japan did not take part directly in the clash but became the stage for heated commercial rivalry and a ruthless cold war between the two partners formally allowed entry to the *sakoku*: the Chinese and the Dutch. The mercantile war being waged throughout the ports and seas of South East Asia became a veritable 'duel' on Japanese territory.[14]

Via the port of Nagasaki, the *sakoku no mado* ('the Window of the Closed Country'), the Japanese archipelago relied on commerce with China above all for the importation and sale of silks (raw and made up), medicinal products and various products of arts and crafts; in exchange it had to export large quantities of silver.[15] This meant a constant drain on national finances, so that the *bakufu* was obliged to take

---

[13] With regard to Zheng Chenggong, see: Xiamen Daxue Lishixi (1982a, 1982b, 1984, 1989); Fang Youyi (1982, 1985, 1987, 1994). Concerning the primary sources, see again: Fang Youyi (1982, 1985, 1987, 1994); see also the collection of documents and historical sources published by the Bank of Taiwan in several series: *Zhengshi shiliao chubian* (*Taiwan wenxian congkan*, n.157) Taibei (1962); *Zhengshi shiliao sanbian* (*Taiwan wenxian congkan*, n.175) Taibei (1963); *Zhengshi shiliao xubian* (*Taiwan wenxian congkan*, n.168), Taibei (1963); *Nan Ming shiliao* (*Taiwan wenxian congkan*, n.169) Taibei (1963). In Japanese: Ishihara Michihiro, *Kokusen'ya*, Tōkyō 1964; *Minmatsu Shinsho Nihon kisshi no kenkyū*, Tōkyō 1945; Inagaki Magobei, *Tei Seikō*, Taibei (1929). Bai Di [Patrizia Carioti], *Yuandong guoji wutaishang de fengyun renwu Zheng Chenggong*, Guangxi, 1997.
[14] See Bugge (1989), pp. 25–44.
[15] NagazumiYōko (2010), pp. 6–9.

precautionary measures and limit traffic from overseas. It is very difficult to give precise estimates as to the number of incoming trading vessels in Nagasaki, and the quantity of goods imported and exported by the Chinese – Zheng Chenggong's fleets in particular – and the Dutch. Also a considerable amount of trade went through 'informal' channels: private commercial transactions, exchanges and retailing and smuggling all went on without any checks or taxation, and thus were not registered.[16] Some evaluations can be deducted from the official registers, such as those belonging to the United Company or the Nagasaki Office of Chinese Interpreters, or from other documents, which constitute the numerous, but generic sources on the activities of the Zheng. Such data are only indicative, but they can provide the basis for some more general considerations.[17]

Nevertheless, archives relating to the Nagasaki trade are extremely long and laborious. Generally, the results can be only partial, related to a limited period, and without any possibility of cross-checking in other documents. For example, the researches can concern a single commodity in a limited period, or be based on a single type of documents and materials (Chinese, or Japanese, or Dutch, etc.) Therefore, we give here only approximate data.

Concerning the first decades of the 17th century, we know that the Chinese merchant ships to Nagasaki avaraged about 30 each year. For the years immediately before the *sakoku*, we have the following data: 36 ships in 1634; 40 in 1635; 64 in 1637; 93 in 1639; 74 in 1640; 97 in 1641. Nagazumi does not indicate how many of these ships belonged to the Zhengs, but calculates that the Zheng ships would have been about 80 per cent. The data of 1637 reveal the first significant rise: that year saw the outbreak of the Shimabara rebellion, and Japanese authorities diverted part of the trade conducted by the Portuguese in Nagasaki up until then to the Chinese fleets; moreover, exactly a year before (1636), Zheng Zhilong had routed Liu Xiang and had settled more firmly on the mainland. In 1639, the Iberians were definitively expelled from Japan, while Zheng Zhilong reenforced his positions: the Chinese ships to Nagasaki rose to 93. In 1640, when Zheng Zhilong became Military Commander of the Fujian, there were 74 Chinese ships to Japan, as Zheng Zhilong had to move the greater part of his organization from Taiwan to Anping. In 1641, the VOC was

---

[16]   Not only by the Chinese, for agents of the Dutch Company were also not averse to pursuing activities that were not named in reports back to Batavia. See Nagazumi Yōko (1998), pp. 147–172. The topic is certainly extremely fascinating, but also very complex, as the flux of 'private' trade had to escape any official report.
[17]   See Nagazumi Yōko (1987), pp. 8–9; Bugge (1989), p. 27, *passim*; Yang Yanjie (1984), pp. 221–235, esp. p. 224.

moved from Hirado to Deshima: the Chinese ships reached the highest number, 97; Zheng Zhilong once more came to control the Chinese mercantile activities.

According to the research for the following decade conducted by Bugge, mostly based on VOC documents, during the years 1641–45 the quantity of raw silks imported in Nagasaki by the Chinese and by the Dutch was almost equivalent. Yet, the quantity of manufactured silks imported by the Chinese was roughly nine times that imported by the VOC. In the following five years 1646–1650, the Tokugawa authorities reduced by two-thirds the import of manufactured silks, but the proportion between the Chinese and the Dutch imports remained the same, with a net superiority for the Chinese; the raw silks also mantained the previous proportions. In the years 1651–1655, the Chinese import of manufactured silks to Nagasaki was 20 times higher than that of the Dutch; raw silk import was again slightly advantageous to the Chinese. During the years 1656–1660, raw silk imports went up – the same Chinese-Dutch proportions – but the manufactured silks were again reduced by the *bakufu* – always with net superiority for the silks coming from Chinese traders.

From this data, with regard to silk imports to Nagasaki, the Chinese superiority over the VOC is clear. Concerning the years 1650–1662, during which Zheng Chenggong ran the Zheng organization trades – as well as most of the Chinese commerce with Japan – from the Chinese documents more precise data emerge. During those years, Yang calculates that 649 merchant ships belonging to the Zheng fleets –called *Kokusen'yasen* in the Japanese sources ('the ships of Kokusen'ya', that is Guoxingye), distributed as in Table 3.1 (year:number of the ships to Nagasaki).[18]

THE ZHENG MARITIME NETWORK

From the moment he took command of the Zheng organization in 1651, Zheng Chenggong waged an incessant and protracted campaign of aggression against the Manchus, which was naturally very costly. Part of the costs could be covered by taxes and tribute levied on the regions he conquered, but it was also essential to have a constant and copious supply of incoming funds, especially when the military operations started to run into difficulties. Thus while the offensive against the Manchus remained his prime objective, Zheng Chenggong never neglected the mercantile aspect of his organization, being fully aware that the strength of his military

[18] Yang Yanjie (1984).

Table 3.1   Zheng's merchant ships to Nagasaki

Year	ships	Year	ships
1650	70	1657	51
1651	40	1658	43
1652	50	1659	60
1653	56	1660	45
1654	51	1661	39
1655	45	1662	42
1656	57		

and political challenge to the Manchus depended on it.[19] He applied a precise and aggressive economic strategy, making the most of the vast, cohesive organization under his command whose markedly military character made it particularly homogeneous and efficient. This did not mean, however, that the men sailing under his colours merely carried out orders, without seeking any personal gain during their transactions on behalf of the Zheng: on the contrary, they invested their own capital in the operations and thus had every reason to ensure their success. They were at the same time soldiers and merchants.[20]

In addition to the profits from the trade of ships belonging to the family and followers, the mercantile organization of the Zheng was indirectly responsible for virtually the whole of Chinese trade, since even the 'independent' traders who did not sail under Zheng's colours conformed to his economic policy. This was a vital element in the success of his strategies. Moreover, he controlled the access to the Chinese continent: every merchant ship arriving in Xiamen was duly taxed.[21] None of which was satisfactory to the Europeans, who resented the implicit submission entailed by such a policy: the Dutch above all, but not only them.

One more element was highly significant in Zheng Chenggong's economic strategy: the adhesion and cooperation of the overseas Chinese communities. Left to their own devices by the total disinterest of the Chinese authorities, the Overseas Chinese were exploited as a cheap workforce by Europeans, and subjected to laws and regulations which were

---

[19]   Fujian Shifan Daxue Lishixi (ed.) (1982), *Zheng Chenggong shiliao xuanbian*, Fujian: Zheng Chenggong Yanjiujui, pp. 295–298. See also: Yang Yanjie (1984), pp. 221–235; Cheng K'o-ch'eng (1990), pp. 217–244.

[20]   Cheng K'o-ch'eng (1990), pp. 234–236.

[21]   During this period, every merchant ship passing through Xiamen had to pay 3,000 *liang* as duty.

alien and iniquitous. Therefore, they turned to the Zheng organization and on more than one occasion sent appeals and requests for military intervention to Zheng Chenggong.[22]

There were basically two trading routes used by the fleets of Zheng Chenggong: one linking China and Japan directly, and another more far-flung: China – South East Asia – Japan, known as the 'trading triangle'. Both, as can be seen, culminated in Nagasaki, for Zheng Chenggong conducted roughly three times as much trade with the archipelago than with South East Asia.[23]

When, in 1635, the Japanese authorities decided to restrict international trade to the port of Nagasaki and, by 1641, permitted access only to the Chinese and the Dutch, they found themselves giving official sanction to two rival powers and footing the bill for their fierce competition, not least because both organizations were chiefly importing the same product, namely silk. During the first decades, the Chinese enjoyed a definite supremacy, partly thanks to the goodwill of the *bakufu* that viewed the Chinese traders with less suspicion. It was no coincidence that the Japanese authorities lodged the Chinese representatives in the city of Nagasaki, relegating the Dutch to the tiny artificial island of Deshima. The *bakufu* also granted the Chinese interpreters – who were responsible for all commercial, social and juridical dealings between the Chinese community and the Japanese authorities – much greater freedom of movement than the Dutch interpreters, who were subject to strict controls in their access to the closed community of Deshima.[24]

Yet in spite of the privileged position of the Chinese traders, or rather precisely because of this, Zheng Chenggong was careful to extend his keenly competitive market strategies to Japanese territory. For each type of goods imported, the Japanese authorities established a fixed price that, in the interests of stability in the internal market, had to remain unchanged for six months. These prices were generally reviewed in the spring and the autumn, with the arrival of the traders from China. Thus if the Chinese withheld an important commodity such as raw silk, or brought it in quantities far inferior to the demand, the price went up sharply. At that point, the Chinese flooded the market with raw silk, which had to be purchased at the established price. By cleverly alternating these phases, the traders realized enormous profits. Having control over approximately 80 per cent of Chinese vessels, Zheng Chenggong could exert considerable influence

[22] Fu Lo-shu (1966), p. 436, n.115 esp. p. 32.
[23] See Yang Yanjie (1984), pp. 221–238; Cheng K'o-ch'eng (1990), pp. 217–244.
[24] Carioti (2010), pp. 62–75.

on the Japanese economy and throughout South East Asia, gaining a clear supremacy over the VOC.[25]

The latter sought to benefit as much as possible from its exclusive concession on Japanese territory as sole European operator. However, as we have said, in the early years its volume of trade was inferior to that of the Chinese. Another factor played a significant role: most of the bases on which it depended for supplies were partially controlled by the Zheng organization, aggravating the Dutch position of subaltern partner. Therefore, the Dutch did not hesitate to attack and rob Chinese vessels off the Japanese coast, as well as in the trading routes of South East Asia and around Taiwan.[26]

LOOKING FOR ALLIES: ZHENG'S REQUEST TO JAPAN

In such an extremely delicate and difficult situation, Japan could only adopt a careful and prudent strategy, with the purpose of keeping the precarious economic balance established in Nagasaki, on which depended foreign trade and, in part, national trade. The Manchu invasion of China, the collapse of Beijing and the progressive advance of Qing troops on the south gave the authorities considerable concern and recalled attempts of invasion conducted by another 'barbaric' dynasty, the Yuan (1274 and 1281).

At the end of 1645, the first request for intervention in favour of the Ming reached Nagasaki. The bearer, a Chinese merchant called Lin Gao, appeared before the authorities in Nagasaki with two missives from the continent, signed by Cui Zhi, a loyal officer in the service of Zheng Zhilong's militia; in fact, the request was submitted on Zhilong's orders. Troops and arms to support the Ming forces were solicited. The *bugyō* of Nagasaki, Yamazaki Gonpachirō (1593–1650), immediately delivered the messages to Edo, where Hayashi Razan (1583–1680) translated the letters and handed them to the third *shōgun*, Tokugawa Iemitsu (1622–1651). After a series of consultations, it was decided to send an ambiguous reply, in order to gain time and reject the appeal but with formal reasons.[27]

Nagasaki was at the mercy of economic reprisals and, at least in this first phase, had very little room for manoeuvre, above all in the sphere of maritime trading. Actually, in the whole field of foreign policy, the *bakufu*

---

[25] Nagazumi Yōko (1988) pp. 6–13.
[26] *Ibid.*, p. 9.
[27] Concerning the request for aid sent to Japan, see Hayashi Fukusai (1912–1913), pp. 1–98; pp. 390–438; Ishihara Michihiro (1945); Tsuji Zennosuke (1942), pp. 640–660; Kimiya Yasuhiko (1955), pp. 640–647.

had to maintain a carefully pondered balancing act, keeping a close watch on developments in China itself and proceeding with great circumspection in its policy of non-intervention.

Nevertheless, in spite of the failure of previous requests for aid sent either directly or through intermediaries by Zheng Zhilong, the Zheng had not given up making appeals to Japan to launch a military intervention in favour of the Ming. In 1648, Zheng Cai had sent a missive to the authorities of Nagasaki in which he proposed to trade in Chinese medicinal herbs and silk in exchange for Japanese arms. A letter from Zheng Chenggong accompanied this communication in which, stressing the strong links he felt with the archipelago by reason of his birth, Chenggong asked for tens of thousands of soldiers to deploy against the barbarous Manchu.

Towards the end of December 1651 or at the beginning of the new year, Zheng Chenggong addressed himself once again to Japan. This was when he was gaining overall command of the Zheng organization and the powers of resistance of the southern Ming seemed to be gaining strength: Zheng Chenggong emerged victorious from the prestigious campaign launched to succour emperor Yongli. The outcome of the dynastic struggle in China was still in doubt and a complete reversal of fortunes could not be excluded, albeit when Zheng Zhilong defected such a possibility had been considered remote. The authorities of Edo had in fact been considering granting Zheng Zhilong's requests for intervention when they had received the unexpected news of his ill-advised surrender to the Manchu. Continuing to ignore such appeals could have proved a risky and counterproductive policy for the archipelago, especially if Zheng Chenggong finally emerged as victor over the Manchu. It was certainly not a good idea to antagonize this powerful and fearsome commercial partner, especially given that he might one day become a political interlocutor if China ever threw off foreign rule. Moreover, Japan was well aware of the significance of the Chinese traders' role in the international affairs of the archipelago through the community of Nagasaki. The influence of Zheng Chenggong on foreign trade was substantial, and the *bakufu* could not ignore this. This in itself was reason enough not to strain relations by rigid or ostentatious refusals. In answer to his letter, Zheng Chenggong obtained metals and arms to strengthen his armies, but no Japanese troops were sent to swell the loyalist ranks.[28]

The subsequent appeals, in 1658 and 1660, were dealt with in the same way, the authorities in Edo preferring to remain nominally neutral while giving token help to Zheng Chenggong. This position was dictated for their own ends rather than signaling a changed attitude towards the

[28] Hayashi Fukusai (1912–1913), pp. 1–98, 390–438; Ishihara Michihiro (1945); Tsuji Zennosuke (1942), pp. 640–660; Kimiya Yasuhiko (1955), pp. 640–647.

Ming, with whom, in spite of the constant efforts of Ieyasu, it proved impossible to re-establish official contact. Thus Japan sought to support Zheng Chenggong without compromising itself: more than once, acting on explicit orders, the Japanese officials responsible for vessels in transit in the port of Nagasaki turned away those few Chinese traders who owed allegiance to the Manchu (recognizable by the humiliating pony-tail), thereby in practice granting Zheng's ships a monopoly.

The discriminating caution adopted was an accurate reflection of the delicate circumstances in which the archipelago found itself. Quite apart from the risks involved, direct intervention by the Japanese in the Chinese conflict in favour of the Ming and alongside the Zheng would inevitably have modified relations with the Dutch and thus would have led to total dependence on Chinese traders and hence Zheng Chenggong. Conversely, a rift with the Zheng would have left Japan at the mercy of the policies of the United Company, giving the latter a dangerous hold over the economy. For if, on the one hand, Japan was obliged to entertain two competing powers in Nagasaki, with all the awkward consequences, on the other hand this represented a position of force: one could be played off against the other to the benefit of the archipelago.

With great skill and foresight, Japan pursued its policy of equilibrium, refusing to intervene in the military struggle on the continent. A clear taking of sides, for or against the Ming, would have upset the delicate balance imposed by the simultaneous presence of the Chinese and Dutch in Nagasaki.[29]

SOME FINAL REMARKS

The birth and later the formal establishment of the Chinese community of Nagasaki, was directly connected with the *bakufu* political positions regarding the foreign relations and sea trade. The control on the maritime commerce carried on by the Overseas Chinese in Japan was in fact essential for the central authorities, from many points of view. On the other hand, the Chinese community of Nagasaki was an important element to balance the Dutch VOC in Deshima. This important role of mediation lasted for the whole of the so-called *sakoku* period. Moreover, the complexity of the Nagasaki community's structure and organization demonstrates without doubt Tokugawa authorities' deep concern toward the Overseas Chinese in Japan.[30]

[29] Carioti (1998), pp. 89–106.
[30] See Carioti (2006c), pp. 1–34.

The Overseas Community of Nagasaki, on which the Zheng organization could exert a deep influence, played a fundamental role in the economic, political and military decisions taken by the Tokugawa *bakufu*. The requests sent by the Zhengs – or by other Ming supporters – for Japanese military intervention in favour of the Ming continued to reach Japan: there were 17 in total, the last being sent in 1686. In 1683, with the Qing conquest of Taiwan by Shi Lang, the collapse of the Zheng regime on the island had meant the pacification of China under Manchu rule. Soon after, in 1689, the Chinese community of Nagasaki was formalized into the *Tōjin Yashiki* ('Residence of the Tang people') of Nagasaki.

The *bakufu* intended to limit the enourmous flux of Chinese migration into Nagasaki, due to the establishment of the Qing empire. Therefore, the Japanese authorities imposed severe restrictions to the arrival of the Chinese ships, and confined the Chinese community into a limited area. They imposed strict control over the overseas Chinese, their activities and their sea trade, in order to reduce the import flux and finally free the Japanese inner market from the dependence on Chinese commerce.

PART II

High value-added services and metropolitan dynamism

4. Regional Headquarters for Multinational Enterprises in Chinese cities: strategies for location

Christine Hung

INTRODUCTION

In an attempt to attract the Regional Headquarters (RHQs) of Multinational Enterprises (MNEs) to Mainland China, the Central Government (Beijing) is not only faced with competition from regional hubs, such as Singapore and Hong Kong, but also from well-established internal rivals, such as the Shanghai and Guangzhou municipal governments.[1]

More and more MNEs have been heading towards Chinese cities such as Shanghai, Guangzhou, Shenzhen and Beijing. The 'Headquarters Economy' of these cities 'extensively attracts the MNEs, international financial centers, enterprises, and groups to set up the head offices and the R&D, operational and procurement centers in order to develop the Headquarters Economy'.[2] Understanding the location strategies and decision-making of MNEs is a key task for developing their global markets. The main questions revolve around localisation and local competitiveness of enterprises, the impact of regionalism, conglomeration and industrial clustering, mode of entry, strategic location choice,[3] relocation and public functions in China.

The RHQs that have been set up are between the global headquarters of MNEs and national markets; they enable overseas MNEs to better understand, for example, local consumers or business practices. American, Japanese and European MNEs, such as GE, Siemens, Hitachi and Rhodia have located their RHQs in a number of different Chinese cities.

In this chapter, the location strategies of RHQs of MNEs in different Chinese cities will be examined. It consists of three main sections. The first

---

[1]   Kroymann (2005), pp. 67–94.
[2]   Beijing Central Business District Administration Commission (2005) 'Headquarter Economy in Beijing'.
[3]   Wanner (2006), with modifications.

describes the relationship between the headquarters of MNEs and their RHQs in China. The following section examines the complex nature of the advantages of location for MNEs. The final section analyses the location strategies of RHQs in China and evaluates the important effects for setting up 'RHQs' of MNEs in different Chinese cities.

THE RELATIONSHIP BETWEEN MNEs AND THEIR RHQs IN CHINA

The Definition of RHQ

An RHQ is often defined as an entity at the top of the regional unit, including all activities of the various business units, to take full responsibility for the overall profitability and success of this regional unit.[4] The RHQ has opened new possibilities for an MNE to coordinate and centralize the location of its business activities in China.

In 2002, for example, the Shanghai municipal government signalled its intent to establish the city as the preferred location for RHQs of MNEs by issuing 'Tentative Provisions on Encouraging the Establishment of Regional Headquarters by Foreign Multinational Corporations'. The Tentative Provisions include a provision for lowering the threshold for establishing an RHQ in Shanghai and have made it a more attractive base for the 'mind and management' of MNEs with projects in Asia.

In Shanghai, the Ministry of Foreign Trade and Economic Cooperation has given the definition of an RHQ as follows: (1) an investment or a management 'Foreign-Invested Enterprise' (FIE) (typically in the form of a 'Wholly Foreign Owned Enterprise (WFOE) approved by the Shanghai municipality; (2) one that is invested in by an MNE; (3) one that becomes the only organization in the region authorized by the MNE to exercise overall management and service over such MNEs' other subsidiaries in the region; and (4) the authority of which is obtained through its investment in such subsidiaries or through the delegation of power by the MNE. The Provisions require that a Shanghai-based RHQ is the only one in China or the region, thus placing Shanghai[5] in direct competition with Beijing,[6] Guangzhou and other cities in Asia.[7]

---

4   *Ibid.*
5   Cai (2003), pp. 1–4.
6   Leong (2008).
7   Wang (2003), pp. 1–4.

The Role of RHQs

Barlett and Ghoshal raise two theoretical approaches which focus on the role of administrative and managerial functions.[8] The first theory developed by Stopford and Wells[9] draws on the strategies of organizations and it is argued that the MNE with products sold internationally would need an organization based on a product line. Those with a high percentage of sales abroad would prefer an organization based on a geographical area, for example, an RHQ, while those with both large product diversity and a high volume of sales abroad would choose a matrix organization.

The second theoretical approach, as formalized by Doz and Prahalad explains the management of the RHQ as a balancing act between two environmental influences: global integration and local responsiveness.[10] It can be illustrated by the fact that General Motors has established its RHQ in Shanghai, in recognition of how important China has become in its plans to expand GM's global industry leadership and has had a strong presence for this dynamic market growth. GM headquarters have been interested in the areas of finance, product planning, communications, human resources, purchasing, public policy, legal and information systems and services throughout the vast region of China.

Regionalization between Globalization and Localization

Lasserre[11] describes development strategy and regional integration as the core tasks of RHQs that are in charge of shaping the regional perspective, initiating business, and setting and controlling targets (see Table 4.1).

The influences of the RHQ on the region correspond to the power of the headquarters and the national units as Morrison et al.[12] and Blackwell et al.[13] have confirmed. RHQs can therefore contribute to shaping a regional perspective. The decision to set up an RHQ as a special organizational unit can also be interpreted as a deliberate transfer of the regional leadership to the MNE managers assigned to it.

Two trends have been observed in the study of the regionalization of MNEs and RHQs. The first is the result of the strategic and organizational shift in large and diversified MNEs towards a combination of global and local strategies alongside a more centralized organization with

---

[8] Barlett and Ghoshal (1991), pp. 5–16, with modifications.
[9] Stopford and Wells (1972).
[10] Doz and Prahalad (1987).
[11] Lasserre (1996), pp. 30–37, with modifications.
[12] Morrison et al. (1991), pp. 17–29, with modifications.
[13] Blackwell et al. (1992),pp. 31–43, with modifications.

the locus of power mainly exercised at the headquarters. If MNEs have difficulties in implementing these globally oriented strategies, they will start to pay more attention to regional strategies and this, in turn, has required an intermediate organizational solution – the establishment of RHQs.[14]

In 2008, for example, General Electric set up five RHQs in China to further tap into a huge market that boasts enormous business potential. The move was in line with its new strategy because China is not only a large market; it is also a significant research and development base and therefore a fundamental foothold for GE's future development. The RHQs will help existing functional departments in different regions to further explore the market and to develop more China-oriented products.[15]

The second trend reflects the geopolitical environment in China, particularly political forces and concerns the creation of geographic regions bound together by preferential trade and investment regimes. MNEs have reacted to these signals by increasing regional trade and investment. This is accompanied by an increasing awareness of the similarities of markets in China and the need to exploit these as well as geographic proximity in terms of marketing, manufacturing, finance and so on. To do this more systematically, RHQs are often established to integrate the diverse activities of the local subsidiaries whose influence is limited to the boundaries of the country in which they operate.

Another example, 6WIND multinational enterprise, has been a leader in embedded networking software and has expanded its Beijing office into an RHQ for the operations of sales, customers support, marketing and R&D in East Asia. The MNE's decision to select a city such as Beijing to set up its regional hub was prompted by increasing commitments to partners and customers in the region in recognition of the importance of China and its neighbouring countries for the mid-to-long-term strategic growth of the company.

LOCATION ADVANTAGES FOR MNEs

Dunning's eclectic paradigm has become the leading conceptual framework for the analysis of international business enterprises. The first important contribution of this conceptual framework is that the location-specific characteristics that contribute to competitive advantages are recognized

14 Schütte (1998), pp. 102–137.
15 *China Daily* (2007).

Table 4.1   Location advantages

Outcome of location advantages (Cost, marketing, efficiency and strategic asset)	Unit of Analysis		
	Beijing	Shanghai	Guangzhou
RHQ (L)	1	3	5
Subsidiaries (O)	2	4	6
MNE (I)	7	8	9

Source: Dunning (1992), with modifications.

as varying for different sites, sectors and MNEs.[16] The paradigm thereby allows us to span the three units of analysis (see Table 4.1). It is interesting to observe at the city level how the location advantages appear to include elements such as the MNE's experience with RHQs and the involvement of subsidiaries, distance variables, attitudes to risk diversification and attitudes towards the decentralization of functions such as R&D. GE, for example, has set up five RHQs in Shenyang (northeast), Wuhan (central), Chengdu (southwest), Xi'an (northwest) and Guangzhou (south).[17]

The second contribution is that it allows the identification of the location advantages of four different determinants of international business: cost effectiveness, market, efficiency and strategic assets.[18]

Seeking Cost Effectiveness

Cost effectiveness-seeking for RHQs occurs when MNEs identify specific Chinese locations as an attractive proposition at the lowest real cost. The cost effectiveness based on the advantages of the location shapes the potential for exports to neighboring markets, develops substantial local sourcing capability and reduces production costs. These requirements attract MNEs to sites or areas (see Figure 4.1) where labour costs are low. The most important influence on the cost/supply-oriented investment of MNEs in China is the potential for the development of substantial local sourcing capability in the local market.[19] However, this may in turn improve the location advantages of MNEs and RHQs, both for the production and exports of goods which use imported resources as a high quality input. An RHQ should therefore not be viewed solely as an

[16]   Dunning (1992), with modifications.
[17]   *China Daily* (2007).
[18]   Dunning (1998), pp. 115–136, with modifications.
[19]   Bulcke, Esteves and Zhang (2003), pp. 11–34, with modifications.

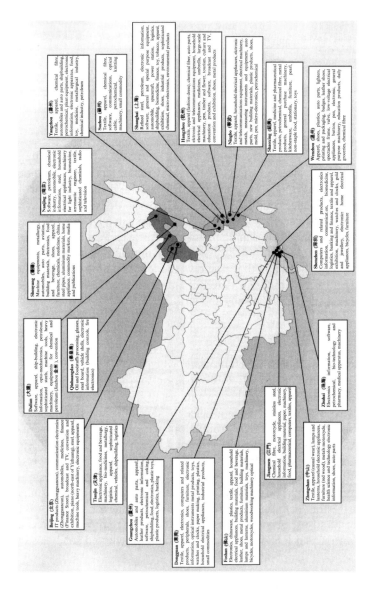

Beijing (北京): IT products (Zhongguancun), communication electronics software, peripherals, shoes, furniture, electronic information, optical instruments, medicines, finance (Finance Street), bicycle and TV, conversion exhibition, piano (north-east of Yizhuang), steel, apparel, machine tools, heavy machinery, electronic equipments

Tianjin (天津): Electronic appliance, food and beverage, machinery, bio-medicines, metallurgy, logistics, apparel, sophisticated chemical, vehicles, shipbuilding, logistics

Guangzhou (广州): Automobiles and auto parts, apparel, leather products, electronic information, software, petrochemical and coking, shipbuilding, food, electronics, household electrical appliances, industrial products, plastic products, logistics, banking

Dongguan (东莞): Textile, apparel, electronics, computers and related products, peripherals, shoes, furniture, electronic information, optical instruments metal products, toys, watches and clocks, paper making, printing, plastics, household electrical appliances, industrial products, small commodities

Foshan (佛山): Electronics, chinaware, plastics, textile, apparel, household electrical appliances, building materials, food and beverage, leather, shoes, metal products, furniture, building materials, lamps and lanterns, aluminium materials, toys, machinery, bicycles, motorcycles, woodworking machinery optical

Zhongshan (中山): Textile, apparel (casual wear), lamps and lanterns, household electronic appliances, furniture (red wood), metals motorcycle, health science and technology electronic information, shoes, auto parts

Dalian (大连): Software, apparel, ship-building, electronic information, opto-mechatronics, petroleum, sophisticated steel, machine tools, heavy machinery, equipments for chemical and petroleum (Jinzhou 锦州), conversion

Qinhuangdao (秦皇岛): Oil and (foodstuff processing, glasses, steel board, vehicle shells, electronic information (building controls, fire electronics)

Shenyang (沈阳): Machine equipments, metallurgy, automobiles, auto parts, aviation, building materials, electronics, food and beverage, shoes, apparel, furniture, chemicals, medicines, china, steel pipes, aluminium materials, home appliance, commodity markets, media and publications

Nanjing (南京): Software, petroleum, chemical industry, automobile, electronic information, steel, household electrical appliances, machinery for light industry, biomedicine, aeronautic engineer, textile, sophisticated chemicals, radio and television

Yangzhou (扬州): Textile, apparel, chemical fibre, electronic and auto parts, shipbuilding, petrochemical, plant equipment, electronic information, electronic apparatus, food, toy, medicine, metallurgical industry, chemical industry, petroleum

Suzhou (苏州): Textile, apparel, chemical fibre, software, communications, optical cable, petrochemical, knitting machinery, small commodity

Shanghai (上海): Refined steel, petroleum, chemical fibre, automobile and auto parts, shipbuilding, power station, shipbuilding, biomedicine, finance, toy, tobacco, apparel, machinery, pen, timber and flower, tourism, culture and education products, software, broadcast and TV, convention and exhibition, shoes, metal products

Hangzhou (杭州): Textile, apparel (fashion dress), chemical fiber, auto parts, software, general and special purpose equipment, household electrical appliances, medicines, umbrella, large-scale metals, measuring instruments and equipment, auto parts, new building materials, plastic products, shoes, mold, pen, micro-electronics, environmental products

Ningbo (宁波): Textile, apparel, household electrical appliance, electronic and telecommunications equipment; electrical machinery, metals, measuring instruments and equipment, auto parts, new building materials, plastic products, shoes, mold, pen, micro-electronics, petrochemical

Shaoxing (绍兴): Textile, apparel, medicine and pharmaceutical products, petrochemical, chemical fibre, metal products, general purchase; household electrical appliances, umbrella, furniture, pearl, non-staple food, stationary, toys

Wenzhou (温州): Apparel, shoes, plastics, auto parts, lighters, printing and packaging, badges, leather shoes, spectacles frame, valve, low-voltage electrical appliance, button, pen, electronic, general purpose machinery, education products, daily groceries, chemical fibre

Shenzhen (深圳): Computers and related products, electronics information, communication, biomedicine, logistics, banking and finance, textile and apparel, exhibition, machinery, watches and clocks, gold and jewellery, electronic home electrical appliances, bicycle, furniture

Zhuhai (珠海): Electronics, information, software, petrochemical, bio-technology, pharmacy, medical apparatus, machinery

Jiangmen (江门): Chemical fibre, motorcycle, stainless steel, household electrical appliances, electronic information, building materials, food, pharmaceutical, computers, textiles, apparel

Source: Ni Pengfei et al., 'Annual Report on Urban Competitiveness', No. 3, Li and Fung Research Centre, Social Sciences Academic Press; M. Enright et al. (2005) *Regional Powerhouse: The Greater Pearl River Delta and the Rise of China*, John Wiley & Sons (Asia) Pte Ltd.

Figure 4.1   Selected industrial clusters in China

outcome of any existing location advantages but it may also be instrumental in the creation of new location advantages.[20]

Seeking a Market

In China, the market-seeking success of an RHQ depends on its foothold gains, the extension of the parent company's geographical market and securing of the dominant share in the market within a specific sector. Furthermore, the market-seeking role of RHQs extends the potential for expanding the exports of the parent company.

The location strategies of RHQs have the major advantage of taking into account the demand of the neighbouring territories. The market-seeking advantages are more complex to reconcile with location strategies because flows of information and goods can often be observed, reflecting sophisticated packages of location advantages and resulting in complex network of linkages among the various RHQs and subsidiaries (see Figure 4.1).

Seeking Efficiency

Efficiency-seeking determines the product/market diversification, learning about market and business management in China, the sharpening of industry structure and norms and, finally, the economies of scale in production. The efficiency-seeking leads to even higher complexity as regards the location advantages of the RHQs involved. This determinant is usually the creation of a strategy at the RHQ and subsidiaries levels because it reflects a rationalization of the operations of an MNE and typically a specialization of the various RHQs and subsidiaries that comprises its internal network, thereby leading to an increase of both intermediate subsidiaries and RHQ.[21] Here, it is important to understand the role of RHQs as 'globally rationalized', with the RHQ performing a particular set of activities in the chain, or a regional or world product mandate.

MNEs are mostly specialized in technology and capital-intensive industries. Their operations in China are often of a 'stand alone' nature and display economies of scale in production. They rationalize their Chinese or even Asian business done from China by creating integrated management tools and structures, for instance, by the establishment of RHQs.[22]

---

[20] Rugman and Verbeke (2005), pp. 223–250, with modifications.
[21] Cantwell (1994), pp. 303–328, with modifications.
[22] Bulcke et al. (2003).

Strategic Asset-seeking

Strategic asset-seeking determines the building of a broader multi-regional or national presence. It also allows strategic responses in order to avoid and/or reduce competition, and the following of key customers in order to maintain relations. For example, the R&D performed in China constitutes the key location advantages for the MNE and the RHQ. To the extent that the acquired assets sourced from a host country, for example China, are also linked to a localized innovation system, the MNE as a whole may get access to spillover effects from that innovation system.[23]

Strategies for avoiding and reducing competition are quite important for MNEs and RHQs, seeking to enter into a new market. The 'follow the leader behaviour' is typical of MNEs, meaning that they have reacted to the increasing presence of their competitors in the Chinese market.

LOCATION STRATEGIES OF RHQs IN CHINA

Table 4.1 provides a simple framework which allows us to classify these different conceptual perspectives on the basis of two key parameters. The first parameter is related to the unit of analysis. Here, the focus is on location advantages of Chinese cities. The second parameter makes a distinction between MNEs, RHQs and subsidiaries as the outcome of specific location advantages. Here, it should be emphasized that RHQs may themselves influence location strategies.

To highlight the location strategies of the RHQs in China, this section is divided into five points that are directly linked: (a) Chinese regional networks and global supply chains; (b) integration, coordination and performance of RHQs in China; (c) headquarters economy development boom in China; (d) strategic decision processes and opportunism, and (e) strategies for the location of RHQs: comparing the efficacy of Chinese cities.

Chinese Regional Networks and Global Supply Chains

The regional network configuration implies that some activities have to be rationalized; others have to be expanded and will be located near the markets being serviced. This demands an integration of the different parts of the value chain on a local, regional and global basis,[24] including:

---

23   Rugman and Verbeke (2005).
24   Vandermerwe (1993), pp. 55–61, with modifications.

- headquarters – centralized, where a Chinese-foreign team can be best located;
- management support centers – attracted to a location with good technical and information infrastructures;
- R&D – where good connections with research and production centers exist;
- manufacturing and logistics – in areas with good infrastructure and utilities, quality and costs of materials, as well as labour and transportation facilities;
- marketing – partly centralized and partly decentralized depending on type of function, including a rather decentralized account management;
- sales and services – regional and local presence required to better serve key customers and end users.

Concerning the location strategies of RHQs of MNEs in China, the former judge their achievements with regard to the choice of location strategies from a regional perspective, the problems concerning the regional integration of the MNE strategies and their use of systems for managing regional operations in China. The analysis of these aspects will allow for an overall assessment of the strength of a RHQ. The perceived usefulness of RHQs and expectations of their role in the future are further explored.[25] Also, the RHQs have an important role in shaping the regional perspective of MNEs but have a negligible influence on the creation of synergies among local subsidiaries.[26]

Field studies conducted by the author in July 2006 suggest the role of RHQs, especially European RHQs, differs widely from the American and Japanese RHQs established in China. For example, American RHQs emphasized their roles as a way to integrate their Chinese activities more actively, and improved efficiency and effectiveness. GM and Ford felt that their local subsidiaries in China could gain significant advantages and benefits from working together and used their RHQs for this purpose. Japanese RHQs, such as Hitachi or Asahi Kasei, felt that their product lines needed to be better tailored to the Chinese market. Thus, RHQs are expected to play a role in coordinating the country-wide organization or in tailoring strategies to a particular regional market.

---

[25] Schütte (1998).
[26] Van Heck and Verdin (2001), pp. 133–134.

Integration, Coordination and Performance of RHQs in China

RHQs are defined as organization units concerned with and involved in the integration and coordination of activities of the MNEs within a given geographical region, and representing the link between the region (subsidiary) and the headquarters. For instance, MNEs intended to move their RHQs to Shanghai and some have even planned to upgrade their Chinese RHQs into Asian headquarters. Another illustration is Dupont, which has overseas R&D centers outside the United States. The Dupont R&D center in China targets the Asian market and is the major component of Dupont global R&D. This stresses the active strategic role taken by the RHQs and de-emphasizes the original rationale for their location that embraced many reasons such as fiscal marketing, financial representative offices, or R&D centers where they were integrating and coordinating different activities across borders (see Table 4.2).

Headquarters Economy Strategies Booming in China

Shanghai
Researcher Chen Wei of the Pudong Reform and Development Institute has noted that the headquarters economy has boomed in China, reflecting the location strategies of the MNEs that have already had footholds in China (see Table 4.3). Beijing, Shanghai and Guangzhou were the first three sites chosen by MNEs for their RHQs. MNEs are the major force pushing forward China's headquarters economy. Kang Hui Jun, Deputy Head of the Pudong New Area (Shanghai) has pointed out that many MNEs intend to move their RHQs to Shanghai, and some even plan to upgrade their China headquarters into Asia headquarters. Simultaneously, China's 'headquarters economy' has been rating 35 major Chinese cities (including, Shenzhen, Tianjin and Wuhan) in accordance with their capability and potential to spur the headquarters economy development,[27] for example, as in the case of Shanghai.[28]

Beijing
In 2008, the first association of multinational headquarters was established in the eastern district of Chaoyang in Beijing.[29] The role of the association is expected to help RHQs and to consolidate Chaoyang's leading position in attracting overseas investments. The association was jointly

---

[27] Xin (2005).
[28] Cai (2003); Wang (2003); Leong (2008).
[29] Guo (2008), p. 10.

Table 4.2   Location strategies for RHQs in China (some examples)

Company	Sector	Regional headquarters	Strategies of location RHQ	Origin
Rhodia	Chemical	Shanghai	It has locally managed the sales, marketing, a profit center and the laboratory of R&D in Asia.	France
Nokia	Mobile phone	Beijing	It has formed the Nokia's largest mobile phone park in the world and has already moved its operational departments, China R&D Center, Product Design and Mobile Phone Production to the new park.	Finland
Ford	Automobile	Shanghai	Ford's China RHQ in Shanghai (Pudong New Area) has been an indication of the growing trend of MNE.	USA
Asahi Kasei	Plastics	Shanghai	Asahi Kasei RHQ (Shanghai) Co., Ltd. (BMS) serves for performing business, management operations, providing services, supporting the advancement and growth of the group and the development of new businesses in China.	Japan
Siemens	Industrial conglo-merate	Shanghai	RHQ integrates departments of management, administration, sales, marketing, R&D, service and training for increasing business in China and Asia.	Germany

Note: The explication from many directors of MNEs and RHQs in China.

Table 4.3   Chinese policies for MNEs to set up RHQs in Shanghai

Conditions	Policies
Achievement	RHQs in Shanghai Pudong New Area: The Area has lured more than 13,000 foreign enterprises from more than 100 countries and regions, with over 100 from the world's top 500 companies, a total investment of US$25 billion.
Forecast	A total of 500 MNEs in 2010.
Rules	The RHQ Rules have demonstrated that the Shanghai government's commitment to compete with other cities in Asia and strengthen Shanghai as a regional management, service and financial centre for MNE. The new legislation is effective to attract more MNE to set up headquarters with national laws and regulations in charge of taxation, customs, and foreign exchange and banking among others, share the same commitment as the Shanghai government.
Functions	Transnational procurement or logistics centers were set up by RHQ to trade internationally, and those with R&D functions for preferential treatments and for the high-technology sector.

Source: Cai (2003), Wang (2003) and Leong (2008).

proposed by the district government together with research institutions and was co-founded by the RHQs of 36 MNEs, firms and companies. The organization aims to provide exchange of information, spread knowledge of the latest regulations and assist communication between companies and governments. Many MNEs have also chosen Beijing Central Business District (CBD) as the place to locate their RHQ. According to this decision, the new title 'headquarters economy' has become a popular phrase in Beijing. The impact has put Chaoyang and CBD in the vanguard of headquarters economy in China. In 2008, 195 Fortune 500 enterprises started operations in Chaoyang, accounting for 43.8 per cent of the total in Beijing, with 85 per cent of those clustered in the CBD. Among them are 17 RHQs recognized by the Ministry of Commerce. The headquarters' operations have contributed to nearly 30 per cent of the district government revenues in 2008. Chaoyang has maintained annual double digit growth over the past few years, topping Beijing's districts in indices ranging from retail sales of consumer goods, fixed asset investment and government revenues. In 2007, Chaoyang district generated about 36.89 billion euros in business revenues that resulted in 11.63 billion euros in profit, an increase of 47.8 per cent and 14.4 per cent over 2006. The sector registered an increase of 18.2 per cent year-on-year in business revenue in the first five months of 2008, when 13.45 billion euros were generated;

profits totaled 3.14 billion euros, three times more than in the same period in 2007.

Strategic Decision Processes and Opportunism

Teece[30] and Williamson[31] make the assumption that the MNE's 'administrative heritage' (such as the establishment of RHQs in a foreign country) of location-investment decisions affects the investment process. This explains why MNEs face similar environmental conditions (for example, Beijing, Shanghai and Guangzhou) and having similar characteristics (design, sourcing, production, marketing, distribution, sales, after-sales services, R&D) in terms of proprietary assets, but may still choose a different site. RHQs have an organizational structure allowing the separation of strategic and operational decisions and prefer to engage in the local economy because of the operational costs advantages (Factor 1) of a large hierarchy. In particular, the structure of MNE-RHQ-subsidiary interactions may substantially affect the outcomes of the investment process (Factor 2). In other words, the important location decision in the RHQ investment process is the design of a decision process which allows an objective assessment of: (1) the costs and benefits (Factor 3) associated with the different location strategies for each project and (2) the relative net benefits associated with the optimal location for all projects under consideration.[32] At a strategic level, decision-making can be centralized (RHQ) and/or decentralized (MNE/Subsidiary) depending upon the optimal location for exploiting the proprietary assets of the RHQ and the MNE.

Transaction costs theory allows us to determine whether or not the strategic location in a RHQ can be considered efficient (Factor 4). This model constitutes an extension of internalization and localization theory since it specifies the conditions to be fulfilled by the investment process in a RHQ in order to guarantee optimal resource allocation (Factor 5) decisions. There are four types of the location-investment of RHQ to be identified (see Table 4.4).

The vertical axis in Table 4.4 measures the degree of centralization and decentralization of the strategic investment processes. These processes include the design, evaluation and choice of investment projects. This axis reflects the execution of specific activities in the investment processes by different levels in the hierarchy of the MNE, including the level of RHQ management.

---

[30] Teece (1985), pp. 21–45, with modifications.
[31] Williamson (1981), pp. 1537–1568, with modifications.
[32] D'Cruz et al. (2005[1995]), pp. 114–117, with modifications.

*Table 4.4   Strategic decision-making processes and opportunism
              (location)*

	Opportunism	
Strategic decision-marketing processes (location)	Low	High
Centralized (RHQ)	1	3 (safeguards, global and local strategic development, benefits of integration, national responsiveness, resource allocation and control)
Decentralized (MNE and Subsidiaries)	2	4 (product-market, requirement of integration, national responsiveness, structure, culture, resource allocation and control)

Source: D'Cruz et al. (2005), with modifications.

Table 4.5   Control over subsidiaries operations in RHQs

Enhancing Factors	Impeding Factors
Technology, management, export marketing, finances	Subsidiaries relationship; extent of autonomy of subsidiary
Shared strategic vision and competitive strategy	Host government regulations
Systems that recognize contributions to global and local strategies	Presence of joint venture partners

Source: Doz and Prahalad (1987), with modifications, p. 166.

The horizontal axis of Table 4.4 deals with the transaction cost concept of 'opportunism' that presents the practice of advantage opportunities (Factor 6). It shows the presence or absence of safeguards (Factor 7) in the structural and cultural context of the organization. Such safeguards are necessary to protect the investment processes against the impact of local rationality. The choice between structural (formal) (Factor 8) and cultural (informal) (Factor 9) coordination and control systems (see Table 4.5) (Factor 10) in RHQs, MNEs and subsidiaries is important.[33]

The main reason for the problem of control is that the case of a centralized and decentralized system aims at the achievement of high national

[33]   *Ibid.*

responsiveness (Factor 11) (see Table 4.5), the knowledge of RHQ managers as to the expected costs and benefits of investment projects is superior to that of the MNE manager. The reasons for this include the information asymmetry between RHQ and MNE managers concerning market characteristics (Factor 12), competitive advantage (Factor 13), investment climate (Factor 14) of the foreign environment, and the geographic distance (Factor 15) between MNEs and RHQs. Then, through cultural safeguards such as extensive socialization (Factor 16) and training (Factor 17), the goals of RHQ managers can be made consistent with the goals of MNE management.

Strategies for the Location of RHQs: Comparing the Efficacy of Chinese Cities

Table 4.5 suggests that within each of its parts normal financially-based net present value measurements about MNEs, RHQs and subsidiaries can be made. In other words, all the usual location investment considerations about taxes (Factor 18), exchange rates (Factor 19), cost of capital (Factor 20), trade barriers (Factor 21) are secondary to the prior critical strategic decision as to which part's location is relevant in order to exploit the proprietary assets of the RHQ.

RHQs positioned in the first part allow the development of global and local strategies aimed at reaping the benefits of integration. The processes (Table 4.4) have been presented in favor of such a centralization of strategic decision-making processes (location), which allows the integration of strategies for RHQs across several local markets in China (Table 4.2).

Concerning the degree of national responsiveness (Table 4.4) of MNEs, this may well have to be initiated at the RHQ level. It should be recognized, however, that the decentralization of strategic location activities towards the subsidiary level may initiate problems of fragmentation if structural and cultural safeguards are not carefully designed. The issue of cultural safeguards in the next section (Table 4.4) is particularly important if regional or world product mandates have been assigned.[34] In this case, resource allocation decisions, taken at the RHQ level, result from an extensive strategic location confrontation between the view of RHQ and MNE managers (Table 4.4).

As a result of the Chinese government's conservation approach, many MNEs have chosen to keep their RHQs in China, HK or Singapore in order to expand their Asian market base. Although there have been

---

[34]   Douglas and Rugman (1986), with modifications.

several highly publicized RHQ relocations to China, most MNEs are not attracted by the current environment there. The reasons include:

1   foreign exchange control requirements on RHQs are as strict as those on any other type of company;
2   import and export control, customs clearance, immigration and visa processes are highly restrictive and complicated;
3   tax and import duties are still very high compared with Hong Kong or Singapore; and
4   infrastructure, freedom of information, rule of law, and quality of life in China are still considered inferior to either Hong Kong or Singapore.

The magazine 'China Law & Practice'[35] shows three factors: economic policies, domestic market size, and infrastructure for the location of RHQs in China (see Table 4.6). Chinese economic policies are seen as the most crucial factor for deciding the location for an RHQ. This chapter has explained the reason why the size of the domestic market is the second most important aspect indicated by MNEs for their location decision-making. Corporations tended to think highly of China's infrastructure and the government policies that have determined their RHQ location decisions. The emergence of the new factor showed that MNEs have a better understanding of the Asian environment and can comfortably operate in different cities (Table 4.6). While regional management still remains an issue, foreign exchange controls in China also need to be more flexible than or similar to those in Hong Kong.

The municipalities of Beijing, Shanghai and Guangzhou, where most of the MNEs operating in China are located, are paying great attention to the above issues. Beijing has attracted the most MNEs. Shanghai, however, has arguably the best chance to compete with Hong Kong and Singapore for RHQs due to the concentration of new foreign investment in the area, the better quality of its infrastructure, work and living environment for foreign employees. For example, the Shanghai municipal government set up a special task force to study the feasibility of policies directed specifically at RHQs. The task force sent delegations abroad, including to Singapore. The Tentative Provisions were presumably formulated as a result of the findings of the task force and the Shanghai government's determination to keep ahead of the national government and the other cities[36] (Table 4.3) in China.

[35]   *China Daily* (2008).
[36]   Cai (2003); Wang (2003); Leong (2008).

Table 4.6   Location strategy factors in three important Chinese cities

No	Conditions/factors	Beijing	Shanghai	Guangzhou
1	Operation Cost	1	2	3
2	Outcomes of investment process	1	1 or 2	3
3	Benefits	1, 2 or 3	1, 2 or 3	1, 2 or 3
4	Efficiency	1 or 2	1 or 2	3
5	Resource allocation	1	2	3
6	Advantage opportunities	1, 2 or 3	1, 2 or 3	1, 2 or 3
7	Safeguards	1	2	3
8	Culture	1, 2 or 3	1, 2 or 3	1, 2 or 3
9	Structure	1, 2 or 3	1, 2 or 3	1, 2 or 3
10	Control	1	2	3
11	Responsiveness	1, 2 or 3	1, 2 or 3	1, 2 or 3
12	Market characteristics	1, 2 or 3	1, 2 or 3	1, 2 or 3
13	Competitive advantage	1 or 2	1 or 2	2 or 3
14	Investment climate	3	1	2
15	Geographic distance	1, 2 or 3	1, 2 or 3	1, 2 or 3
16	Socialization	3	1	2
17	Training	1	2	3
18	Taxes	3	2	1
19	Exchange rates	1	1	1
20	Cost of capital	3	2	1
21	Trade barriers	3	1 or 2	1 or 2

Note: The explication from many interviews with directors, managers and CEOs of RHQs and MNEs in China over three years. 1: more important, 2: important and 3: less important.

Source: Aguilar (1979), Williamson (1981), Teece (1985), Hennart (1986), Douglas and Rugman (1986), and D'Cruz et al. (2005), with modifications.

RHQs are the management core locus represented by the leaders of the enterprises, integrating the strategic planning, accounting statement and decision-making power. In addition RHQs play the key role in the regional economy of China. If a number of RHQs agglomerate in a certain area, it will be more valuable. RHQs have established different development goals, some focusing on profit and others on mid-to-long-term development. Shanghai has the competitive geographic location, the longest history of economic development and an increasing globalized character, which is very attractive to transnational institutions. Shanghai has also been focusing on perfecting its system of business services, which also gave it a competitive advantage. Therefore, those focusing on profit earnings will choose Shanghai.

However, as a political, cultural and economic center, Beijing possesses the unparalleled advantages from the perspective of talent, with a great number of higher-education institutions. Many RHQs have chosen Beijing for political reasons. RHQs also need proper requirements, for example, human resources. Since the reform of the opening policy for foreign investors,[37] the investment environment in China has gradually improved, the physical infrastructure of each city has been making progress very quickly[38] but the differences between cities remain quite large.[39]

The development of the Headquarters Economy has created five categories of economic effects:[40] tax contribution, multiplication of industries, consumption growth, employment and social fund such as for education.[41] Therefore, the Headquarters Economy is a kind of economic model to facilitate simultaneously the benefits of MNEs, the headquarters located in the region, the domestic enterprises and the production base. This is the quadruple-win model of Headquarters Economy that has been suggested by Lou,[42] Han et al.[43] and Zhao.[44] The success of the regional economy depends on the appropriate industrial environment and policies, vigorous innovative enterprises and products as well as the extension of the activities such as transport services.[45]

CONCLUSION

The results of our research have shed some light on the activities, structures and processes of these organizational units within MNEs, RHQs and national subsidiaries. Table 4.2 shows the successful MNEs in China attributed their achievements to their RHQs. These were perceived as useful and are expected to become more powerful and more active in the future. RHQs were therefore seen not as temporary phenomena, but as necessary organizational units.[46]

As a result of local-market consideration and an orientation towards long-term investment options, RHQs considered location determinants such as the orientation-seeking of market size, cost reduction, strategic

37 Cai (2003); Wang (2003); Leong (2008).
38 Beijing Central Business District Administrative Commission (2005).
39 Zhao (2004).
40 Wang and Wang (2008).
41 Guo (2008).
42 Lou (2004).
43 Han et al. (2007).
44 Zhao (2004).
45 Beijing Central Business District Administration Commission (2005).
46 Schütte (1998).

presence and efficiency to be the very important strategies that need to be achieved for location in China.

The added value from RHQs lies particularly in their ability to stimulate regional strategies and finding a more creative and manageable solution for globalization/localization tensions. We look at the global integration process within GM and Ford (US RHQs in China), and the regionalization in Asahi Kasei and Hitachi (Japanese RHQs in China), and suggested that the added value of RHQ is the key in this process. In some instances, the European RHQs in China were even abolished or virtually indicated: that is the RHQs have delivered the expected benefits and that the role had been fulfilled and could now be taken over, by global head offices and/or local subsidiaries on a virtual basis.[47]

On the other hand, the development of the Headquarters Economy is to facilitate a new economic situation for Beijing as well as Shanghai, Guangzhou and other major Chinese cities. The development of Headquarters Economy 'extensively attracts the MNEs' which have set up their RHQs, centers of R&D, operational and procurement activities and are the particular concerns of the Central government. According to the *China Daily* (2007), 154 MNEs had set up their RHQs in Shanghai and 181 in Beijing. Therein lies one important problem: the government should better guide the regional distribution of the Headquarters Economy in order to establish a positive outcome for further attracting MNEs. The Headquarters Economy is a strong catalyst for a service boom and infrastructure improvement. RHQs could generate higher economic growth than an industrial park, as they can help boost a number of related services such as finance, accounting, consulting, hotels and catering and so on.[48]

By holding constant the internal and external factors of influence, the advantage of RHQ location in affecting the profits of MNEs can be investigated in various regions of China, along with the different Chinese cities. Furthermore, by keeping the internal and external environment constant, the RHQs of different origins in the same region, such as the RHQs of Japanese, European and US MNEs in China, have been explored. As a general conclusion, the research reported in this chapter suggests the positive influence of existing economic activity on the location choices for RHQs in Chinese cities, the linking of local and international markets, the expertise of national and MNE management, and the opportunity to make profits.

---

[47] Heck and Verdin (2001).
[48] Lou (2004); *China Daily* (2007); Han et al. (2007).

5. China's tax system on foreign enterprises and its impact on multinational firms' localization strategies

Hu Ying

INTRODUCTION

Over the last 30 years, characterized by opening-up and reform, the fiscal privileges granted to foreign enterprises, especially the privileges on enterprise income tax, have remained a major tool to attract the foreign investments that are believed to play an essential role in China's economic growth. Big Chinese cities, such as Beijing, Shanghai, Guangzhou and Tianjin adopted one after another the policy of attracting foreign direct investments as one of the most important policies for regional economic development. Tax privileges have created and worsened the competition between the different Chinese regions; objectively speaking, that has caused a tax discrepancy among cities and worsened the unfair competition between them. Apart from those special zones authorized by the central government, local governments have created their own with tax privileges and have become rivals. This chapter attempts to give some solutions to this problem through a comparison of the tax privileges offered by certain Chinese cities and an analysis of the competition between regions.

These fiscal privileges evolved over time: from volume incentives to quality incentives, from regional privileges to sectoral privileges, with the development of tax privileges in the central and western parts of China. Such tax policies have borne fruit: foreign investments attraction, economic growth traction and pilot experience used in opening-up expansion. However, these policies have also manifested their limits over time. Examples are: inequitable treatments between foreign and Chinese companies, irrational distribution of foreign capital in various sectors, unbalanced privileges structure, inappropriate management of fiscal privileges, and so on.

EVOLUTION OF THE TAX SYSTEM ON FOREIGN ENTERPRISES SINCE THE OPENING-UP

The tax system in China reflects developments in the economic system and changes in the political structure of the country. Foreign companies only started to invest in China after the 1978 opening-up and economic reform. China uses tax privileges as one of the main ways to attract foreign direct investments. Briefly, the evolution of the tax system on foreign firms can be divided into four periods: the early 1980s, 1984–1993, 1994–2007, and the post-2008 years.

In most cases, the current Chinese tax system dates back to the 1994 reform. This tax reform can be considered as one of the most important and radical reforms that has ever occurred in China, not only by its extent, but also through its impact on social and economic life. It was thus a major step towards the modernization of the Chinese tax system.[1]

This reform is mainly characterized by a better distribution of power and financial resources between the central government and the local communities, through a split between state taxes, common taxes and local taxes. This reform erases discrimination between Chinese and foreign capital enterprises, as well as discriminations between individuals of either Chinese or foreign nationality.

Indeed, the 1994 reform laid a path to tax harmonization:

1. for individuals regardless of their nationality, with the establishment of a unique tariff, though there are still a few variations in the calculation methods;
2. for enterprises, whether Chinese or foreign. While Chinese firms had in the past been taxed at a rate of 50 per cent, their taxes now lined up with those of the foreign enterprises, at a global rate of 33 per cent (except in special tariff zones).

Another effect of the 1994 reform was the unification of indirect taxes by reducing their number. In order to respect the principle of neutrality in indirect taxation, the government set up two major policies:

1. the establishment of a VAT, comparable in principles to the French or other European countries' VAT, and completed by two other taxes, being a tax on turnover (Business Tax) and a tax on consumption;
2. the abolition of existing discriminations between Chinese, foreign and foreign capital enterprises, so that all economic operators would be

---

[1]   Jin Banggui (2000), p. 25.

equally subject to the above-mentioned taxation, regardless of their nationality.

In 1999, the preferential tax treatments granted to foreign investors were oriented towards specific sectors considered as priorities. Productive foreign capital enterprises operating in the sectors of energy development, transport and infrastructures could now enjoy a 15 per cent tax rate.

In 2000, China started intensifying the development of the central and western regions. The government adopted preferential policies and encouraged foreign firms to invest in these regions. As a result, the preferential tax rate of 15 per cent was granted an extra three years extension for foreign capital enterprises established in the central and western parts of China.

Generally speaking, the tax privileges granted to foreign companies result directly from the opening-up and reform of China. They date back to the end of 1970s and the beginning of 1980s, when a market-oriented reform spread all over the country. Within the international context prevailing at that time, and in order to attract investments and speed up their utilization, China chose the way of 'promoting opening-up through preferential treatments'. In terms of taxation, it translated into a series of tax incentives granted to foreign investors, so that they ended up by paying less tax than Chinese enterprises. At that time, the fiscal system applying to foreign capital firms was completely different from the one applied to national firms. The privileged factors were first the investment volume, and second the structure of the company. No real privileges were granted to any given sector or region.

From 1984 to 1993, China promulgated a series of rules aimed at enlarging the scope of tax privileges, and created a spread-out structure of incentives related to the regions in which foreign enterprises were investing: special economic zones, economic and technological development zones, coastal economic open zones, other specific zones and inland zones. This allowed income tax harmonization amongst foreign enterprises, but this system still remained different from the tax system applied to national firms. The number of taxes was reduced and their rates lowered. By that time, tax privileges were thus limited to productive foreign capital enterprises. The eastern region was given priority, as well as the high technology sector.

From 1994 onwards, the Chinese tax system went through a major revolution. One can notice the harmonization of direct and indirect taxes between foreign and national enterprises. Furthermore, the government granted more tax privileges to foreign firms investing in priority sectors and in the central and western regions.

HARMONIZATION OF THE ENTERPRISE INCOME TAX RATE BETWEEN CHINESE AND FOREIGN ENTERPRISES

On 16 March 2007, the National People's Congress released the 'Enterprise Income Tax Law of the People's Republic of China' (the 'EIT Law'). The EIT Law unifies the application scope, the tax rate, tax deductions and preferential tax policies for both foreign capital enterprises and domestic enterprises. It is the first law in Chinese history that imposes an income tax on all forms of enterprise.

The EIT Law provides a unified income tax rate of 25 per cent. A reduced rate of 20 per cent may be applied to small or low-profit enterprises. The withholding tax rate is now 10 per cent on interest, royalties, capital gains and dividends, according to the detailed implementation rules.

As indicated by the statistics in Table 5.1, compared with ten other countries, in the year 2000, the income tax rate (33 per cent) on the foreign enterprises in China was below the average level, 2.4 per cent less than the average tax rate of the ten countries. Since 2002, the Chinese income tax rate has been higher than the average level. From then on, the income rate on foreign enterprises in China has continued to grow. Thus, the rate of 33 per cent, which was competitive in 1994 when China made the tax reform, has become less attractive. The rate of 25 per cent in the New Tax Law is favourable for continuing to attract foreign investments because it is lower than those of the first ten countries which invested in China.

Table 5.1   Comparison of the enterprise income tax rate among different countries

	2000	2001	2002	2003	2004	2005	2006
Hong Kong	17.5	16.5	16.5	16.5	16.5	16.5	16.5
China	33.0	33.0	33.0	33.0	33.0	33.0	33.0
Japan	40.9	40.9	40.9	40.9	39.54	39.54	39.54
USA	39.4	39.3	39.3	39.4	39.3	39.3	39.3
South Korean	30.8	30.8	29.7	29.7	29.7	27.5	27.5
Singapore	26.0	25.5	24.5	22.0	22.0	20.0	20.0
U.K.	30.0	30.0	30.0	30.0	30.0	30.0	30.0
Germany	52.0	38.9	38.9	40.2	38.9	38.9	38.9
France	37.8	36.4	35.4	35.4	35.4	35.0	34.4
Netherlands	35.0	35.0	34.5	34.5	34.5	31.5	29.6
Canada	44.6	42.1	38.6	36.6	36.1	36.1	36.1
Average	35.4	33.5	32.8	32.5	32.1	31.4	31.1

The EIT Law abolishes most of the geography-related tax rate reductions and incentives offered to manufacturing and export foreign capital enterprises, including: a two-year tax exemption and a three-year 50 per cent rate reduction for manufacturing enterprises and a 50 per cent rate reduction for export enterprises.

The major tax incentives now offered under the EIT Law include:

- reduced tax rate of 15 per cent to advanced technology enterprises nationwide;
- tax exemption or reduction for enterprises that engage in infrastructure projects, agriculture, forestry, fishery, energy and water preservation, environmental protection businesses and transfers of qualified technology;
- reduced taxable income in proportion to the investment of venture capital;
- accelerated tax deduction for R&D expenses for developing new technology, new products and new processes.

The EIT Law is a landmark piece of legislation in Chinese tax history. It not only unifies the foreign capital enterprises income tax law and the interim EIT regulations, but also introduces new concepts and provisions. The Minister of Finance highlighted 'four unifications': unification of the income tax law applicable to both domestic and foreign-funded enterprises, unification of the tax rates, unification and standardization of the deductions in computing taxable income, and unification of the tax incentives.[2] Most of the new provisions deal with international tax avoidance transactions, such as thin capitalization, transfer pricing, and foreign corporations located in low-tax jurisdictions.

ANALYSIS OF THE EFFECT OF CHINA'S TAX SYSTEM ON FOREIGN ENTERPRISES

Since 1994, China has established a tax system that is compatible with a market-oriented economy. The current system includes 29 tax categories, of which 14 are applicable to foreign capital enterprises and foreign tax payers.[3] Table 5.2 gives an overview of China's tax system. The various taxes, duties and levies to which foreign capital firms, foreign firms and foreign individuals are subject are: the Value-Added Tax (VAT), the

[2]   Jin Renqing (2007).
[3]   Liu Zuo (2005), p. 10.

Consumption Tax, the Business Tax, the Foreign-Invested and Foreign Enterprises Income Tax, the Urban Real Estate Tax, Land Appreciation Tax, the Purchasing Vehicle Tax, the Vehicles and Vessels Usage Plate Tax, the vessel tonnage tax, the Stamp Duty, the Deed Tax, the Slaughter Tax, the Agricultural Tax and the Customs Duty.

After the 1994 tax reform, foreign capital enterprises and Chinese enterprises became subject to the same tax system regarding VAT, the Business Tax and the Consumption Tax.[4]

However, before 2008 foreign capital enterprises still had their own tax system regarding income tax. Established with the aim of attracting foreign investments, this system is much more profitable than the one used for Chinese firms.

Current Income Tax System on Foreign Enterprises

The tax system applicable to foreign firms depends on whether or not they have created a legal structure in China. Foreign enterprises having a legal structure in China are considered as Chinese residents and are subject to full (or unlimited) taxation, wherever their income comes from. They are thus subject to taxes on all incomes derived from Chinese and from foreign sources. This concerns three types of enterprises: Chinese-Foreign Equity Joint Ventures (EJV), Chinese-Foreign Contractual Joint Ventures (CJV) and Wholly Foreign Owned Enterprises (WFOE). These firms are established according to Chinese Law and their legal entity is of Chinese nationality. As a common rule, the income tax of these companies attracts a 30 per cent rate, plus a local tax of 3 per cent, except when specific privileges are applicable. But these privileges (see later in this chapter) are so numerous that the common law rate actually becomes a fictive rate.

If the foreign enterprises have no legal structure in China, their taxation will depend on whether or not they have a stable establishment in

---

[4] **VAT:**
For imported or commercialized products: applicable rate of 17%.
For agricultural goods, papers and magazines: applicable rate of 13%.
For agricultural products directly sold by producers: VAT exemption.
Business Tax:
Transport: 3%, building industry: 3%, insurance & finance: 5%, post & telecommunication: 3%, culture.
& sports: 3%, entertainment: 5% to 20%, services: 5%, transfer of intangible assets: 5%, sales of real estate: 5% .
Consumption Tax:
For luxury items (tobacco & cigarettes, wines & alcohol, cosmetics, cars) and polluting items (petrol, diesel): applicable rate of 5 to 45%.[/list]

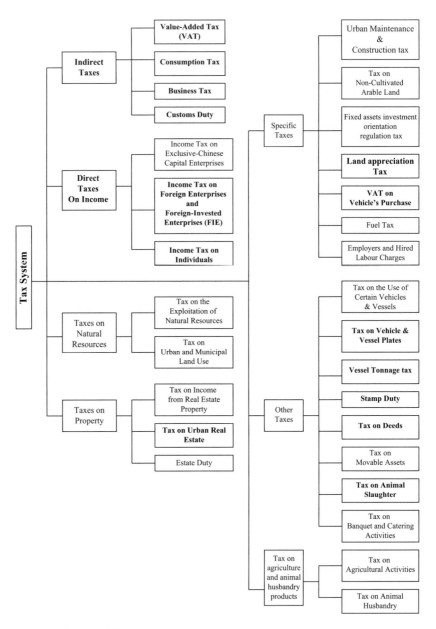

Source: Liu Zuo (2005).

Figure 5.1   China's tax system

China. A foreign enterprise operating with a stable establishment in China will be taxed the same way as a foreign capital enterprise having a legal structure in China, or (see above) a Chinese enterprise. But it will only be subject to a limited taxation and will thus only pay taxes on income derived from Chinese sources. If it has no stable establishment, a foreign enterprise will be taxed according to a 20 per cent pay-as-you-earn system, this rate having currently been reduced to 10 per cent[5] for each income category.

Preferential Tax Treatments Granted to Foreign Enterprises

From the very beginning of China's opening-up, foreign investments have enjoyed some preferential tax treatments as opposed to the tax system applicable to Chinese enterprises. These preferential tax treatments are linked to the activity area, the location and sometimes to the Chinese-foreign contract duration.

By identifying and combining all the tax measures in their favour, the enterprises can achieve a certain tax optimization. These preferential tax treatments which allowed a tax exoneration or a tax reduction are generally granted, during a determinate period of time, to those enterprises operating in economic sectors or the locations where the foreign investments are encouraged by the state. Table 5.2 shows us the different rates according to different enterprises.

Comparative Study of the Preferential Tax Treatments in Five Chinese Cities: Beijing, Shanghai, Shenzhen, Tianjin and Hong Kong

The preferential tax treatment given to specific regions is the most important part of tax policy system on the foreign investments. Based on a general preferential tax treatment, different tax rates are applied to different regions. As indicated in Table 5.2, the income tax is levied with progressive rates 15 per cent–24 per cent–30 per cent corresponding to the investments' locations: special economic zones economic and technological development zones, coastal economic open zones, other specific zones and inland zones. The tax rate on foreign capital enterprises is decided by the investment's location and those who enjoy the low tax rate are mostly in the coastal region. We will compare the preferential tax treatments in five big cities in China.

---

[5] See the basic text of taxation in the People's Republic of China, China's Fiscal Affairs Press, Beijing, 2001 p. 145.

Table 5.2 *EIT rate on foreign enterprises*

Enterprise Activity Area	Normal EIT Rate	Special Economic Zones	Development Zones		Free Zones	Coastal Economic Open Zones
			Economic and Technical Development Zones	Development Zones for High and New Technology Industry		
EIT Rate Productive Enterprises	30%	15%	15%	15%	15%	24%
High or Advanced Technology Enterprises	30%	15%	15%	15%	15%	15%
Exporting Entreprises	15%	10%	10%	10%	10%	12%
Finance Establishments (capital ≥ 10 millions $, operating period ≥ 10 years)	30%	15%				
Enterprises operating on ports and quays construction; energy, transport, etc.			15%	Agreed by the State Council 15%		

Comparison between Shanghai, Beijing, Shenzhen and Tianjin

While comparing the preferential tax treatments granted in Shanghai, Beijing, Shenzhen and Tianjin, we noted some similarities regarding the recipients and the tools used. Tax privileges and a preferential policy regarding land use are the main political tools used in attracting foreign investment. The recipient firms are multinational companies, their regional offices and 'advanced technology' enterprises.

The most common incentives are: exemption and reduction on the enterprise income tax (EIT), exemption and reduction on customs duties, exemption on exports and redemption speed up. Tax privileges also concern indirect taxes, but they usually enjoy rate unification, as is the case for VAT, Business Tax and Consumption Tax. The tax differences and competition between cities thus occur mainly in terms of EIT and Redemption Tax. Table 5.2 shows that Shenzhen grants a more profitable EIT than the other cities, with an exemption of local tax and a reduction on income tax.

In order to attract the 'advanced technology' enterprises, each city has created its own panel of tax incentives.

For instance, Shenzhen grants the newly established firms a two-year tax exemption followed by a 50 per cent tax reduction for eight years. For the existing ones, the city grants a two-year tax exemption followed by a six-year 50 per cent tax reduction, this being extended by another two years. The firms owning intellectual property rights enjoy EIT tax exemption and Business Tax exemption for five years, as well as a 50 per cent reduction on local VAT.

Beijing's policy is more in favour of the R&D expenses incurred by high technology enterprises. For instance, expenses linked to the development of a new product, new technology or new process, and expenses linked to the buying of R&D equipment, can be imputed in running costs as long as they increase by 10 per cent from the previous year, thus leading to a direct 50 per cent reduction on EIT. 'Advanced technology' enterprises working in an activity area encouraged by the State can enjoy an exemption on customs duties and import duties when they import equipment for their own use. During their first three trading years, these companies can also benefit from the rebate of the local tax.

Shanghai has set up a series of tax policies aimed at reducing the implementation costs of technological improvements. 'Advanced technology' firms settled in Shanghai can enjoy a local subvention consisting of the full rebate on their Business Tax and local EIT for three years, followed by a 50 per cent rebate on these taxes for two years. Companies owning intellectual property rights enjoy a full rebate for five years and a 50 per cent rebate for three years. All enterprises working on technology transfer and technology development, with their related advice and services, benefit from Business Tax exemption.

Comparison between Hong Kong and the four cities in continental China

Regarding preferential tax treatments, the differences between Hong Kong and the four cities mainly occur at form and principle levels. Unlike in other cities, there is no tax discrimination in Hong Kong: foreign and Chinese enterprises are subject to the same tax system and rate. The preferential tax systems are not discriminatory and do not differentiate foreign firms from inland Chinese companies or local companies. Tax privileges are granted in conformity with WTO regulations and international usage. The preferential tax treatment follows a general principle, thus creating a fiscal environment that is just and equitable. In contrast, in continental China, there is discrimination between foreign and Chinese enterprises. The preferential tax treatments depend on the activity area, the location and the length of the Chinese-foreign contract.

There are two forms of preferential treatment: one on direct taxes and the other on indirect taxes. The four mainland cities of China prefer to use direct preferential tax treatments that allow tax exemption or tax reduction, thus implying that the beneficiaries must make a profit before enjoying these privileges. Hong Kong on the other hand uses the indirect method that allows a reduction of the investment cost, based on redemption speed-up, tax credit for investments, expenses deduction, and so on. The more they invest, the more the companies benefit from these incentives. Indirect methods are more interesting for 'advanced technology' enterprises. Indeed, such firms often lack capital at the beginning of their activity and their expenses overtake their income. In this context, the indirect method allows them to instantly reduce their investment cost, which bears more results than the direct method.

MAIN PROBLEMS OCCURRING WITHIN THE TAX SYSTEM ON FOREIGN ENTERPRISES

The objectives of the current preferential tax treatments are imprecise, the sectorial orientation is simplified and the foreign investments repartition is not adequate. One must keep on re-adjusting the preferential policies granted to certain sectors.

The objectives of preferential tax treatment policies are not precise enough. As a result, priorities are not obvious. Generally speaking, the tax privileges granted to foreign companies express the requirements of

Table 5.3   *Comparison of tax systems*

City	Enterprise Income tax (EIT)	Local Tax
	30%	3%
	Exemption and Reduction	
Shanghai	1. "Production type" enterprise: tax rate: 24% (**Pudong** 15%) 2. Tax exemption during the first 2 years followed by 50% tax reduction for 3 to 8 years 3. 'Advanced technology' enterprises: 3 years extension for their 50% tax reduction 4. 'Exporting' enterprises, whose exports value reaches at least 70% of the total production value: 50% tax reduction	1. Local tax: 3% 2. Exemption during the first 2 profit-making years 3. Exemption for exporting enterprises 4. 'Advanced technology' enterprise owning intellectual property rights: 5 years local tax subsidies (= tax exemption) on Business Tax and local EIT, then 3 years local subsidies (= 50% tax rebate)
Beijing	1. 'Production type' enterprise with operating period > 10 years: tax rate: 24% 2. Tax exemption during the first 2 years followed by 50% tax reduction for 3 to 5 years 3. 'Advanced technology' enterprises: 15% tax rate, with 3 years tax exemption followed by 3 years 50% tax reduction 4. 'Exporting' enterprise : 50% tax reduction 5. Finance establishment with exploitation period > 10 years and capital > 10 millions $: 15% tax rate, with 1 year exemption followed by 2 years 50% tax reduction	1. 'Advanced technology', 'new technology' and 'exporting' enterprises: tax exemption 2. 'Production type' enterprise with operating period > 10 years: 5 years tax exemption and 5 years 50% tax rebate 3. Regional office of multinational enterprises: tax exemption
Shenzhen	1. Tax rate: 15% 2. 'Production type' enterprise: 2 years tax exemption + 3 years 50% tax reduction.	Tax exemption

Table 5.3   (continued)

City	Enterprise Income tax (EIT)	Local Tax
	30%	3%
Shenzhen	'Service type' enterprise: 1 year tax exemption + 2 years 50% tax reduction 3. 'Exporting' enterprise : 10% tax rate 4. 'Advanced technology' enterprises: 10% tax rate, with 2 years tax exemption followed by 6 years 50% tax reduction	Tax exemption
Tianjin	1. 'Production type' enterprise: tax rate: 24% If operating period > 10 years: tax rate 15% with 2 years tax exemption + 3 years 50% tax reduction 2. 'Advanced technology' enterprises: 15% tax rate + 3 years extension for their 50% tax reduction 3. 'Exporting' enterprise: 50% tax reduction 4. Finance establishment with exploitation period > 10 years and capital > 10 millions $: 15% tax rate, with 1 year exemption followed by 2 years 50% tax reduction	
Hong Kong	1. Enterprises: 17.5% 2. Organizations other than enterprises: 16%	

the sectorial policies up to a certain level. However, since their implementing provisions are rather global, the sectorial orientations are not properly highlighted. Indeed, as all the tax incentives are a very wide-ranging, foreign enterprises can benefit from several privileges and this compromises the structure and the regional repartition of foreign investments. For instance, the fact that privileges are granted to all foreign enterprises of 'productive type' has weakened the orientation role of the sectorial policies. Coastal regions receive more privileges than western and central regions, and regional disparities have been increased.

In the first years of opening-up and reform, China offered tax privileges to attract a large number of FDI (Foreign Direct Investment). Nowadays, the objective is the proper use of these investments in order to promote an increase in industry range and industrial restructuring. However, the tax system on foreign enterprises defined implementing provisions for only a few sectors and the general provisions apply in all other sectors, so that the sectorial orientation is not precise at all. There is a strong sectorial divergence regarding FDI repartition. Most of the FDI is engaged in the manufacturing sector: foreign enterprises represent 68 per cent of the car industry, 70 per cent of the lift industry and a large part of the agro-food, paper-making, pharmaceutical sectors, and so on.[6] In contrast the foreign capital share is pretty weak in agriculture, energy and transport, although China needs to reinforce these sectors. This lead to the following problems:

1   Unfavourable environment for Chinese enterprises. While China gives up a part of its tax income to attract FDI, foreign firms, due to their experience, grab a large market share of certain products. On the other hand, some Chinese companies are bankrupt and most of the national firms find it difficult to develop.
2   Large number of FDI in the manufacturing sector. This is considered as no help for the global improvement of China's economic development.
3   Loss of tax income for the Chinese government, due to preferential tax treatments. And in the meantime, some countries do not accept the deduction of preferential tax, so that when their incomes are repatriated, foreign investors are subject to double taxation and do not, in the end, enjoy a real tax privilege.

Time seems ripe for an adjustment of the 'General tax privileges' (two years EIT exemption and three years EIT 50 per cent reduction) conferred to foreign capital enterprises engaged in productive activities.

---

6   OCDE (2004).

The Preferential Tax System: Simplified Forms, Unbalanced Structure

As already stated, the preferential tax systems can be of two forms: direct or indirect. The direct form concerns tax exemption, tax reduction and tax rebate; it is a clear, simple and secure form. The indirect form entails redemption speed-up, tax credit for investments and expenses deduction; it is a flexible form. The direct method is generally interesting for short-term projects involving a low to medium-sized capital investment; it is not very useful for long-term projects with large investments. The direct method is also interesting for production activities involving high labour charges, but it does not benefit 'advanced technology' enterprises and intensive capital enterprises since their assets are intangible and their investments on equipment are heavy.

Since direct preferential tax treatments have time limits (two years tax exemption and three years tax deduction), some foreign investors try to escape taxation or extend their tax privileges by re-registering or modifying the registration of their company. Some Chinese enterprises also register overseas in order to benefit from tax privileges. Obviously, the direct form encourages fraud while the indirect form incites enterprises to improve their production and their exploitation. China must thus give priority to indirect preferential tax treatments and decrease the direct preferential tax treatment.

Although more and more importance is given to incentives such as redemption speed-up and tax credit for investments, regular tax exemption-reduction and preferential tax rates still remain the main incentives for foreign enterprises. We also note that there are some stringent conditions attached to redemption speed-up: only firms playing a major role in the national economy, with 'advanced' technology and fixed assets, can access this privilege under specific conditions. As for tax credit on investments, this incentive was only set up at the end of 1999 and is still in its trial period.

The negative effects of the incentives linked to regular exemption-reduction and preferential rates can be felt in the sectorial orientation of foreign investments. Countries that are competitive in terms of tax privileges prefer to go first for indirect incentives, and complete the system by direct incentives. In contrast, in China, more than 95 per cent of the tax privileges are in direct form, and less than 5 per cent are indirect incentives. Indirect tax privileges thus still play a major role in China.

Confusion and Disorder in the Management of Preferential Tax Treatments

A management share between the central government and the local authorities does not seem sufficient. The management power should also be distributed between the legislative, the administrative and the fiscal authorities. In fact, the management power related to fiscal privileges is mainly in the hands of the central government, and not in the local authorities' hands.

To solve the problems that can only be addressed at the local level, the local authorities then have to overstep their powers in order to establish some favourable policies. At the central government level, only 10 per cent of tax privileges are managed by the legislative authorities, the rest being managed by the administrative authorities, especially the fiscal authorities. Moreover, the government's department of economic management also manages a part of fiscal incentives.

China is still suffering from a non-performing system of income redistribution. There are several categories of taxes and administrative charges. According to estimations, the taxes and general charges, including administrative charges, additional charges, adjustments and levies, are comparable to real taxes and represent 19 per cent of GDP.[7] Foreign enterprises are heavily affected by dozens, if not hundreds of different taxes and charges. And in order to attract foreign investments in their own areas, the local authorities have overstepped their power by setting up several tax privileges, resulting not only in confusion, but also in a loss of confidence for foreign investors in China.

CONCLUSION

The preferential tax treatment system granted to foreign enterprises was created at the beginning of China's opening-up and reform. The context and the needs of those times have determined the orientation and the priorities of the system. Tax incentives played an important role during the earlier years of economic development by helping attract FDI to China. However, the negative impact of the tax incentives and the discriminative policy against domestic enterprises has become more serious in recent years. Such a tax system is clearly revealing its limits. In order to resist the increasingly fierce competition that followed China's adhesion to WTO, the preferential tax treatment linked with the investment's nature and location will be replaced gradually by sectorial tax policies.

From the viewpoint of taxation optimization and strategic restructuring of foreign investments, this chapter studied and analysed the tax system applied to foreign enterprises, and proposed an optimization plan consisting of the modification of the tax system through the fiscal structure,

---

[7] Yang Congchun (2005).

the tax incentives and the tax management. We offer a route towards the reform of the tax system applied to foreign enterprise, with the aim of setting up a system adapted to the current context of globalization and the market-oriented economy. The final result should be a better tax deployment, foreign capitals of increasingly good quality and the promotion of China's economic growth.

6. Hong Kong and Shanghai: rivalry or complementarity among Asia's international service hubs?*

Sung Yun-Wing

INTRODUCTION

Hong Kong and Shanghai share a common history. They are two of the five trading ports along the coast of China forcibly opened by the West under the Treaty of Nanking in 1842, following the end of the First Opium War. From obscurity, both ports rose rapidly to prominence under Western influence because of their strategic location. Before World War II, whereas Hong Kong was a regional port handling the South China external trade, Shanghai had already been a global city. In the 1920s, Shanghai was known as the Wall Street of the Far East.

When the Communists came to power in China in 1950, the service sector of Shanghai shrank because of Marxian bias against services. On the one hand, industrial development continued. The growth of Shanghai was above national average, and it was the number one sub-central city/ province in terms of GDP, industrial output and exports in the pre-reform era (Sung 1999: 1). On the other hand, Shanghai was no longer a global city because it was cut off from the world market.

The eclipse of Shanghai as a global city provided an opportunity for Hong Kong. Many Shanghai capitalists fled to the then-British colony, providing the capital and skills for the export-oriented industrialisation of Hong Kong. The demand for services from the manufacturing sector stimulated the development of banking and business services. In the 1970s, Hong Kong began to emerge as an international financial centre.

Hong Kong took advantage of China's opening in 1978 to build a 'world factory' in the Pearl River Delta (PRD). Whereas Guangdong raced ahead, growth of Shanghai, as well as that of its neighbouring provinces in the

* The author wishes to acknowledge research support from the Hong Kong Institute of Asia-Pacific Studies and the able research assistance of Jessie Pang.

Yangtze River Delta (YRD), fell behind. Shanghai was burdened by state-owned enterprises and conservative bureaucrats trained in the tradition of the command economy. The GDP of Guangdong surpassed that of Shanghai in 1983, its exports in 1986, and its industrial output in 1989 (Sung 1999: 2).

The 'world factory' that Hong Kong entrepreneurs built in Guangdong was largely supported by producer services sourced from Hong Kong. With the opening of China, Hong Kong became a global service hub. From 1992 to 2004, Hong Kong had been the world's busiest container port (except for 1998). Hong Kong airport was also the world's number two in terms of air cargo from 2002 to 2009. Hong Kong also vied with Singapore to be the largest international financial centre in East Asia. In the mid-1990s, Hong Kong handled approximately 60 per cent of China's trade, and was the source of over half of China's foreign direct investment (FDI) (Sung 2006: 152–169).

The dominance of Hong Kong in the trade and investment of China has declined since the mid-1990s as China developed its producer services. For instance, the port of Shenzhen developed rapidly (with the help of Hong Kong investment), and cargo was diverted from the Hong Kong port (Sung 2005: 77–78). Moreover, with the opening of Pudong in 1990, China shifted the regional emphasis of its developmental policy from Guangdong to Shanghai.

Since 1990, Shanghai has enjoyed favourable policies and has grown much faster than the national average. Its container throughput and stock market turnover surpassed those of Hong Kong in 2007. However, despite the rapid development of Shanghai, Hong Kong remains ahead as a financial centre and services hub.

With the 2008 Financial Crisis and the economic decline of the United States, China has had to play a more active role in the international finance community. Beijing is determined to gradually allow the Chinese renminbi (RMB) to become an international currency. On 29 April 2009, Beijing unveiled a master plan to transform Shanghai into an international financial and shipping centre by 2020, in line with Chinese economic power and the growing importance of the RMB (Hang Seng Bank 2009).

The opening of the capital account of China will be gradual because its financial system is not yet sufficiently robust to handle large and volatile capital flows. Hong Kong is the only Chinese city to have a fully open financial system. Moreover, its system has successfully weathered the financial crises of 1997 and 2008. In pursuing financial liberalisation, China can benefit greatly from Hong Kong's experience and financial infrastructure. To further its reform and opening, China has adopted a 'dual financial centres' model that utilises the comparative advantages of both Shanghai and Hong Kong (Bank of East Asia 2009).

The rest of this chapter is organised as follows. The following section compares the macroeconomic indicators of Hong Kong and Shanghai, as well as those of the PRD and YRD, the hinterlands of the two hubs. The next two sections compare the two cities as transportation and trading hubs, followed by the examination of the two hubs as financial centres, and the final section concludes the chapter.

MACROECONOMIC INDICATORS OF HONG KONG AND SHANGHAI

Shanghai has a much larger area and population than Hong Kong, and its GDP surpassed that of Hong Kong in 2009. However, the per capita GDP of Hong Kong was nearly 2.7 times that of Shanghai's in 2009, and will remain higher for a long time (Sung 2011).

The 2009 Hong Kong exports, at US$ 319 billion, were slightly lower than that of Shanghai at US$ 325 billion. Comparing the trade of Hong Kong and Shanghai is very tricky statistically, as detailed below. Hong Kong continues to have a huge lead over Shanghai as a service hub. For the share of the tertiary sector in GDP in 2008, that of Hong Kong was 86 per cent, whereas that of Shanghai was only 54 per cent. In 2008, the inward FDI of Hong Kong was over four times that of Shanghai, whereas the outward FDI of Hong Kong was over 50 times that of Shanghai. In mid-2009, Hong Kong had 1,252 multinational regional headquarters, whereas Shanghai only had 260 (Sung 2011).

However, the growth rate of Shanghai is much higher than that of Hong Kong because economies with a lower level of development tend to grow faster than mature economies. The growth of Shanghai is likely to slow down as it reaches a higher level of development. The fact that Shanghai is currently growing faster does not imply that Shanghai will inevitably surpass Hong Kong in the level of economic development.

The hinterland of Shanghai, the YRD, is much bigger than that of Hong Kong, the PRD, in terms of area and economic size. For instance, in 2008, the area, population, and inward FDI of the YRD were respectively 3.8, 1.6 and 1.4 times that of the PRD, which gave Shanghai an advantage over Hong Kong.[1] However, the per capita GDP of the PRD was 22 per cent higher than that of YRD (Sung 2011).

---

[1] Here, Shanghai is excluded from the YRD as we wish to compare the hinterlands served by Shanghai and Hong Kong. The YRD covers 15 cities: Suzhou, Wuxi, Changzhou, Zhenjiang, Nanjiang, Yangzhou, Taizhou (泰州), Nantong, Hangzhou, Ningbo, Jiaxing, Huzhou, Zhaoxing, Zhoushan, Taizhou (台州). The PRD covers 13 cities and counties

HONG KONG AND SHANGHAI AS HUBS OF TRANSPORTATION

Hong Kong and Shanghai are not direct competitors in transportation because they serve different regions: Hong Kong serves the PRD, whereas Shanghai serves the YRD. Shanghai is recognised as the leading transportation hub in the YRD, whereas the status of Hong Kong as a transportation hub in the PRD is challenged by Shenzhen and Guangzhou. Transportation costs in Shenzhen and Guangzhou are cheaper, and these ports are closer to the source of the cargo in the PRD.

The Shenzhen and Shanghai ports have developed with the help of Hong Kong investment, and their container throughputs have approached or surpassed that of Hong Kong. Delivering containers to the Hong Kong port is expensive because the Hong Kong government forbids mainland Chinese container trucks to drive in order to Hong Kong to protect the jobs of its truck drivers. Another problem is that container terminals and container yards are land-intensive and Hong Kong is short of land. Unsurprisingly, Hong Kong will lose out to Shenzhen and Guangzhou in container throughput in the long run.

The lead held by Hong Kong air transportation is likely to last longer. In comparison with sea transportation, air transportation has higher value added and is less affected by high labour costs. As late as 2001, airfreight and passenger traffic handled by Hong Kong's airport were over twice that of Shanghai. In fact, in 2002, the airfreight handled by the Hong Kong airport was as large as all the 147 airports in mainland China. However, airports in the mainland are developing extremely rapidly. Shanghai, for instance, is closing in on Hong Kong in both air cargo and passenger traffic.

Hong Kong faces intense competition in the PRD in terms of air transport. Four international airports serve the PRD area: Hong Kong, Shenzhen, Guangzhou and Macau. Guangzhou is a formidable competitor because it is one of three major air hubs (Beijing in the north, Shanghai in Central China and Guangzhou in the south) of mainland China. The capacity of the newly opened Guangzhou Baiyun International Airport is as large as that of the Hong Kong airport. Moreover, a third runway is currently being constructed in the Guangzhou airport, which will be completed by 2012. Given the limited land resources of Hong Kong, building a third runway for its airport will be very expensive, especially as, should the government decide to build it, it would only be ready by 2021 at the

(districts): Guangzhou, Shenzhen, Zhuhai, Foshan, Jiangmen, Dongguan, Zhongshan, the urban districts of Huizhou, Huidong County, Boluo County, Zhaoqing, Gaoyao and Sihui.

earliest. Guangzhou has reserved land for five runways for its airport, whereas the Hong Kong airport only has space for three.

Presently, the airport of Hong Kong has a significant advantage over Guangzhou airport in terms of quality of service and international connectivity. In terms of international airlinks, Hong Kong has over 110 versus Guangzhou's 60. However, Guangzhou's airlinks are growing very rapidly. Given the much larger population of the YRD relative to the PRD, the air traffic of Shanghai is likely to surpass that of Hong Kong. The air traffic of Guangzhou is also likely to surpass that of Hong Kong in the long run because of Hong Kong's limited land to build additional runways.

As airports and container ports are land intensive, Hong Kong will lose out in services that are directly related to the physical movement of cargo (e.g., shipping, air freight, trucking and warehousing). Hong Kong has to concentrate on its area of comparative advantage: logistics, headquarter functions and trade support services not directly related to movement of cargo (e.g., intermediation, trade finance and insurance). Such services are not land-intensive as they can be housed in high-rise buildings.

HONG KONG AND SHANGHAI AS TRADING HUBS

We compare the shares of China's trade handled by Hong Kong and Shanghai, two rival hubs in handling China's trade.[2] They do not compete much in non-China-related trade. We distinguish between the following three types of trade in our analysis:

1 trade arising from producers and users in Hong Kong (Shanghai);
2 trade arising from producers or users outside Hong Kong (Shanghai), but transported via Hong Kong (Shanghai); and
3 trade arising from producers or users outside Hong Kong (Shanghai) using the intermediary services of traders in Hong Kong (Shanghai).

The determinants of the three types of trade are different. The first is relatively small in Hong Kong because its manufacturing has largely relocated to the mainland. However, Hong Kong continues to largely service its manufacturing base in the mainland. As a result, the second and third

---

[2] Comparison of total trade of the two hubs is misleading because Hong Kong is a separate customs territory. Flow of goods between the mainland and Hong Kong would be counted as external trade; however, the same flows would not be counted as external trade in the case of Shanghai.

types of trade are relatively large for Hong Kong. These can be used to gauge the roles of Hong Kong or Shanghai as transportation and trading hubs, respectively.

Hong Kong as a Trading Hub

Table 6.1 shows China's trade handled by Hong Kong through *re-exports* and *offshore trade*. The first type of trade is not included in the table because it is small (i.e., less than 1 per cent of mainland's trade since 2003). We focus on the role of Hong Kong in serving 'outside trade' (trade arising from producers and users outside Hong Kong). *Re-exports* (or entrepôt trade) include re-exports of mainland goods via Hong Kong to third countries, as well as re-exports of third-country goods to the mainland via Hong Kong. *Offshore trade* does not go through Hong Kong customs; however, Hong Kong traders function as middlemen in the trade.

Re-exports involve both transportation and intermediation. Goods are transported via Hong Kong; they go through Hong Kong customs. They are also sold to a Hong Kong trader who resells the goods outside Hong Kong.

Similar to re-exports, offshore trade uses Hong Kong traders as intermediaries. The China-related offshore trade of Hong Kong is nearly as large as its China-related re-exports. Statistics on Hong Kong's offshore trade are obtained from surveys conducted by the government. Statistics of offshore trade are less detailed than those of re-exports because offshore trade does not go through Hong Kong customs.

Table 6.1 ignores mainland trade trans-shipped via Hong Kong that does not involve intermediation by a Hong Kong trader. Mainland traders may trans-ship goods via Hong Kong to take advantage of Hong Kong's frequent shipping schedules, even though Hong Kong firms do not play a role in the intermediation. The value of such trans-shipment is not known because it does not go through Hong Kong customs. Table 6.1 thus understates the share of the China trade handled by Hong Kong.

Table 6.1 shows that the China trade via Hong Kong in the form of re-exports grew much faster than the total China trade in the early reform era. Its share of the total China trade rose from 4 per cent in 1979 to over 40 per cent in the mid-1990s; in absolute terms, it has grown nearly a hundred times in the period. The very rapid rise of the Hong Kong mainland-related entrepôt trade is partly due to the relocation of Hong Kong manufacturing to Guangdong, which generates a huge amount of outward processing trade. Hong Kong firms supply their subsidiaries in the mainland with raw materials, parts, and components, and the processed output is often sold back to the parent firms in Hong Kong for re-export to the final market.

Table 6.1   Hong Kong's mainland-related re-exports and offshore trade

	Value of trade (US$mn)			Percentage share of China's total trade		
	Re-exports	Offshore trade	Total	Re-exports	Offshore trade	Total
1991	51,952	12,122	64,074	38.3	8.9	47.2
1992	61,263	–	–	37.0	–	–
1993	80,772	–	–	41.3	–	–
1994	94,819	35,611	130,430	40.1	15.0	55.1
1995	111,636	–	–	39.7	c	–
1996	119,771	–	–	41.3	–	–
1997	126,758	67,006	193,764	39.0	20.6	59.6
1998	118,642	–	–	36.6	–	–
1999	118,567	–	–	32.9	–	–
2000	140,632	111,422	252,054	29.7	23.5	53.2
2001	139,318	128,433	267,751	27.3	25.2	52.5
2002	155,837	145,626	301,463	25.1	23.5	48.6
2003	185,149	152,968	338,117	21.8	18.0	39.7
2004	220,760	190,469	411,229	19.1	16.5	35.6
2005	253,637	212,542	466,179	17.8	14.9	32.8
2006	288,697	238,533	527,230	16.4	13.5	29.9
2007	322,265	282,056	604,321	14.8	13.0	27.8
2008	341,267	371,976	713,243	13.3	14.5	27.8
2009	309,616			14.0		

Source: Hong Kong External Trade, Census and Statistics Department, Hong Kong, various issues.

Moreover, Hong Kong also handles a substantial amount of 'pure re-exports' (i.e., re-exports not related to outward processing). The demand of mainland China for intermediation has increased with the decentralisation of China's foreign trade system. This demand is often channelled to Hong Kong due to its efficiency in intermediation.[3]

However, with the further opening of China, the share of the China trade via Hong Kong in the form of re-exports declined from a peak of 41 per cent in 1996 to 14 per cent in 2009. This rapid decline can be attributed to two factors. First, as mentioned above, the Shenzhen container ports developed rapidly with Hong Kong investment, and cargo was diverted from Hong Kong to Shenzhen. Second, with Deng Xiaoping's 1992 his-

---

[3]   For a detailed account of the entrepôt role of Hong Kong in the mainland's trade, see Sung (2005: 77–94).

toric southern tour, other provinces emulated the export-oriented model of Guangdong, and China exports shifted northward from Guangdong towards the Yangtze Delta and the northern coastal areas. Trade in the northern areas is usually served by Shanghai or other hubs in the north, rather than Hong Kong. The total share of China trade handled by Hong Kong (as re-exports and as offshore trade) declined from a peak of 60 per cent in 1997 to 28 per cent in 2008.

The decline of Hong Kong as a middleman in the China trade is relative, rather than absolute. The value of China trade handled by Hong Kong as re-exports and offshore trade has grown quite rapidly. From 1997 to 2008, the China trade handled by Hong Kong has grown at the average rate of 13 per cent per year, whereas total China trade has grown even faster at the average rate of 21 per cent per year during the same period.

Shanghai as a Trading Hub

Table 6.2 shows the following three different types of trade related to Shanghai in *China Customs Statistics*:

1   imports and exports through Shanghai customs (i.e., 'trade via Shanghai customs');
2   imports and exports of consumers/producers located in Shanghai, or for brevity, 'trade originating in Shanghai' (more than half of 'trade via Shanghai Customs' is 'trade originating in Shanghai'); and
3   imports and exports of importers/exporters located in Shanghai (i.e., 'trade handled by Shanghai traders').

From the above three types of trade, we can derive 'outside trade via Shanghai customs' (i.e., trade originating outside Shanghai that goes through Shanghai customs), as well as 'outside trade intermediated by Shanghai traders' (i.e., trade originating outside Shanghai in which Shanghai traders act as intermediaries). 'Outside trade via Shanghai customs' is defined as the difference between trade via Shanghai customs and trade originating in Shanghai.[4] 'Outside trade intermediated by Shanghai traders' is defined as the difference of trade handled by Shanghai traders from trade originating in Shanghai.[5]

---

[4]   We assume that all 'trade originating from Shanghai' goes through Shanghai customs, rather than the customs of other cities, because Shanghai is the foremost port in the YRD.
[5]   We assume that all 'trade originating from Shanghai' is handled by Shanghai traders because Shanghai is the foremost trading hub of the YRD.

Table 6.2 Shanghai's trade

	Trade via Shanghai Customs				
	Total (1)	Trade originating in Shanghai (2)	Trade handled by Shanghai traders (3)	Outside trade via Shanghai Customs	
				Total (4)	Intermediated by Shanghai (5)
1992	25,145	15,364	11,691	9,781	–
	(15.2)	(9.3)	(7.1)	(5.9)	–
1993	30,931	17,549	14,501	13,382	–
	(15.8)	(9.0)	(7.4)	(6.8)	–
1994	36,242	20,154	18,062	16,088	–
	(15.3)	(8.5)	(7.6)	(6.8)	–
1995	48,137	25,897	24,358	22,240	–
	(17.1)	(9.2)	(8.7)	(7.9)	–
1996	52,870	27,892	27,137	24,978	–
	(18.2)	(9.6)	(9.4)	(8.6)	–
1997	58,683	30,365	29,800	28,318	–
	(18.0)	(9.3)	(9.2)	(8.7)	–
1998	63,638	31,172	31,344	32,466	172
	(19.6)	(9.6)	(9.7)	(10.0)	(0.1)
1999	76,151	38,053	38,618	38,098	565
	(21.1)	(10.6)	(10.7)	(10.6)	(0.2)
2000	109,311	54,706	54,711	54,605	5
	(23.0)	(11.5)	(11.5)	(11.5)	(0.0)
2001	120,488	60,707	60,893	59,781	186
	(23.6)	(11.9)	(11.9)	(11.7)	(0.0)
2002	142,501	72,276	72,276	70,225	0
	(23.0)	(11.6)	(11.6)	(11.3)	(0.0)
2003	201,201	110,530	112,355	90,671	1,825
	(23.6)	(13.0)	(13.2)	(10.7)	(0.2)
2004	282,575	156,803	160,019	125,772	3,216
	(24.5)	(13.6)	(13.9)	(10.9)	(0.3)
2005	350,678	181,509	186,344	169,169	4,835
	(24.7)	(12.8)	(13.1)	(11.9)	(0.3)
2006	428,754	221,239	227,825	207,515	6,586
	(24.4)	(12.6)	(12.9)	(11.8)	(0.4)
2007	520,909	273,988	282,913	246,921	8,925
	(24.0)	(12.6)	(13.0)	(11.4)	(0.4)
2008	606,557	313,926	322,103	292,631	8,177
	(23.7)	(12.3)	(12.6)	(11.4)	(0.3)
2009	515,298	273,408	277,751	241,890	4,343
	(23.3)	(12.4)	(12.6)	(11.0)	(0.2)

Note: Figures in bracket represent percentage to China's total trade.

Source: China's Customs Statistics, various issues.

The rise in the share of trade via Shanghai customs to the national total since 1991 is because of the rapid growth of both 'trade originating in Shanghai' and 'outside trade via Shanghai customs'. The share of 'trade originating in Shanghai' to the national total rose from the low of approximately 9 per cent in the early 1990s to over 13 per cent in 2004 because of the rapid growth of production and consumption in Shanghai.

'Outside trade via Shanghai customs' also soared. Its share of the national total rose from 6 per cent of the China trade in 1992 (when data were first available) to a peak of 12 per cent of the China trade in 2005 (however, it declined slightly thereafter). This shows the success of the Shanghai port in serving trade originating outside Shanghai. However, the share of 'outside trade via Shanghai customs' intermediated by Shanghai traders to the total trade of China was negligible (0.2 per cent in 2009). Shanghai is a hub of transportation rather than intermediation for 'outside trade'.

In the pre-reform era, a substantial share of the exports was handled by state-run trading companies (12 per cent in 1978) in Shanghai in accordance with the central plan (Sung 1996: 192). However, in the early reform era, many neighbouring provinces developed their own trading companies, and trade originating outside Shanghai was diverted from the Shanghai trading companies. Outside exports intermediated by Shanghai trading companies fell to negligible amounts. Unlike Hong Kong, Shanghai is not a big hub of intermediation for outside trade.

Shanghai and Hong Kong Compared

Figure 6.1 compares China trade handled by Hong Kong and Shanghai as trading and transportation hubs. The share of the mainland trade handled by Hong Kong rose in the early reform era to a peak in the mid-1990s, and then declined sharply. Hong Kong traders continued to handle a large volume of mainland trade, amounting to 28 per cent in 2008.

The data shown for Hong Kong deals entirely with 'outside trade' (i.e., trade originating outside Hong Kong). However, including trade originating in Hong Kong would not change the overall picture because such trade is small (i.e., less than 1 per cent of mainland trade since 2003).

For Shanghai, the trade originating in Shanghai is approximately as large as Shanghai 'outside trade' because Shanghai is a large manufacturing centre (unlike Hong Kong). The share of 'outside trade via Shanghai customs' to the total China trade doubled from 6 per cent in 1992 to 12 per cent in 2006. Including the trade originating in Shanghai, the share of total trade via Shanghai customs to total China trade rose from 15 per cent

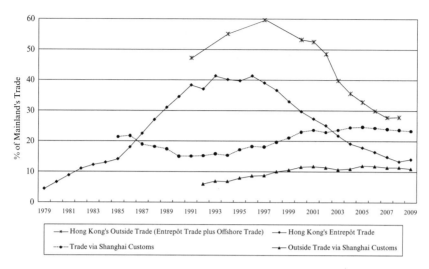

Source: Hong Kong External Trade, Census and Statistics Department, Hong Kong. China's Customs Statistics, various issues.

Figure 6.1   Hong Kong and Shanghai as trading hubs

in 1992 to nearly 24 per cent in 2008.[6] Although the share of Hong Kong (including offshore trade) remains higher than that of Shanghai, the share of the latter is likely to exceed that of Hong Kong in future because the trend of decline in the Hong Kong share has been quite sharp.

Hong Kong's prominent intermediary role in 'outside trade' cannot be entirely accounted for by outward processing. Approximately half of the Hong Kong mainland-related entrepôt trade is 'pure re-exports' that does not involve outward processing. Hong Kong is clearly an important hub of intermediation for 'outside trade', whereas the role of Shanghai as a hub of intermediation for 'outside trade' is insignificant.

Unsurprisingly, Shanghai has greater success as a transportation hub than as an intermediation hub. With the help of foreign investment and

---

[6]   Apart from 'outside trade', we should also look at total trade, which includes trade originating locally. Hong Kong's 'outside trade' is biased upwards because Hong Kong is much smaller than Shanghai in area. Approximately half of the mainland-related entrepôt trade of Hong Long is outward-processing trade (i.e., trade involving the relocation of Hong Kong manufacturing to the mainland) (Sung 2005: 88–91). Shanghai is six times larger than Hong Kong in area and is roughly the same size as Hong Kong, Shenzhen and Dongguan combined. The relocation of Hong Kong manufacturing to Shenzhen and Dongguan is analogous to the relocation of manufacturing from the urban centre in Shanghai to the less urbanised periphery of Shanghai. A substantial portion of 'outside trade' for Hong Kong would still be classified as 'trade originating locally' in the case of Shanghai.

expertise, Shanghai has been able to expand its port facilities extremely rapidly. However, trading and intermediating require entrepreneurship and the accumulation of soft skills in marketing, logistics and networking.

The remnants of the command economy in the mainland have also retarded the development of intermediary services in Shanghai because local governments in the YRD tend to protect their own trading companies. However, with further marketisation and reform of the Chinese economy, Shanghai may play a more significant role in intermediation for trade originating outside Shanghai in the future.

HONG KONG AND SHANGHAI AS FINANCIAL CENTRES

Although Hong Kong was already developing into an international financial centre in the 1970s, Shanghai's re-emergence as a financial centre only began in 1990 with the opening of Pudong. However, its development has been extremely rapid.

In 1993, when data for Shanghai were first available, Shanghai's stock exchange turnover was only a quarter of that of Hong Kong. However, from 2007 to 2009, the Shanghai stock exchange surpassed that of Hong Kong in both turnover and market capitalisation. However, in 2010, the Hong Kong stock exchange jumped ahead of Shanghai in market capitalisation, ranking fifth in the world, just behind London. Shanghai's rank slipped from sixth to seventh. Hong Kong was also the world's number one in capital raised through Initial Public Offering in 2009 and 2010 (Sung 2011).

Hong Kong has a very small bond market because of its conservative fiscal policy. In 2009, the value of bonds listed in Hong Kong was only 2 per cent of the United Kingdom's value and 1 per cent of the United States. Shanghai has a much larger bond market due to the activist fiscal policy China. At the end of 2008, the value of bonds listed in Shanghai was over six times that of Hong Kong.

Given the vast size and rapid growth of the Chinese economy, the Shanghai financial markets are expected to surpass those of Hong Kong in scale. However, the Hong Kong financial markets perform much better than the markets of Shanghai. This is reflected in the much higher scores and rank of Hong Kong in the Global Financial Centres Index (GFCI) compared with Shanghai. Hong Kong has a huge lead in the rule of law, in free flow of information, in transparency of regulations and in free and fair arbitration to resolve business disputes.

The GFCI is a semi-annual study launched by the City of London

Corporation in early 2007. In the eight studies conducted thus far (Z/Yen Group 2010) Hong Kong and Singapore ranked consistently in third or fourth place after the two global leaders, London and New York. In the first four studies from early 2007 up to the 2008 financial crisis, Hong Kong's rating was approximately 80 points behind the two global leaders. In the GFCI 8 released in September 2010, Hong Kong was only 10 points behind London and New York and 'Hong Kong has joined London and New York as a genuinely global financial centre' (Z/Yen Group 2010).

From GFCI 1 to 8, Shanghai jumped from 24th to 6th, and its rating rose from 576 to 693, still approximately 70 points behind Hong Kong. In GFCI 8, Shanghai and Beijing are classified as 'Global Specialists – they do not yet offer a sufficiently developed and diversified service to be global leaders'.

Although the Shanghai financial markets are quite large, the city lags far behind Hong Kong in international finance because the RMB is not convertible on the capital account. For instance, at the end of 2008, Shanghai foreign currency deposits were only 7 per cent of Hong Kong's and Shanghai foreign currency loans were only a third of those of Hong Kong. The Shanghai foreign exchange market turnover was only 5 per cent of that of Hong Kong in 2007.

As previously mentioned, China plans to gradually liberalise capital controls and internationalise the RMB. China has taken trial steps in this direction, utilising the financial markets of Hong Kong. Since early 2004, China has allowed the development of offshore personal RMB business in Hong Kong, and Hong Kong residents could open RMB accounts, with daily exchange limits of RMB 20,000. Since mid-2007, China has allowed its financial institutions, including the Ministry of Finance, to issue RMB bonds in Hong Kong. This would help establish a benchmark yield for the government debt of China, as well as stimulate the development of the Hong Kong bond market. In April 2009, China allowed the mainland branches of Hong Kong banks to issue RMB bonds in Hong Kong (Bank of East Asia 2009).

In July 2009, China started a pilot scheme to use RMB for trade settlement in five cities (i.e., Shanghai, Guangzhou, Shenzhen, Zhuhai and Dongguan, and Hong Kong). Apart from facilitating the mainland China–Hong Kong trade, the scheme would also enhance the status of RMB, and promote the development of Hong Kong as a major offshore RMB business centre (Tse 2009).

The RMB is likely to be convertible on the capital account in the medium term, and Shanghai will be able to develop its international financial business more rapidly. However, the development of international financial business is highly dependent on free flow of information and a clean, transparent and even-handed regulatory environment. Given the corrupt and cumbersome bureaucracy in China, the development of a reputable legal framework and a transparent and fair regulatory environment is likely to require political reforms that are more time-consuming and risky than economic reforms. As long as Hong Kong can maintain its world-class standard in market regulation and quality of financial services, it will have an edge over Shanghai.

Although Hong Kong has a big lead over Shanghai in quality of regulatory environment and institutions, Hong Kong cannot match the size of the Shanghai financial markets in the long run. The competition between Hong Kong and Shanghai in financial services will be very intense once China achieves capital account convertibility. Unlike transportation, in which the natural hinterlands of Hong Kong and Shanghai are separated, geographical distance is not significant in financial transactions. Time zone is a factor in financial transactions; however, Hong Kong and Shanghai are in the same time zone.

To avoid head-on competition with Shanghai, Hong Kong should specialise in niches such as derivatives, wealth management and re-insurance. Hong Kong is significantly ahead in derivatives, not only because of superior financial expertise, but also because it has a freer market than Shanghai. The Chinese government tends to put various restrictions on financial markets due to political and social considerations (e.g., China continues to restrict short-selling and restrict the magnitude of stock price movements). Hong Kong will have an advantage in derivatives for a long time to come.

The Hong Kong advantage in rule of law and protection of property rights is especially important in business insurance and re-insurance, which involve complicated contracts. Secure property rights is also important in wealth management. The many emerging millionaires in mainland China prefer to place their wealth in Hong Kong. That the Hong Kong fund management business rose from 1,485 billion to 9,631 billion from 2000 to 2007, increasing by 549 per cent, is no accident (Sung 2011). Hong Kong has become an important regional fund management centre, especially for mainland funds. The Hong Kong fund management business is highly international, involving many non-Hong Kong investors and very substantial amounts of assets outside Hong Kong/China, as well as outside Asia.

Finally, capital account convertibility of the RMB poses threats, as well as opportunities, for Hong Kong. With a convertible RMB, Hong Kong will face intense competition from Shanghai in international financial business. However, Hong Kong will gain as a wealth management centre as mainland wealth will be able to flow freely to Hong Kong. Although wealth management business has suffered a great deal from the financial tsunami as investors have abandoned complicated structural products for 'plain vanilla' products, the willingness of investors to take risks will return with economic recovery (Hong Kong's fund management business fell by 39 per cent in 2008, but rebounded by 45 per cent in 2009) (Hong Kong Securities and Futures Commission 2010).

CONCLUSION

In comparison with Hong Kong, Shanghai has an important advantage in location because it is the hub of the YRD, which is substantially larger than the PRD in economic size. However, the Hong Kong pre-eminence appears when the rule of law, clean and transparent governance and fair regulation are taken into account. Quality of institutions is a most important long-run determinant of the level of development.

Presently, Shanghai has a much higher rate of economic growth. However, its growth rate will probably slow down as its level of economic development approaches that of Hong Kong. Shanghai needs to greatly upgrade the quality of its economic institutions. If Shanghai can achieve the level of quality of Hong Kong institutions, it may surpass Hong Kong in economic development because its natural hinterland is larger in terms of economic size than that Hong Kong.

Since the early 20th century, London and New York have been the only global financial centres. Given the size and dynamism of East Asian economies, and the significal difference in time zone between East Asia and Europe or America, there is obviously the scope for a third global finance centre to emerge in East Asia. Presently, Hong Kong and Singapore are the leaders among East Asian financial hubs. However, in the long run, Shanghai will be a serious contender. The crucial barrier to the realisation of the potential of Shanghai is the quality of its institutions.

In political and economic governance, Shanghai is part of the mainland system whereas Hong Kong is separated from the mainland under 'one country, two systems' principles. This means that Shanghai has better access to the mainland market. Moreover, Beijing is likely to favour Shanghai over Hong Kong in China's national development strategy because Shanghai is politically more trustworthy and reliable.

However, the fact that Shanghai is part of mainland's system imposes severe constraints on Shanghai's ability to reform and upgrade its institutions. Shanghai cannot change its legal system and political governance unless China does the same. The road to rule of law, clean government

and transparent regulation in China will be lengthy and perhaps tortu-
ous as political reforms are likely to be more difficult and more risky than
economic reforms.

With the rise of China, Beijing is determined to make the RMB an
international currency. China has adopted a 'dual financial centres' model
that would utilise the comparative advantages of both Hong Kong and
Shanghai. The liberalisation and internationalisation of China's financial system will provide many opportunities for both Hong Kong and
Shanghai. For instance, both cities are involved in the 2009 China trail
scheme to use the RMB for trade settlement. Several leading Hong Kong
firms, including HSBC, are planning to list in Shanghai (*South China
Morning Post*, 30 April 2009).

In short, Hong Kong and Shanghai are the only Chinese cities that can
aspire to be global service hubs. With the rise of China, the prospect of the
two cities as global service hubs has an important bearing on the role of
China in the future world economy.

7. Hong Kong: an upgraded gateway for China trade

James J. Wang

INTRODUCTION

This chapter focuses on how Hong Kong has been upgrading itself as a value-added gateway for China's trade in the past three decades. For about 150 years, Hong Kong has been regarded as an entrepôt to Mainland China and plays a pivotal role as a commercial center linking China with the rest of the world.[1] In recent literature on world city studies, Hong Kong has been ranked among the 10 Alpha-level world cities in 2000, 2004, and 2008.[2] Although its status as a world city is weighted heavily by its being a financial center and regional headquarters for transnational corporations (TNC), its port as the busiest hub in the world is also considered as a key factor for its worldwide connectivity. Similar classification and ranking are found from Master Card annual report, which ranks Hong Kong among the top world cities, largely due also to its port throughputs and airport connectivity.[3]

A basic theoretical underpinning in the literature, particularly those from the Globalization and World Cities (GaWC) Research Network, a group of geographers at Loughborough University, UK, is that the formation of a global urban system must be defined by its worldwide connections; at which level a city is positioned in the global urban hierarchy depends largely on the power of control and command it has over the networks of TNCs. The ranking of a city in the world city hierarchy is therefore a reflection of its global and regional influences through a multi-

---

[1] See, for example, Tsai, Jung-Fang (1995); Frankel (1997), pp. 101–102; Leung (2002), pp. 33–36.

[2] Alpha world cities are supposed to be full-service world cities, which are among a roster of 55 world cities considered by the Globalization and World Cities (GaWC) Research Network. They include 10 cities, namely, London, New York, Paris, Tokyo, Chicago, Frankfurt, Hong Kong, Los Angeles, Milan and Singapore. See Taylor (2004).

[3] See Master Card (2008) Worldwide Centers of Commerce Index, at www.mastercard-worldwide.com/insights (accessed May 2010).

layer multiple-center network structure. This conceptual framework has been challenged by Short et al.[4] because it may exclude many cities that are also involved in globalization in one way or another. To bring these cities into the research as they are in the real world, Short et al. defined very loosely the concept of a gateway city as '. . . to refer to the fact that almost any city can act as a gateway for transmission of economic, political and cultural globalization'. This argument has triggered intensive discussions in recent literature in association with many new issues facing many cities that are not considered as 'world city' in this globalization era but are one way or another affected by globalization.[5] In the discussion, Short realized that such loosely defined gateway cities can be better termed as 'globalizing cities'[6] because they are not really gateways. Indeed, it seems that little attention is given to the fact that most well-known and well-studied world cities themselves are also gateway cities. These studies on these cities have been more and more focused on the intangible aspects, financial transactions and networks in particular, as these aspects are considered a proper reflection of power and control. The tangible counterparts, such as transport and logistics for trade in kind, have not received the same amount of attention because it seems that the time to focus on trade in kind is over. Consequently, we tend to forget that all major financial market cities such as London, New York and Chicago were once the major gateway cities in their region, and their financial center status today stemmed from their being gateways of trade in kind in the past.

Interestingly, Hong Kong seems to be still in the transition from a hub for trade in kind to a gateway with more control and operation for intangible transactions. This chapter intends to reveal the process of how such transformation or upgrading takes place. In particular, from a transport geography point of view, we are interested to know, during this process, how Hong Kong selectively keeps its gateway to China as a 'spatial quality' in positioning itself in the era of globalization.

As the central matter here is the gateway city and its transformation, it is necessary to conceptualize the term first. When the concept of gateway city was first formally theorized by Burgardt,[7] it was regarded as a contrast to the concept of a central place. Revisiting Burgardt's conceptualization should therefore be a proper starting point before we turn into our study of how Hong Kong is upgrading itself into a new type of gateway.

4   Short et al. (2000), pp. 317–340.
5   See, for example, Eliana and Taylor (2006), pp. 515–534. The intention of this paper is to insert Brazilian cities into the world city context.
6   See a discussion in Short (2004), pp. 21–46.
7   Burgardt (1971), pp. 269–285.

REVISIT OF BURGARDT'S THEORY OF A GATEWAY CITY

Burgardt defines a gateway city as one in command of the connections between the tributary area and the outside world. Using disaggregate employment data in North America, he argues in some cases that a gateway city tends to be more heavily committed to transportation and wholesaling than serve as a central place. He then proposes a hypothesis describing the dynamics on how an existing gateway city may be challenged:

1   The gateway will be shorn of much of its original hinterland, and will be reduced to the position of a central place with a service area not much larger than that of its newer competitors.
2   However, the former gateway will retain its transport nodality, and hence will probably remain one level above its competitors in the central place hierarchy.
3   If the former gateway is located between areas of markedly differing intensities of production, the extended hinterland may be rotated from the productive area previously controlled into the more sterile area.
4   The final state, after a long period of time, will be an approximation of the classical central place distribution and hierarchy of centers. (Burghardt, 1971)

Burghardt collected some cases to prove this hypothesis (including Winnipeg as a gateway for middle and west Canada, Cincinnati for the Appalachian region in USA), although the results were not very convincing because he could not exhaust all the development possibilities of how gateway cities may change. These points were suggested almost 40 years ago, so it is not surprising that the theory does not take the impacts of globalization into consideration. It is expected, however, that Burghardt's theory does not discuss much on institutional barriers which in fact are equally important, if not more important, in creating and conditioning gateway cities located at boundaries between two politically or economically divided countries or geographical systems. Indeed, in the cases of Cluj as a gateway for Transylvania (in challenging Budapest in the early 19th century) and Cincinnati as a gateway for central USA in modern history, the relative accessibility and transportability in terms of distance and physical barriers. It seems that these gateway cities gained popularity through their role in the process of military and political occupation for the period studied, and this may be the reason why Burghardt overlooked the trading conditions and institutional barriers relating to trade.

Another drawback of the theory comes from its urban systems approach, as it fails to point out how a gateway as a node in transport networks differs from other nodes. From a transport geography perspective, the major difference between a central place and a gateway city is that the former is of centrality with regard to spatial quality, while intermediacy is the spatial quality of the latter.

According to Fleming and Hayuth (1994), centrality and intermediacy are identified as the

> spatial qualities that enhance the traffic levels of transportation hubs, and hence indicate which places are strategically located within transportation systems. The local, regional, national, continental or hemispheric centrality of a city has a fundamental impact on the city's own size and function and on its traffic-generating powers. Intermediacy, while it may reflect a natural geographical 'in betweenness', is a spatial quality that needs to be defined in the specific context of contemporary or prospective transportation systems and networks. Intermediate places can be given extra traffic if they are favoured by transport carriers as connecting hubs or relay points in the system.

With the cases drawn from the United States and other counties, they proved that such spatial qualities led to various ways of formulating transportation hubs, and many large hub cities possess both spatial attributes at various scales or levels. In another paper, Fleming and Hayuth used container hubs such as Rotterdam and Hong Kong to illustrate how the shipping lines in the 20th century reinforced these places as great gateways due to the ever-increasing global trade and their routing and business strategies.

From the world city theory to the theorization of transport hubs based on the concepts of centrality and intermediacy, we see a major difference: the former focuses on the spatial organization of intangible networks, while the latter emphasizes the impacts of physical movement and the strategies of the movers/carriers. For a trade-based city, the questions left unanswered are as follows. First, how can such a world city with both centrality and intermediacy be affected when its intermediacy or gateway city status with multi-modal hub (airport and port) is partly taken over by nearby cities? Second, how will the city react to this kind of change? These questions deserve serious inquiry with real world cases. Hong Kong is going to be investigated for this purpose.

THE CASE OF HONG KONG

Hong Kong as a major commercial gateway to China has witnessed many changes in the past few decades. Before 1978 when the country started implementing its open-door policy with economic reforms, Hong Kong was regarded as the only gateway to handle the trade between China and

Western countries and the global market at large. After 1978, particularly after the establishment of the Shenzhen Special Economic Zone (SEZ), most Hong Kong industrial enterprises moved and/or expanded north to Shenzhen SEZ and gradually towards nearby cities in the Pearl River Delta (PRD) region such as Dongguan and Huizhou. From the mid-1980s to the mid-1990s, a new spatial model, the 'front-door back-factory' (*qian dian hou chang*), was set up, meaning there is a spatial division of labor in the manufacturing sector with headquarters and design units in Hong Kong and the production in PRD.[8] Taking both the trade network ability of Hong Kong firms and the low costs of labor and rent in PRD, the model was a great success, making PRD as one of the world's leading manufacturing bases for labor-intensive products such as electronic goods, toys and clothing.

One consequence of this model was the increasing cross-border traffic of containers between the Hong Kong port and PRD factories. A rational solution to this, as understood by both the market and the state, was to have more container terminals on the mainland. Joint ventures between the Shenzhen government and private container terminal operators in Hong Kong therefore acted in time to erect new large container terminals first in Shekou and Yantian in Shenzhen from the early 1990s, and later in Nansha in Guangzhou, in order to reduce the land trucking costs and thus keep the cost-led competitiveness of the region in the world market.

This process of port regionalization[9] with new hubs/main ports in other cities eased cross-border traffic but also significantly diminished the future growth potential of Hong Kong as the most important container hub in the region. For about 10 years from 1995 to 2004, the government of the Hong Kong Special Administration Region (SAR) has made a variety of efforts, such as reducing the border-crossing time of trucks, in order to keep the port competitive.[10] However, existing major terminal operators show no intention of expanding port activities in Hong Kong because they have all invested in Shenzhen or Guangzhou ports, the two competitors of the Hong Kong port. Moreover, their expertise has helped the two mainland ports to improve significantly in all aspects, which not only led to more international shipping lines providing direct services but also effectively affected the performance of the customs, which has been regarded as a major disadvantage for ports in the mainland. The shrinking performance gap between the ports across the border raises two critical questions about the role of Hong Kong in South China at large or the PRD in particular:

---

[8] See a detailed discussion in Sit (1998), pp. 880–904.
[9] See Notteboom and Rodrigue (2005), pp. 297–313.
[10] See McKinsey & Company (2003).

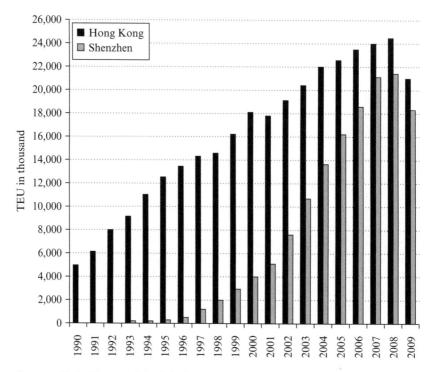

Source: (1) the Census and Statistics Department of the Hong Kong SAR Government, (2) Transport Bureau of the Shenzhen City Government.

Figure 7.1   Growth of container throughputs in Hong Kong and Shenzhen

Will Hong Kong follow the path of London and New York to become a financial and cultural center and see its shipping and logistics hub being relocated to or replaced by other cities? If this were the case, would Hong Kong still function as a gateway to China or be marginalized to a regional central place as suggested by Burgardt's theory?

To answer these questions, we need to separate the two aspects of the Hong Kong gateway for analytical purpose. The first is how it serves the region of the Pearl River Delta, and the second is how it contributes to Hong Kong's own economy, that is, how the city gains from being a gateway. In the following section, we shall first examine how the port role has been changing by providing more transshipment services to the region while handling a smaller share of import-export cargo, which may lead to fewer opportunities for value-added logistics. We shall then examine the key data in the gateway trade – the re-export of Hong Kong in relation with China – in order to see what kind of role Hong Kong plays as an intermediary between China, and how it is played through the two major intermodal gateway interfaces, the port and the airport.

The definition given by the Hong Kong Government is as follows:

> Goods imported into Hong Kong or exported/re-exported from Hong Kong are classified as direct shipment, whereas goods transshipped in Hong Kong under a *through bill of lading* (as distinguished from those imported into Hong Kong for subsequent re-exportation) are classified as transshipment. Goods in transit through Hong Kong are not included in the statistics.[11]

In other words, transshipments are defined as those goods that go through Hong Kong territory purely for transportation purpose as trade between two other countries, and are not included in Hong Kong trade figures but are counted as part of transportation figures such as port throughput. According to this definition, we notice that 56 percent of the total containerized cargo handled at the Hong Kong port, or 10 million TEUs[12] out of a total of 19. 3 million TEU laden containers were through bills of lading, implying that they did not involve any value-added activities other than port services provided in Hong Kong. In other words, for these cargoes, Hong Kong is a 'stopover' place purely for vessel relay to complete their entire journey (see Figure 7.2).

Among these cargoes, 48 percent of inward transshipment was from mainland China, and a total of 68 percent of the outward transshipment were going to non-mainland China destinations, indicating the transshipment hub function of Hong Kong in linking China and other countries.

In a comparison to the pattern of transshipments and that of waterborne imports and exports in Hong Kong, the similarities are found both in the origin structure in the inward/import side and the destination structure in the outward/export side, which may imply the overall trade characteristics of South China (Pearl River Delta region in particular). The major difference lies in the fact that Hong Kong seems to have more exports (including re-exports) with America and Europe than those transshipped in Hong Kong.

The laden containers to and from mainland China are estimated at 3.78 million TEU, which is equal to 20 percent of the total laden container throughput of the Hong Kong port. Considering that 39 percent of waterborne imports were from China and 27 percent of the exports/re-exports

---

[11]   The definition is taken from the Web site of the Census and Statistics Department, Government of the Hong Kong Special Administrative Region.
[12]   TEU stands for Twenty-foot Equivalent Unit, which refers to the size of a 20-foot-long container set by the International Standard Organization.

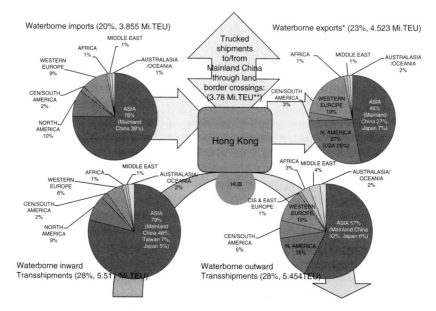

Note: Data with * and ** are estimated by the author.

Source: Compiled by the author, with the data collected from various ports in the Pearl River Delta, and the Census and Statistics Department, Government of the Hong Kong Special Administrative Region.

Figure 7.2   Hong Kong Port: shares of waterborne laden containers by shipping direction, 2006

were from China, at most, 6 million TEU of China-related containerized cargo could have been involved in the value-added logistics in Hong Kong (except for loading and unloading at container terminals), which was only about one-fourth of the total throughput of the Hong Kong port (23.539 million TEU in 2006, including empty containers handled). From these calculations, we may infer that the huge total throughput number could be misleading, and further growth by handling more water-borne container traffic may not contribute as much to Hong Kong's economy as it first appears.

Let us turn now to the issue of those re-exports that may involve value-added logistics activities. According to the Hong Kong government:

> Re-exports of goods refer to products which have previously been imported into Hong Kong and which are re-exported without having undergone in Hong Kong a manufacturing process which has changed permanently the shape,

nature, form or utility of the product. Their values are recorded on f.o.b. (free-on-board) basis.[13]

As intermediaries in entrepôt trade, Hong Kong firms trade a large number of Chinese goods in terms of re-exports, that is, simple processing such as sorting or packaging, or service activities such as marketing or transport. They also intermediate re-exports to China. In 1996, the re-exports of Hong Kong accounted for 47 percent of China's total imports.[14] Enright et al. (1997) estimated that in 1994, export-import services accounted for 18 percent of Hong Kong's GDP.[15]

Another fact is highlighted in a recent survey[16] on the changing transport services of Hong Kong's re-export business: since 2002, air transport has become the most important mode, replacing maritime shipping, in terms of total re-export values. By 2007, air transport handled 37 percent of the total re-exports of Hong Kong in trade value. Most firms gained in the transport, and the logistics during this period were air-transport related. Noting that maritime shipping and air transport handle different types of cargo, the former dealing with large-volume, time-definite goods while the latter with small-volume, time-sensitive goods, we would like to examine further if such a modal shift means a change in foreland market.

Using time-series data on Hong Kong re-exports as a percentage of its total trade value, the top eight destination countries/territories are compared in Figure 7.3. The following facts are worth noticing:

● From 1972 to 2008, the total re-export ratios fluctuated within a range of 5 percent–32 percent between Hong Kong and its major Asian trade partners, namely, Taiwan, Singapore, Japan and South Korea. In contrast, those ratios between Hong Kong and European and North American countries such as USA, Germany and the UK changed dramatically in a normative 'S' shape – from 2 percent–3 percent in the 1970s before China's economic reforms and up to 60 percent–70 percent after 1994 when Shenzhen began to operate direct container shipping routes to major markets in the world.

● Assuming that Hong Kong has had a constant proportion of imports and exports from each of its trade partners for its own consumption during this period, the divergent trend between the intra-Asia market and the long-distance market may reflect an important fact:

[13] See   http://www.censtatd.gov.hk/hong_kong_statistics/statistics_by_subject/concept/external_trade/index.jsp (accessed May 2010).
[14] Sung, Yun-Wing (1997). See also Young (1999).
[15] Enright et al. (1997).
[16] Wang and Cheng (2009).

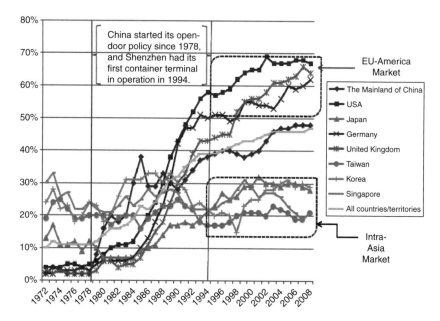

Source: Census and Statistics Department, Government of the Hong Kong Special
Administrative Region.

*Figure 7.3   Hong Kong re-exports as a percentage of total trade:
                comparison of the top eight destination countries/territories*

from the middle of 1990s, Hong Kong began to focus its gateway
role in linking China with EU and North American markets, while
its focus on the intra-Asia market was only secondary.

These facts seem to confirm that since China entered the world market
as a major producer, the gateway role of Hong Kong has changed substantially and North America and Europe became more important for
Hong Kong. The shift in the past 10 years towards the greater use of air
transport rather than maritime shipping has reinforced this trend in a
special manner: as a higher percentage of re-exports are time sensitive and
are handled by air transport to/from the same group of markets (mainly
USA and EU) from/to China, Hong Kong can still gain in its value-added
logistics despite seeing a slowdown, negative growth or greater transshipment in its port throughout.

Indeed, two things seem to contribute to more transshipment in Hong
Kong port. First, as more Chinese coastal ports have been involved in
global trade and the interlining services by foreign shipping lines are not

allowed within Chinese mainland ports, it becomes common practice for these liners to use Hong Kong as their transshipment hub for overbooking and interlining operations. Second, when the labor and land become more expensive in the coastal China, some global supply chains have begun to explore a 'multi-hinterland strategy', that is, to have different components produced in low-labor-cost Asian coastal cities (especially those of ASEAN members such as Vietnam and Indonesia), and then assembled somewhere in China before shipping to Europe or North America. These two causes mean a more integrated Asian economy as a whole, and therefore more intensified intra-Asian trade than global trade is anticipated.

CONCLUSIONS

In this chapter, we argue that an upgraded logistics and trade gateway is in the making in Hong Kong. This process started in the early 1980s when China re-entered the world market and opened up more and more gateways along its long coast. The process is not yet complete as large re-export activities are still currently taking place through the port of Hong Kong, an indicator of gateway for trade-in-kind, although air transport has become more critical than maritime transport. In relation to the theory of the gateway city, the case of Hong Kong sheds light on the following two points. First, gateway functions may be shared by more than one city in a region of huge trade and logistics demands. When container port business became regionalized, Hong Kong upgraded its gateway role using its air transport, together with many other advantages in global trade. Good infrastructure for multi-modal gateways is a foundation for a gateway city to upgrade itself to high-end trade and logistics. We have seen that the spatial diffusion of gateway functions in the Greater Pearl River Delta region and the intermodal upgrading of the gateway in Hong Kong happened as two sides of one process, a process of building a regional gateway hierarchy. This is clearly different from the central place hierarchy suggested by Burgardt.

Second, the hub-and-spoke structure of shipping lines and airports may be one of the reasons for a hub city to favor distant markets. Cities with hub port and/or airport have much better connectivity with all other cities, within their region or beyond. However, nearby cities in the shadow of a hub may suffer from such a 'one-hub-in-a-region' arrangement by shipping lines or airlines. In other words, since it is not possible for non-hub cities to compete on trunk services between hubs, they may focus on secondary markets through direct services, which will in turn makes hub cities more focused on the major market at a distance. The re-export business in Hong Kong having become more focused on North America and Europe is a good example.

To put these two points into a broader context, we can compare the case of Hong Kong with Amsterdam, London and New York in the past, and Shanghai and Dubai in the future. Centuries ago, Amsterdam and London as two major European trade and transport hubs gradually lost their dominance in making trade in kind and in their maritime hub status; however, both have retained and further developed their financial market, and most importantly, their air transport hubs in Europe. A similar evolution can be said to have happened in New York, which was the most important trade gateway for the entire North America up until half a century ago. Since the 1960s when port business gradually moved away to the New Jersey port due to high land rents in Manhattan,[17] and since 1990 when the global order-placing center for garments and toys moved to Hong Kong due to economic globalization and the China factor, financial services and many other tertiary services and activities became the core business in New York. All these high value-added non-trade-in-kind activities stemmed from the previous role of the city as a cargo hub, and relied much as before, if not more, on the global connectivity provided by air transport and telecommunication.

In the future, we will probably see Shanghai and Dubai go through similar gateway upgrading processes. Shanghai, for example, has become the world's busiest port by total cargo throughput since 2007, and it is now achieving its new goal to be a top international financial center[18] while port cities nearby such as Ningbo compete for the flow of international trade in kind.[19] A similar objective is pursued by Dubai.[20]

From a global perspective, we may see these cities (London, New York, Amsterdam, Hong Kong, Shanghai and Dubai) among the top ranks in the gateway city hierarchy because of where they are located and the role they play. However, there has been little research done on the similarities and differences between these gateway cities, the needs and possibilities for

[17] See Levinson (2006), Chapter 5.
[18] As announced on March 25, 2009, the State Council of China gave the green light to speed up the process of turning Shanghai into a major international financial and shipping center by 2020. It urged Shanghai to be developed into a multi-functional financial center by 2020 to keep up with 'China's economic influence and the yuan's international position'. For more details, see the *China Daily* website: http://www.chinadaily.com.cn/china/2009-03/26/content_7617756.htm (accessed May 2010).
[19] See Wang and Olivier (2007), pp. 193–197.
[20] The Dubai International Financial Center (DIFC) opened in September 2005, considering itself 'the world's fastest growing international financial center'. It aims to develop the same stature as New York, London and Hong Kong. See http://www.difc.ae/ (accessed May 2010).

the region to develop a hierarchy of gateway cities, or the division of the gateway role among a few cities in the region. As today's advancements in telecommunication may allow further separation of money transactions and physical movement of cargo for trade-in-kind, research on gateway hierarchy and gateway upgrading is imperative for many cities to position themselves properly in an increasingly globalizing world.

If Hong Kong could do anything to distinguish itself from the afore-mentioned cities, it must still be its role between China and the rest of the world. 2009 and 2010 witnessed four ASEAN+1 free trade agreements (FTAs). A free trade Asia is anticipated to appear in the near future. When the tariff barriers are gone in this region, non-tariff barriers will be more sensitive to the operators of global supply chains using Asia as production base. It would be a great challenge for Hong Kong to make itself a leading Asian trade hub by further reducing non-tariff barriers, particularly those related to Mainland China.

8.   Singapore in the new economic geography: from geographic location to the relocation of economic dynamics

Loïs Bastide

Singapore was founded as a node within the extensive network of trading routes that developed across the British Empire. The settlement's value laid in its highly strategic location between Europe, India, China and the Malay Archipelago at the most convenient crossroads for goods and merchants operating within these geographical sub-systems against the background of the geo-political interplay between the Dutch and the British in Asia. Indeed, its location was the only resource underpinning Singapore's growth (Huff 1997: 7). This early advantage of geographic location was very significant within the particular patterns of trade and geo-politics of the early 19th century and, supplemented by free port status, facilitated Singapore's growth as a major entrepôt for trade within both the British Empire and Asia.

This early asset was instrumental in producing economic growth at a time when transport was slow, making distance a critical economic parameter. Yet, this 'natural edge' was to become less relevant following the drop in transportation costs and the marginalization of distance as a crucial economic constraint as a result of the rapid development of telecommunications and the widespread use of containerization (Trace 2002) and air transportation. However, in a context in which geography alone can no longer support Singapore's growth, the city has succeeded in securing its pivotal position within new economic geographies largely framed by the organizational logics of transnational corporations' production networks (Veltz 1997) and changes in patterns of capital flows. We suggest that this success, as fragile as it may look, can be seen as a result of Singapore's ability to re-create location effects in a context in which distance has been marginalized as a determining factor of patterns of economic activity. In this respect, we wish to show that Singapore, through detailed policy planning, has substituted or at least supplemented geography with a sophisticated 'built environment' in order to retain its position as an important trading hub within a new economic system.

The chapter will be organized in three sections. In the first section, we will look at the city's early history. Through a brief overview of its shifting position within changing pre-independence patterns of economic activity, first as an entrepôt within the British Empire and also for the junk trade and then as a staple port, we will show that location underpinned the city's economic growth until the 1960s.

In the second section, we will show how, as distance became less important as a structuring feature of global trade, Singapore took advantage of the international expansion of Western and Japanese firms to secure its position within the expanding transnational system of production organization by adopting an aggressive policy designed to capture and channel foreign direct investment. By attracting foreign enterprises, Singapore carved out a position for itself within the expanding geographies of transnational corporations.

In the last section, we will show that the country's endeavor to rise up the value chain and become a preferred site for transnational corporations' high-end operations required the crafting of a carefully designed material and immaterial environment, which re-produced location effects relevant to the configurations of the new economic geographies.

EARLY HISTORY: LINKING TRADE SYSTEMS

The founding of Singapore in 1819 was a strategic move by the British East India Company (EIC) both to secure its China trade and to penetrate the Malay Archipelago trade systems against a background of fierce competition with Dutch traders bent on advancing their mercantilist interests in the region. Indeed, the island of Temasek, where the settlement was established, was strategically located in terms both of maritime security and its central position between different trading systems and maritime zones (Hamashita 2003). Its location at the southernmost tip of the Malay Peninsula, at the crossroad between India and China and between mainland Asia and the Malay Archipelago, gave Singapore a natural edge to become a bulk-breaking and redistribution center for the region and made it a convenient place for regional trading networks to join long-distance shipping routes. Thus from its inception Singapore fulfilled a double function within the broader framework of the British Empire's commercial interests: the colony was used as a connecting hub between regional and world shipping routes where cargo could be consolidated and then transported further along several trading sub-systems, serving different destinations and operated by different merchant communities, and as a port of call on long shipping routes (Trocki 2005; Huff 1997). Thus Singapore's geographic location served as a 'switch' between different trading zones, facilitating communications within the broader framework of the British commercial and imperial enterprise.

As mentioned, maritime trade systems and trading routes which crisscrossed maritime spaces and linked ports in the East Asian region and connected the region to the West through India were not homogenous. They were distributed between different maritime zones, trading communities and networks[1] and trading systems which communicated within global economic systems in which they operated in ways that were both articulated and discontinuous, with each community specializing in terms of economic zone and adopting distinctive trading practices.[2] Among these overlapping networks, Singapore came to have two main functions. The city soon emerged both as a bulk-breaking station for British manufactured goods, from where they were then forwarded and distributed throughout the region by local and regional merchants, and as a collecting point for Straits produce from the Malay Peninsula and Dutch India, which was then shipped towards Europe or China (Jones 2000; Jones and Wale 1998; Kratoska 2006; Trocki 2005). In this sense, Raffles'[3] vision of making the colony into a strategic trading outpost within China's trade system proved unsuccessful. Instead, European ships running the India-China trading route would typically stop for bunkering and to load small amounts of local bulk, mainly cargoes of Straits produce consolidated in Singapore by Chinese and merchants from the archipelago, before proceeding eastward or westward. As a result, Singapore actually became the gateway for the Malay region (Huff 1997). It also emerged as a major logistical platform for the junk trade (Hamashita 2003), functioning as an entrepôt for regional trade in East Asia, notably for Straits products, raw materials, rice and opium.

However, Singapore's position was to change greatly from the 1870s

---

[1]   Let us mention Western merchants and agency houses, trading Straits produce against manufactured goods, Chinese merchants running the junk trade, who had a strong hold on Straits produce and staple production and were very active in the opium trade, and regional traders such as the Bugis, who supplied the archipelago.
[2]   A good example is the very different commercial practices that distinguished the tributary system, which linked East-Asian countries, from the treaty ports system (Preston 2007; Latham 1994; Hamashita 2003).
[3]   After having served the EIC as Governor General of Java between 1811 and 1815, during the British takeover of the Dutch East Indies in the context of the Napoleonic Wars, Stamford Raffles had been appointed Lieutenant Governor of Bencoolen – now Bengkulu – in West Sumatra in 1817, when he founded an outpost in Singapore in 1819.

onwards, because of two historical circumstances. First, industrialization in Europe was to give rise to a booming demand for regional staples,
first tin, then rubber by the turn of the 20th century, and later petroleum
(Huff 1997; Jones and Wale 1998; Ramasamy 2007; Booth 2008). This
new demand for raw materials produced in the Malay Peninsula and in
Dutch India re-positioned Singapore as a staple port for its Malay hinterland, from where locally extracted staples were exported to the West
(Tan 2007, 2008), thus reinforcing both Singapore's regional ties with
the Malay region and its strategic position within the British Empire.
Second, the revolution in transportation triggered by the advent of steam-
ships and the opening of the Suez Canal reinforced Singapore's position
as a port of call, not only for Southeast Asia but notably for the China
trade, as all ships that had previously sailed through the Sunda Straits
subsequently passed through the Malacca Straits, thus sailing through
Singapore waters (Ken 1978; Frost 2004). Steamship navigation only
reinforced Singapore's increasingly central position within multi-layered
trade systems, as the port became a major stop for bunkering, where ships
could both break bulk and fill up empty cargo space at a low marginal
cost.In this context of expanding trade systems, rising demand for regional
staples tied to industrialization in the West and slow transportation, location proved a highly strategic resource in Singapore's pre-independence
period. However, this geographic advantage was subsumed within a set
of economic and geo-political forces whose rationale lay outside the city
itself, mainly in the greater interests of British mercantile enterprise and
the regional junk trade system, within which Singapore functioned as an
entrepôt. Since Singapore had practically no domestic industry or staple of
its own, the economic outcomes of location were dependent upon global
economic circumstances, which lay far outside the control of its authorities and depended heavily on the shifting nature of demand for imports in
Western countries. After 50 years of rather slow growth as a gateway for
the Malay region (Huff 1987), Singapore found some economic stability
and high growth potential through consolidation of its 'natural' Malay
hinterland and its position as a staple port. This situation lasted until the
colony gained independence in 1965.

SINGAPORE: FOREIGN DIRECT INVESTMENT AND THE NEW GEOGRAPHIES OF TRADE AND PRODUCTION

In 1965, when Singapore was separated from Malaysia, the political split
was soon followed by a deep restructuring of the city's economy and a

qualitative shift which affected its position within economic geographies. To borrow Saskia Sassen's formulation, political sovereignty, along with emerging reorganizations within the global economy, marked a *tipping point* (Sassen 2006: 9)[4] in Singapore's history, heralding a period that would see both a radical restructuring and the maintenance of continuities in the city's economy and its integration into global patterns of economic activity. To understand this shift, it is useful to consider both the path taken by Singapore after independence to develop its domestic economy and the historical context in which this process unfolded.

At independence, the country's economic position as a staple port for the region was under serious threat, as Singapore had been both severed from its Malay hinterland, which provided the bulk of its staple inputs, and deprived of a viable market for industrialization based on import substitution (Huff 1997: 34; Trocki 2005: 166). Soaring unemployment made the situation even more volatile. In these uncertain times, Singapore faced two main risks: first, the city was exposed to disruption of its trade and, as a result, to economic collapse because of its over-dependency both upon a few staples and on a region that was turning dangerously unfriendly. Second, the situation carried a high potential for political and social unrest under strained economic and labor market conditions. In order to address these threats, the government identified economic growth as the essential precondition for nation-building if the incipient state was to survive as an independent polity (Castells 1992; Low 2001; Yao 2007).

Economic development was to be based on an export-oriented growth strategy that would allow Singapore both to bypass the region as its main trading partner and to compensate for a small domestic market. This economic strategy took advantage of historical circumstances. From the late 1950s onwards, US companies had started to 'go international', adopting transnational relocation strategies that would thereafter increasingly rearrange global patterns of economic activity. An increasing number of companies then started to disperse their operations and value chains across different countries, thereby rearranging the geographic landscape of industrial production to form what Pierre Veltz has termed the 'archipelago economy' (Veltz 1996). Singapore took advantage of these dynamics in order to make up for the lack of domestic capital and technical know-how, by backing its export-oriented growth strategy with inflows of foreign capital. In order to secure foreign capital inflows, the government shaped the city into an attractive environment with cheap labor, favorable

---

[4] S. Sassen defines a *tipping point* as the time-space where institutions, taken in a broad sense, tip into new historical circumstances and are reframed accordingly, both developing into new patterns and retaining historical continuities.

tax regimes and good infrastructures, making it appealing to foreign firms wishing to locate offshore assembly plants in Asia (Mirza 1986; Rodan 1989; Chia 1997; Perry et al. 1997). In the context of the 'new international division of labor' (Fröbel et al. 1980), the foreign capital thus attracted provided the means for fast industrialization and helped to absorb a growing workforce. More importantly, it positioned Singapore as a strategic site within the fast-expanding economic geographies of transnational firms and capital (Rodan 2004). In this respect, foreign capital played a decisive part in diversifying Singapore's economy: by integrating the city into transnational corporations' production networks and the regional trade in parts and components (Athukorala 2008), trade in manufactured goods moved the economy away from its narrow focus on a few staples. Moreover, the global span of transnational corporations' geographic organization lifted Singapore out of its confinement in its immediate geographic and geo-political setting in the Malay world.

The volume of foreign direct investment (FDI) was to grow rapidly. In 1972, Singapore's cumulative stock of foreign direct investment stood at US$547 million (Mirza 1986: 9). In 2007, it reached US$250 billion, an eightfold increase over 1990, making Singapore the world's second largest recipient of inward FDI per capita, just behind Hong Kong (UNCTAD 2009a). In the wider region the country has been consistently capturing a 50 percent share of FDI in Southeast Asia since the 1980s and in 2009 it was only outpaced by China and Hong Kong in Pacific Asia. Critical also in terms of political stability, foreign enterprises accounted for around 50 percent of employment in Singapore's manufacturing sector in 1999 (Ruane and Ugur 2004). Moreover, they accounted for between 70 percent and 75 percent of the country's manufacturing output from 1970 onwards (Blomqvist 2000) and for between 70 percent and 88 percent of Singapore's manufacturing exports (Athukorala 2006; Dent 2003), showing the critical importance of foreign companies not only as engines of industrialization but also as major contributors to Singapore's trade. However, analysis of the impact of foreign capital on Singapore's economy requires a more qualitative approach, as the nature of FDI 'absorption' by the country has shifted over time. Indeed, as transnational companies' corporate organization became more sophisticated and they spread their operations and value chains throughout Pacific Asia against a background of 'production fragmentation' and 'fragmentation trade' (Athukorala 2008), Singapore's central position within pre-war trade patterns shifted as it repositioned itself as a regional control and business center and a manufacturing and assembly offshore platform within the geographies of transnational corporation networks (Yeung et al. 2001). Through this process, Singapore was able to secure its position as a trading hub and logistical platform as it became fully integrated into the emergent geographies of offshore production.

However, Singapore's government did not base their FDI strategy on 'laissez-faire' economics, as was the case in Hong Kong. Indeed, Singapore had to deal with the critical issue of nation-building and this was to have a profound influence on the city-state's political economy in what is arguably the most significant difference with Hong Kong which, as a British and then a Chinese territory, did not have to face this question. This situation has sustained the idea, in Singaporean politics, that close political management of the economy is necessary in order to attune economic development patterns to the perceived political needs of nation building and national survival (Yao 2007). Through the political fine-tuning of the city's economic, social, legal and infrastructural environment, by means of a continuous re assessment of global economic circumstances and dynamics (Siong and Chen 2007) and also through the engineering of various incentive packages (Dent 2003; Soon and Stoever 1996), the government fought both to attract foreign capital and to channel FDI in order to maintain control of economic and development policies. As a result, after a first phase when, in the messy times of independence, foreign direct investment was left to flow in without any clear planning policy and served mainly to sustain the growth of a burgeoning electronic industry and the development of the petroleum sector, the government took a more strategic approach to foreign capital (Huff 1995).

As early as the mid-1970s, not only were economic policies carefully designed in order to embed Singapore into the geography of transnational capital flows but they were also increasingly aimed at enhancing and securing Singapore's functions within the web of shifting economic geographies. In this respect, foreign capital was channeled in such a way as to enable Singapore's industries to rise up the value chain in the international division of corporate operations (Lai-To 2000) by reducing the share of labor-intensive industries and specializing in knowledge, capital-intensive and fully-integrated niche economic sectors such as the wealth-management, bio-pharmaceutical (A*Star 2009) and petro-chemical sectors (Ramasamy 2007; Pillai 2006). In practical terms, the development strategy was to position Singapore both as a services hub, a coordination center and a sophisticated platform for high-end manufacturing processes. This was achieved by identifying specific services and manufacturing sectors on the basis of their high growth potential and by upgrading existing sectors in order to focus on high-end operations throughout the value chain, from research and development to finance and merchandizing. This move is clearly perceptible in the shifting sectorial composition of foreign direct investment. In the manufacturing sector for instance, investments have been redirected to a very significant extent. FDI in electronics has evolved from 36 percent of total manufacturing FDI in 1989 (Chia 1997) to 50 percent in 1997 (Singstat 2007) and 25 percent in 2007 (Singstat 2010) as it has been redirected towards high-end production processes, shifting from personal computers towards industrial electronics. At the same time, investments in the bio-pharmaceutical sector have rocketed, accounting for 41 percent of total manufacturing FDI in 2007, a huge increase over 1995 when it accounted for only 8.3 percent of total sectorial inflows.

This strategy somehow succeeded in moving Singapore into the upper stratum of transnational corporate organization, as a location for higher functions within transnational commodity chains. Indeed, the city has emerged, with Hong Kong, as one of the two preferred locations in East Asia for transnational corporations to set up regional headquarters performing regional coordination and finance operations. Transnational corporations are increasingly dividing their operations between East and Southeast Asia and tending to refine their coordination structures by locating regional headquarters in both cities.[5] Over and above their efforts to shape the city into a major regional control hub, the government also tried to retain some control over transnational corporations' relocation strategies, as they moved their labor-intensive production operations outside of Singapore. As part of this strategy, the Indonesia-Malaysia-Singapore Growth Triangle (IMS-GT), a cross-border economic zone, was created in the 1990s in cooperation with the city's two big neighbors, in a configuration somehow reminiscent of its old Malay hinterland. This transnational territory was conceived of as an integrated economic space, highly compressed within a short distance from Singapore, where transnational corporations could locate their entire value chains. Differentiated national territories could be taken advantage of and linked within flexible global value chains, in which Indonesia would undertake the labor-intensive, low-skill production stages and provide cheap land, Malaysia would accommodate intermediate operations and Singapore would be the hub for high-end production processes and services in a transnational organization of labor, natural resources and capital (Yeoh et al. 2009; Pereira 2009a; Grundy-Warr et al. 1999; Perry 1992). Moreover, the goods produced by the relocated labor-intensive industries would continue to feed Singapore's trade economy, since the city would be the natural gateway for goods entering international commodity supply chains and the location for corporations' higher functions. Although it is yet to

---

[5]   In this emerging geography of regional coordination operations, the position of Hong Kong is somehow uncertain, as it is challenged by mainland China cities such as Beijing and, in a lesser extent, Shanghai (Yeung et al. 2001; Phelps 2007; Ho 2009).

prove fully effective, this strategy was later expanded with the creation of industrial estates in China, Vietnam and India, where foreign corporations could relocate or set up industrial plants. Singapore itself was presented as the natural site for the most sophisticated operations within transnational value-chains, thus strengthening its position as a node within the new economic geographies of transnational companies (Phelps 2007).

As Singapore became integrated into the emerging geographies of expanding transnational corporations, its historical role as an entrepôt, trading hub and financial center underwent a change as a result of the new production and trading patterns. The city's position shifted from that of a commercial outpost within the British Empire trading system to a renewed and carefully politically designed location as a city-state, with a strong development policy, within the patterns of transnational corporation networks. To stick to Saskia Sassen's formulations, Singapore's *capabilities* as a historical entrepôt – say physical and 'soft' infrastructures – have been re-positioned to fit into the new economic configuration of expanding transnational corporations' geographies and organizational logics.

FROM GEOGRAPHIC LOCATION TO RE-LOCATING ECONOMIC DYNAMICS

Singapore's trade patterns today are framed by their integration into these new geographies of transnational production spaces, as the city's historical role as a linking point between an intra-Asian trade system and trans-continental trade patterns has changed to fit into the new organizational framework of transnational corporations. The geo-morphological continuity in this process is evident, as Pacific Asia as a whole still accounted for almost 60 percent of Singapore's total trade in 2007 and there were still evident imbalances in the intensity of its trade with Southeast Asia and more specifically its historical Malay hinterland, now split between Malaysia and Indonesia.[6] However, whereas this geographic position used to reflect Singapore's role as an entrepôt both in the framework of the British Empire and as a strategic crossroads for Asian merchants sailing between China and the Southern Seas, it is now embedded within the 'fragmentation trade' system. In this new configuration, Singapore is now used both as a logistical platform with a pivotal role in forming

---

[6] In 2004, Singapore's trade intensity indexes with commercial partners were 1.68 with East Asia, with a strong bias towards China and Hong Kong (3.28). With ASEAN countries the ratio was 5.63, whereas the persistence of Singapore's trade integration with its historical Malay hinterland is clearly shown, with respectively 11.52 for Indonesia and 10.93 for Malaysia (compiled from Asia Development Bank's data sets).

supply-chains in the region, as a high-tech manufacturing platform and as a services and control center for transnational corporations' operations dispersed throughout the region (Aminian et al. 2007; McKendrick et al. 2000). Thus although it is still strongly focused on Southeast and East Asia, Singapore's physical trade has now to be explained in relation to global production networks and global organizing logics.

Within the broader framework of transnational corporations' operations, the consolidation of an East-Asian trade system is to be understood as the result of the dissemination of production processes throughout Pacific Asia, mainly in the electronics industry. In this configuration, Singapore has secured a position as a logistical hub for linking, coordinating and servicing fragmented production operations in Southeast Asia (Aminian et al. 2007), as a center for dispatching parts and components produced within ASEAN countries to China for assembly and as a high-tech assembly and capital-intensive offshore production platform. Thus although there are obvious strong morphological resemblances with pre-war trade patterns in terms of geographic span, the fact remains that Singapore's position as a linking point between different commercial networks has been reconfigured to fit into the integrated value chains that link offshore production plants with final markets within transnational corporations' networks. And this shift in Singapore's position within new economic patterns is underpinned by a radical re-arrangement of its first historical resource endowment, namely geographic location.

Singapore's ability to become a major trading hub resulted, as already noted, from its physical location. This advantage was supplemented by the attribution of free port status, thus turning the city into the first iteration of a new economic doctrine founded on private trade, which was then growing in importance (Ken 1978). Before independence, free trade, technological advances in transportation and external economic circumstances had driven the growing volume of cargo passing through Singapore, as the city became the gateway for regional raw materials entering transcontinental trading routes. In order to be sustained, this continuous growth required a continuous overhauling of Singapore's 'soft' and physical infrastructures. As infrastructures developed, what was originally a geographic advantage was turned into an increasingly sophisticated logistical infrastructure which, in turn, strengthened Singapore's position within trade networks and made it less reliant on sheer geographic coordinates. At independence, Singapore was endowed with a comprehensive mix of infrastructures, with one of the busiest ports in the world, a sound legal system and a well-developed trade finance sector. This infrastructural depth was to offset the decreasing relevance of space as an organizing economic principle and played a significant part in attracting foreign capital to the newly independent country. Moreover, the government was fast to take a pro-active approach in upgrading these increasing resources in fixed capital: the continuous upgrading of physical infrastructures to support and sustain the increasing inflows of foreign capital was indeed undertaken mainly by the state (Perry et al. 1997; Trocki 2005: 167), working through government agencies or 'government linked companies' (GLCs), and they have proved very efficient in accommodating foreign companies by channeling large volumes of national savings and, later, budgetary surpluses into infrastructure building.

However, the government's strategy of advancing up the value chain within the regional organization of transnational companies' operations required not just enhanced physical infrastructures. As organization became an increasingly important factor in firms' competitiveness (Veltz 1996), 'soft infrastructures', in the form of support services, developed rapidly. In turn, economic sectors grew out of historical services such as trade finance and insurance which, although originating in the entrepôt trade, had become detached from physical trade per se, thereby reducing their historical dependency on geography. Thus the financial sector increasingly grew away from its origins in trade finance. The opening in 1968 of the Asian Dollar Market,[7] an offshore euro-dollar market, has allowed Singapore to develop both as the world's fourth biggest foreign exchange market, the second in Asia after Tokyo, and into a major wealth management center, deeply embedded in the constellation of offshore markets.[8] In the same way, the growth in business and financial services and a growing pool of skilled labor were used to leverage Singapore's position as a major trading hub for physical trade in order to promote the growth of local merchanting and merchandizing activities, which sparked off a fast growth in offshore trading.[9]

As a result, Singapore's economy changed from being a logistical platform and low-cost offshore production plant for transnational corporations looking to relocate their labor intensive operations at the turn of the 1970s and instead became a comprehensive services platform and high-tech manufacturing center, thus gaining in depth and diversity. As these changes occurred, Singapore's critical position within the shifting

[7]   On the Asian Dollar Market, see Lee and Tse 1991; Bernauer 1983.

[8]   Among the top ten sources of FDI in Singapore for 2006 were Switzerland, British Virgin Islands, the Bahamas, Bermuda and the Cayman Islands, all well-known offshore financial centers. Symmetrically, this integration is also shown by Singapore's FDI abroad, where the first destination is the British Virgin Islands, ahead of China, and where Mauritius (which is often used as a channel for investments in India) and Bermuda (the world's leading offshore insurance center) also enter the top ten.

[9]   Offshore trade reached a total volume of US$465 billion and contributed US$7.8 billion to GDP through business spending (Channel News Asia, 20 May 2008).

configurations of economic geographies changed, turning a fragile yet powerful assemblage of geography and political status – that of a free port – into a highly constructed position. In this respect, the city has come to rely less on distance and location than on an intricate and carefully designed 'ecosystem' that encompasses physical infrastructures and immaterial goods, such as a highly reliable legal system, a well-developed financial sector and liberal immigration policies toward skilled immigrants, and such intangible elements as a clean atmosphere, now a significant differentiating factor in the competition with Hong Kong to attract foreign companies,[10] or a strengthening reputation for providing one of the best 'living environments' in the region.[11] This complex urban ecology, which has driven Singapore on the path towards global city status (Sassen 1991; Olds and Yeung 2004), has succeeded in changing Singapore's historical position and embedding it in the new geographic regimes of globalizing economic forces. This shift from a strong reliance on geographic coordinates within an economic geography structured by Euclidian distances towards the more complicated time-spaces of the new economic geographies is maybe best epitomized by Singapore's changing position as an oil trading center.

During the interwar period, Singapore had been used by oil companies as a place to collect and blend petroleum extracted in Dutch India and British Borneo. Operations in Singapore were then restricted to handling, storage and shipping. At independence the government took a very liberal stance toward the petroleum trade, basically sticking to the British free port policy. Moreover, geography and tax policies were complemented by heavy investment in physical infrastructures: in the 1980s the government reclaimed a large area of land by merging several islets off Singapore's Southern coastline to form Jurong Island, where it invested heavily in infrastructures in order to facilitate oil companies' operations.[12] This move efficiently supplemented geography as an important incentive for oil companies to make Singapore their preferred base in Asia for oil trading (Ramasamy 2007).

Investments were planned with two objectives in mind: on the one hand, to integrate as much as possible of the industry's value chain within Singapore and, on the other hand, to use the oil industry to develop and

---

[10] See for instance *The Straits Times*, 5 January 2009.

[11] A territory's ability to emerge as an important location within the circuits of transnational capital does not rely so much now on the physical geography of Euclidian distances but rather on the depth of an integrated blend of human capital, cultural goods and physical infrastructures among others (Sassen 1991, 1998).

[12] As at 2009, Jurong Island had received about 30 billion Singapore dollars of cumulative investment in fixed assets (SEDB 2009).

strengthen adjoining economic sectors. This development strategy positioned Singapore as a major player in the offshore oil extraction industry,
as a high-tech logistic platform for handling oil cargo and as the third
largest oil refining center worldwide (Tong 2007). At the same time, infrastructures and its geographic location between the Middle East and Pacific
Asia and between Southeast Asia and East Asia helped secure Singapore's
position as the first processing and trading center for petroleum products
in Asia in a fast changing environment: as countries throughout the region
developed their own refining plants, Singapore kept pace with these new
organizing logics by occupying an economic niche as a regional swing sup-
plier. Moreover, the gradual erosion of oil production has been countered
by the rapid diversification of processing industries into a booming petrochemical manufacturing sector, which has consistently contributed 30
percent of the city's total production output and which accounted for 11
percent of total value of exports in 2003 (Pillai 2006). Lastly, Singapore's
position as an oil trading center in turn generated a thriving commodity
exchange and derivatives market, the value of which had surpassed that
of physical trade by 2004 (298 billion and 260 billion Singapore dollars
respectively) (Hong 2007). Singapore's position has thus shifted over time
from that of an oil entrepôt to that of an integrated energy hub with integrated value-chains, from extraction, industrial development to shipping,
from research and development to legal, insurance and financial services
(Hong 2007, Pillai 2006).

   More generally, just as the petroleum cluster has come to sustain a broad
range of industrial and services activities, so Singapore's attempt to move
up the value chain within transnational corporations' operations in order
to retain its position as a trading hub has produced an increasingly sophisticated and integrated economic environment, which has proved able to
generate service sectors less dependent on geographic location. The point
is that this growth in business and financial services has, in turn, nurtured
and reinforced Singapore's position as a major trading hub and its appeal
for transnational corporations wishing to settle in the Pacific Asia region.
In this regard, Singapore has succeeded in reinventing its initial resource
– location – within economic logics predicated upon new time-space com-
pression regimes. The city is now both less reliant on old spatial economies
and more closely integrated into the emerging 'archipelago economy'.

CONCLUSION

By anchoring its early economic development in foreign capital, Singapore
became the center piece of a then emerging 'archipelago economy'. This

strategy has shaped the country's economic development ever since. As Singapore's political and economic elites continuously re-invented the city to keep pace with the fast shifting needs of global capital, the metropolis came to offer an increasingly sophisticated environment, which now arguably makes it a 'global city' (Sassen 2001, Olds and Yeung 2004). In the process, Singapore reduced its historical dependency upon geographic location as it came to rely on this integrated environment in order to consolidate its position within economic geography and to move up the value chain within the networks of transnational companies' disseminated operations. This process of economic restructuring has now entered a new phase, as some of Singapore's enterprises, backed by the government, have started to venture abroad, thus entering the field of transnational corporations (Pereira 2009) in a move to lessen the city's historical reliance on FDI. Indeed, for a country so reliant on transnational capital, seeking new forms of relevance within the global economy is somehow a never-ending and stressful process, into which Singapore has been throwing all its energies for the past 45 years. In this endeavor, the city has succeeded in turning what could have been a critical weakness, namely its economy's over-reliance on external economic and political dynamics, into a viable economic model, as it was able to shape itself into an important node within the new layouts of a globalizing economy.

And yet its deep embeddedness in transnational capital circuits still leaves Singapore overexposed to exogenous political and economic circumstances. This fragility is deeply lodged within the political thinking of the political and administrative elites (Siong and Chen 2007). This anxiety has fueled the endless rush for competitiveness within the shifting global logics of capital accumulation, which has driven Singapore's efficient and successful attempts to move up transnational value chains, the rapid diversification of the entrepôt economy and the strong growth of a national industry that has cleverly leveraged on foreign transnational corporations to grow both in assets, as Singaporean corporations, mainly government linked companies, captured vast amounts of public capital invested in infrastructures, and in skills, as public policies favored joint ventures with foreign companies. Nevertheless the question remains whether the city's growing economic depth, an increasingly distinctive combination of hard and soft infrastructures and the broad range of its trading links is enough to offset its enduring reliance on external trade. If the ongoing economic downturn can be said to provide any clues, it is worth noting that, after slow growth in 2008 and a contraction in economic activity of 2 percent in 2009, Singapore is forecast to be the world's second fastest growing economy in 2010, just after Qatar.

Another puzzling challenge is that of the region's increasing economic polarization around China, which is reorganizing Pacific Asia's economic geographies. In this regard, it is difficult to anticipate what the outcomes of this move are going to be for Singapore. It is still largely disputable whether being close to China but outside China's political grip is going to give Singapore a competitive edge or, conversely, undermine Singapore's regional and global position.

Finally, from a more political point of view, the coercive stance the government has adopted towards its citizens since independence is also at issue. Indeed, it is both a crucial factor in the city's ability to keep pace with global economic dynamics through fast and sometimes painful social and economic restructurings and, increasingly, a source of weakness as the balance between social discipline and economic achievement is being questioned more and more. What is at stake is Singapore's ability to adjust its position as it has done so far in order to keep up with the fast pace of global economic reorganizations and to make acceptable the associated social and political costs its citizens inevitably bear.

9. The factors of competitiveness of Greater Chinese cities: the case of the localization of foreign research and development in Beijing and Shanghai

Du Debin and Pierre Miège

INTRODUCTION

Within Greater China, major cities are competing for the title of the leading metropolis of the region. In a globalizing economy, multinational companies and organizations create worldwide networks as well as complex supply chains, and choose major cities as hubs for their global activities. Until recently, the concept of 'competitiveness' was attached only either to individual firms (Krugman, 1994) or to nation-states. However, the new economic context of globalization, sub-national local governments and, most notably, major cities (Ash and Thrift, 2007), appear to play a crucial role in attracting capital, enterprises and skilled labour (Gordon, 2003). In China, as in the rest of the world, cities have to rethink their positioning in a 'web of flows' (Burger et al., 2008), at the regional, national and global level.

Innovation represents a crucial factor in the economic development and competitiveness of a city or a region, and contributes to the construction of the images of the modern, high-tech and 'creative cities' (Landry, 2008). Since the beginning of the economic reform at the end of the 1970s, China has adopted vigorous policies to encourage technical and scientific innovations in order to accelerate the production process from assembling and manufacturing to innovation and the conception of new products.

Despite these policies, Chinese domestic firms mostly rely on the transfer of knowledge and technologies from foreign partners, therefore departing from the development models observed in East Asian economies (Arvanitis et al., 2006). China has become a leading production base for some sectors such as information technology (IT) and the manufacturing and exporting of DVD players, computers and mobile phones, but this massive industrialization has been accompanied by the limited expansion of domestic innovation capabilities (Zhao and Arvanitis, 2008). Different studies have shown that foreign-owned firms and Sino-foreign joint ventures have contributed massively to the increased sophistication of Chinese exported goods (Moore, 2008; Breslin, 2005). Their share in China's total exports have risen steadily from 31 per cent in 1995 to more than 58 per cent by 2005 (Wang and Wei, 2007). This increase includes around 90 per cent of electronics and information technology exports (Moore, 2008). At the national level, spending in research and development (R&D) has grown by around 20 per cent a year since 1995, reaching 1.70 per cent of GDP in 2009, but most Chinese enterprises spend less than 0.6 per cent of turnover on R&D activities (Leadebeater and Wilsdon, 2007) and rely on imported technologies. Only 0.03 per cent own the intellectual property rights of the core technologies they use. Though patent applications from domestic enterprises have increased steadily since the early 2000s, in 2007 they still amounted to less than 41 per cent of total patent applications, against for example 50 per cent in Japan's high-tech sectors, foreign companies and lead domestic companies (Zhou and Stembridge, 2008).

In such a context of 'catching-up', the establishment of R&D centres by foreign companies does contribute significantly to the expansion of production capacities in technological and innovative sectors. Since the late 1990s, the number of foreign R&D centres in China has steadily grown, but due to the specificities of national and local statistical systems it is difficult to assess their number. According to a survey conducted by the National Administration of Science and Technology, a total of 1,223 R&D centres were set up by multinational corporations (MNCs) by June 2007 (Du, 2009). Beijing and Shanghai are the two main localizations of such investments and host almost half of the R&D organizations created by foreign MNCs. According to statistics provided by National Administration of Science and Technology, by June 2007, the number of R&D institutions set up by MNCs in Shanghai and Beijing was 296 and 278 respectively, representing 24 per cent and 23 per cent of all foreign R&D centres in the country (Du, 2009).

In recent years, a considerable number of rankings have been proposed to evaluate and compare competitiveness of cities in world, such as the Global Urban Competitiveness Reports. The Chinese Academy of Social Sciences (CASS) regularly publishes surveys on the relative competitiveness of Chinese cities (for example, Ni, 2009). Most of these studies place Shanghai above Beijing, in terms of general competitiveness and attractiveness, for R&D and other high-tech related investments, contradicting the fact that Beijing hosts more domestic and foreign R&D centres than its main rival of the south. Such studies propose series of indexes and factors to evaluate and compare competitiveness of nations, regions and cities. Most of these try to explain activities and policies from both the national and the local levels simultaneously, as well as the territorial endowments and resources of each place (Webster and Muller, 2000). Some of statistical data used for such rankings are questionable, for example, some studies have demonstrated that most new patent applications filed in China are for a new design appearance or new models, therefore not requiring technological innovation (Walsh, 2003).

This paper presents the results of research conducted in Beijing and Shanghai and analyses the evolving factors of competitiveness of the two cities. To do this, interviews were conducted with managers of 20 R&D centres situated in Shanghai and Beijing in order to understand the factors that have led foreign MNCs or small and medium enterprises (SMEs) to choose Beijing or Shanghai to set up such centres. This methodology enables researchers studying competiveness to depart from utilizing purely quantitative factors, and to question instead the way foreign managers perceive the different cities and evaluate their competitive advantages. Of course, foreign R&D centres only represent one element of the competitiveness of a city, but in the context of economic globalization and Chinese economic development, their localization highlights some of the strengths and weaknesses of the two main Chinese metropolises.

In the first section, the specificities will be presented: the contrasted economic and social evolutions of Shanghai and Beijing since the 1950s, which have endowed them with different comparative advantages as well as weaknesses. The second section will present the results of the interviews conducted with foreign R&D centres managers. The factors they put forward to explain their choices of localization are different from the factors usually favoured by international rankings. Such apparent singularity will be discussed in a third section in the light of the specificities of Chinese economic and social development.

BEIJING AND SHANGHAI: TWO METROPOLISES WITH CONTRASTING ECONOMIC DEVELOPMENT PATHS

Economic development does not depend solely on national state policies; on the contrary with the opening of countries to foreign investments and trade, regions and cities are increasingly exposed to global forces (Utis and Webster, 2000). As Schmitz and Nadvi have stressed, local governance must be taken into consideration because public actors act as catalysts or mediators in the context of globalization (Schmitz and Nadvi, 1999).

The most obvious contribution of municipal governments concerns infrastructures, which cities can build or improve, but also the setting up of special zones, which offer domestic and/or foreign companies with preferential conditions to operate, recruit and export. Cities can also participate in the expansion of educational institutions, favour mobility of labour and facilitate recruitment of high-skilled personnel.

In the context of the transition from a planned-economy to a market-led economic system, Chinese municipalities such as Shanghai and Beijing have been granted considerable power, through a more favourable sharing of tax revenues and the devolution of some decision-making power. The consequences have been far-reaching, especially for high-tech activities and industries, for example, the emergence of Zhongguancun in Beijing and Shenzhen as the main IT bases of the country was led by market forces and active policies from municipal governments, contradicting some strategic planning from the central government (Wang and Tong, 2005). Under the transformative effects of decentralization and globalization: 'The range of competitiveness factors that are directly or indirectly within the purview of local urban authorities is increasing rapidly in many, probably most, developing urban regions' (Webster and Muller, 2000).

Another important factor explaining the capacity of a city to attract foreign investments in research and other high-tech activities is too often left aside: the image of a city. Shanghai and Beijing have both deployed extensive, and usually effective, methods to offer the image of developed, modern, high-tech and international cities. The Olympic Games organized in Beijing in 2008 gave the municipal government the opportunity to present the national capital as 'the country's largest science, technological, and cultural hub', 'the hot spot for entrepreneurship and investment in China's high technologies', or 'the fertile land to breed and gather high quality talents', to quote the website of Beijing Municipal government (as retrieved in August 2008). The preparation of the Shanghai World Expo 2010 in the southern metropolis is analogous to the role of the Olympic Games in Beijing. Webster and Muller, though they do not fully integrate this element in their ranking models, insist that: 'A city's image very much affects the behaviour of investors. Investors usually only consider a very few places in making investment decisions, thus you must be on their radar screens' (Webster and Muller, 2000). Certainly, Shanghai and Beijing appear more consistently on 'radar screens' of potential investors than other Chinese cities.

Such a factor also plays a role when MNCs plan to transfer expatriates, and have thus to worry about the quality of life they and their families can expect to have in their new location. As a foreign banker mentioned, foreign multinationals which transfer many of their executive staff from North America or Europe favour Hong Kong, Shanghai and Beijing over, for example, Guangzhou or Chongqing (interview in Beijing, August 2006). Indeed, they consider the existence of international schools and the diversity of cultural events in English as necessary to ensure successful expatriations.

Beijing and Shanghai have benefited from the national policies that have supported technical innovation and scientific research since the late 1970s. But their different economic, social and political histories have given them divergent 'path dependencies'. After the founding of the People's Republic of China in 1949, under the planned economy, Beijing has worked to develop an industrial basis, favouring investments in sectors such as iron and steel, electronics and textiles. More recently, the national capital has also benefited from the creation of high-tech industrial development zones, and other industrial clusters, which have been promoted by the central government since the launch of the Torch Program in 1988 (Arvanitis and Jastrabsky, 2006). Zhongguancun in Beijing is certainly the most famous and most acclaimed of the more than 150 of such special zones which have been created all over the country. More than 15 multinationals, including Microsoft, IBM, Siemens, Motorola, Nokia and Samsung, have set up manufacturing facilities and/or R&D centres there.

The rapid growth of this high-tech zone has been enabled by another legacy from the recent past: the domination of the national capital in terms of number of universities and public research institutions. According to the 2006 edition of the Educational Statistics Yearbook of China (China State Statistical Bureau, 2007), among 1,867 higher education institutions, 80 were situated in Beijing (including 39 universities) against 60 in Shanghai. The national capital also hosts more than 200 public research laboratories. When the figures of enrolment are considered, the contrast is even more marked: the number of post-graduate students reaches 46,540 in Beijing (18.2 per cent of the national total) and 19,931 (7.8 per cent) in Shanghai, including 9,462 PhD graduates in Beijing (26.1 per cent of the national total) and only 3,925 in Shanghai (10.8 per cent).

Around 15,000 domestic small and medium high-tech enterprises have mushroomed in Zhongguancun, many of them either spin-offs from universities or research centres, or operating through collaboration with researchers and scholars. Confirming these trends, the Second National Survey on Basic Units, published in 2002, found that Beijing hosted 4,679 firms specialized in software development (almost a quarter of the national total), employing more than 100,000 people, against only 2,353 enterprises in Shanghai, employing 47,500 (Wang and Tong, 2005).

Shanghai offers a very different economic and social history. Already a major industrial and financial centre before 1949, it has remained an important manufacturing city, hosting a diversified and solid industrial structure. From 1992, new central policies granted more autonomy to the city, and the creation of the Pudong New Area became the symbol of its renewed economic and financial strength (Wu, 2003). Thun and Segal have stressed the importance of Shanghai's local government, which (more so than in Beijing) has played an active role in promoting the development and modernization of the city's industry since the early 1990s. The large state-owned conglomerates have benefited from increased financial resources after 1992 when the city government was allowed to retain a greater share of its fiscal resources. In 2006, there were twice as many large and medium-size industrial enterprises in Shanghai than in Beijing (China State Statistical Bureau, 2008). Unlike the IT sector, which requires more flexibility and small units, the manufacturing sector benefits from such a strong impulse from the local state on already solid local (often public) companies (Thun and Segal, 2001). The municipal government has given priority to the strengthening of manufacturing sectors such as petrochemical and fine chemical industries, equipment and automobile manufacturing and the biomedical sector. The Zhangjiang High-Tech Park has not been created to rival Zhongguancun, but targeted already well-established local manufacturing industries (Wang and Tong, 2005).

Building on its industrial capacity – the Yangtze River delta region produces almost 20 per cent of the national GDP and 30 per cent of national industrial output – Shanghai has managed to attract more foreign direct investments (FDI) in manufacturing capacity than any other mainland Chinese city. In 2005, Shanghai alone received 11.4 per cent of all FDIs. Furthermore, domestic and foreign enterprises in Shanghai employ more engineers and scientists than in Beijing. In 2006, there were close to 600,000 employees in this category in the Yangtze River delta region, 20 per cent more than in the Beijing-Tianjin conurbation (China State Statistical Bureau, 2009).

LOCALIZATION OF FOREIGN R&D CENTRES APPEARS AS MOSTLY LINKED TO PARTNERSHIPS WITH CHINESE PRIVATE AND PUBLIC INSTITUTIONS

The main reason given by our interviewees to explain why their company chose to move to Beijing is the need to remain close to government agencies to develop their activities. Some multinationals need to remain close to government offices and bureaus, for example pharmaceutical companies which need to negotiate the launch of new drugs with the State Food and Drug Administration (SFDA). For this reason, a European pharmaceutical enterprise has chosen to locate its production units in other cities in the south of the country, but all other activities, including research and development, have been set up in Beijing (interview in Beijing, March 2008).

Some companies involved in internet-related technologies and services have also insisted on the fact that they participate in international cooperation between the Chinese government and European or North American institutions, and have therefore chosen Beijing to conduct their R&D. It is the case of a European SME, specializing in the design of internet services, which opened R&D facilities in the capital because it was collaborating with a Chinese public laboratory under the funding of a bilateral research agreement (interview in Beijing, July 2006). Companies engaged in software industries also need intense contacts with central institutions which set up crucial industrial standards. As the manager of a European home appliance company told us, many cities can be considered to open manufacturing units, but 'companies choose Beijing when they really need to stay close to the government' (interview in Beijing, August 2006).

Interviews in both Beijing and Shanghai reveal that the second factor that managers took into consideration for choosing a city for their R&D activities was the localization of their Chinese partners. This factor is directly linked to the different economic specializations of these two cities. In Beijing, the managers of R&D centres of MNCs involved in IT and software designs insist on the number of potential partners for collaboration in research and development. Such partners emerge from both a large network of private small and medium enterprises and the concentration of universities and public research institutions. In Shanghai, R&D centres studied are involved in sectors well developed in Shanghai and the surrounding provinces, such as machinery, pharmaceuticals and chemistry.

The third motive addressed by the interviewees in the two cities is their perception of the market they target. Beijing and Shanghai are both extremely big cities, with more than 15 million people. But Shanghai appears, to many foreign MNCs, as the centre of a much larger market, which covers the fast-growing neighbouring provinces of the great Yangtze River delta (Jiangsu, Zhejiang and Anhui). Except in the IT sector, foreign enterprises which have chosen a more developmental and adaptive market strategy prefer to set up R&D facilities in Shanghai to benefit from its larger and more diversified market. Therefore, in 2005, the Shanghai-centred Yangtze River delta region received 46 per cent of all the FDI of the country, making it the manufacturing core of multinational corporations

(China State Statistical Bureau, 2007). It is therefore not surprising that manufacturing oriented R&D activities from foreign enterprises are found more often in this region. In the interviews conducted in Shanghai, half of the interviewees explained that the main reason for choosing this city to set up an R&D centre was to support their manufacturing activities by developing new products. For example, a European multinational specializing in high-tech material used for construction explained that it chose to set up a R&D centre in Shanghai, where it already has production units, in order to serve directly and efficiently its manufacturing needs (interview in Shanghai, July 2007).

Interviewees in Beijing have not always insisted, as much as their counterparts in Shanghai, on the quality of the local market, except for companies engaged in IT and software sectors which consider Beijing as a more attractive market for their products. A foreign software development firm sees Beijing as a more mature market for high technologies. As one manager explained, in the national capital there are more internet users than anywhere else in China, and a remarkable concentration of young professionals working in fields related to high-tech, media or culture. Many of them have studied or worked in North America or Europe, and are passionate consumers of technological innovations in computers, software, or communication tools such as mobile phones (interview in Beijing, July 2006).

Interviews included questions about other potential factors, especially the quality and availability of the labour force and the perception of local governments' policies toward foreign investments. In both cities, the latter factor is seen as not crucial in deciding the localization of a R&D centre, as these two cities appear to have relatively comparable policies and regulations concerning foreign investments. Similarly, even though Beijing has more universities and engineer schools than Shanghai, this comparative advantage is presented as not decisive. Indeed, for the managers interviewed, Shanghai benefits from the mobility of new graduates from other provinces, and from a larger presence of young foreign professionals. For example, a prominent European software enterprise based in Shanghai recruited in 2007 for its new R&D activities: 50 per cent persons from Shanghai, 7 per cent from Beijing, 4 per cent and 3 per cent respectively from neighbouring Jiangsu and Zhejiang provinces and 19 per cent from other cities; 15 per cent of its staff were young graduates returning from Western countries (interview in Shanghai, March 2009).

Therefore, interviewees seem to perceive as secondary the factors usually put forward by international surveys and competitiveness rankings, such as the volume of a skilled labour force, the quality of infrastructure or more favourable tax system. This outcome may appear to contradict the quantitative factors often used to measure competitiveness of cities and regions. In fact, these interviews with managers show rationality in the choices of localization for their R&D activities, and reveal some of the actual strengths and weakness of the two major metropolises linked to their development path.

ANALYSING THE IMPACT OF THE 'PATH DEPENDENCY' OF BEIJING AND SHANGHAI TO UNDERSTAND THEIR COMPETITIVENESS

In order to understand the motivations behind the choice of a city by foreign multinationals in the particular field of R&D, it must be stressed that most of the R&D activities in China, both foreign and domestic, are in reality mainly development activities (Walsh, 2003). Many foreign MNCs are eager to adapt products such as mobile phones and computer software to the local markets, especially in the IT sectors. However, a second factor plays a crucial role: the majority of foreign R&D in China is adaptive, developmental,and tactical in nature (Sun and Huang, 2006). A representative of a foreign economic ministry in Beijing explained that, with the Chinese market being particularly responsive, an increasing number of foreign MNCs choose Beijing or Shanghai to test new versions of their products not just in preparation for the Chinese market, but before an international launch in Asia and beyond (interview in Beijing, July 2006).

Even in Zhongguancun, many foreign and domestic enterprises do not engage in much research. Cong Cao identifies some factors explaining the relative weakness of Zhongguancun in terms of R&D: lack of clear ownership, especially for spin-offs from state-controlled universities or laboratories; lack of private venture capital; and government-sponsored venture capital which prefers to invest in the stock market, rather than in technology start-ups (Cong, 2004).

Other researchers have also noticed the difficulty for small non-state firms to finance their investments and research projects (Yu, 2005). In contradiction to this, the representative of a foreign venture-capital company interviewed stated that, according to his own experience, the funds available still exceed the number of really innovative small enterprises (interview in Beijing, July 2006).

To these factors must be added the poor protection of intellectual property rights, which seriously limits incentives to conduct innovative research. For Yu Zhou, this leads to a lack of trust of potential partners, and limits the capacity of domestic enterprises to benefit from innovations originating from foreign MNCs or SMEs present in China (Yu, 2005).

Therefore many, including local managers, now doubt that the expression 'China's Silicon Valley' is relevant to describe Zhongguancun. But such an analysis of the weakness of domestic and international research capabilities can be extended to other Chinese cities.

Overall, foreign investments mainly concern development of products for Chinese – and increasingly for regional and international – markets. Therefore, factors such as quality of infrastructure, size of the labour force or relevance of local economic and fiscal policies are not considered as the most crucial. In this respect, the experience of FDI in R&D in Chinese cities reflects the experience of other countries, such as R&D centres set up by Japanese firms in the US which are mainly located near sites of production (Florida and Kenney, 1994).

A singularity arising from these interviews is the fact that Beijing is not immediately described as having a better labour market. In the last decade, China has steadily increased the number of students enrolled in universities and technical schools, in order to provide its growing economy with skilled labour: as a consequence, the number of new graduates grew from 1.8 million in 2001 to 5.59 million in 2008 (Xinhua News Agency, 2008). Beijing has benefited more than others from this evolution as it hosts the greatest number of institutions of higher learning in the country. As we have already noted, a little more than a quarter of all PhDs in China are obtained from universities situated in Beijing.

Recent studies have pointed to the relative scarcity of highly-skilled personnel in China. A McKinsey survey released in 2005 insisted on a paradoxical 'shortages amid plenty' (Farrell and Grant, 2005). Even though many new students graduate every year, only a small number meet the qualifications required of foreign multinationals. Lack of practical knowledge and personal creativity appear to be the main reasons explaining the difficulty for foreign MNCs in recruiting young professionals. Low proficiency in English is also seen as a problem for many foreign enterprises. Other studies, based on interviews with managers, have also concluded on a relative scarcity of suitable candidates for foreign MNCs or SMEs, especially in high-tech sectors and R&D activities (Wang and Tong, 2005). Some managers interviewed insisted on the difficulty faced when trying to find young graduates capable of autonomy and creativity. They often resort to keeping some expatriates and to hiring 'returnees', young people just returning from studying and/or working abroad. The Ministry of Education estimates that 1.21 million returned between 1978 and 2007. It must be noted that 'returnees' also face difficulties in integrating within foreign and domestic companies in China (Leadebeater and Wilsdon, 2007).

Another aspect of Chinese job market is the relatively low mobility of the skilled workforce. The McKinsey report notes that only one-third of all Chinese graduates move to another province to find a job, as opposed to half in India. The problem is increased by local regulations concerning the registration system (*hukou*). In Beijing for example, a domestic research centre indicated that they would have to lose three of their 30 employees born outside of the capital and who still had a rural *hukou*. These three young professionals would face many difficulties if they stayed in Beijing, especially in terms of access to health services and education for their children (interview in Beijing, December 2008). Such regulations contribute to the relatively low mobility of workforce in China, even though local situations vary. Shanghai offers easier procedures than Beijing to obtain local registration (Chan and Buckingham, 2008).

If overall Beijing appears to suffer less from this relative scarcity of highly trained personnel, interviewees evaluate differently the strengths and weaknesses of local labour markets differently depending on their sector of activity. Not surprisingly, firms in the IT sector perceive the capital as a place where it is easier to recruit suitable local personnel. However a manager of a European pharmaceuticals R&D centre in Beijing admits that it is more difficult to hire well-trained staff than it would be in Shanghai where such a sector is better developed (interview in Beijing, March 2008).

A final factor must be stressed. Beijing and Shanghai have followed very different economic paths, but both currently host a solid industrial base, though in different sectors. This indirectly explains why, when following their local partners, foreign MNCs and SMEs tend to set up their R&D activities in either city. Around Zhongguancun, Beijing has seen the emergence in the 1990s, and the strengthening in the 2000s, of a large pool of companies of different sizes and capabilities, offering a wide range of potential partners, both private and institutional. In the capital, foreign investors also indirectly benefit from more state funding to domestic R&D actors: Beijing receives five times more state funding for R&D than Shanghai (Wang and Tong, 2005). Shanghai, with its diversified manufacturing sectors, enables foreign enterprises to find suitable partners for manufacturing-oriented R&D. When foreign managers insist that they have not really compared different cities but followed their actual or potential partners, they indirectly point to the different paths followed by the industrial and economic development of these two metropolises.

CONCLUSION

Our interviews with managers of foreign R&D centres show how Beijing and Shanghai have benefited from their distinct economic development since the 1950s. Managers interviewed do not put forward traditional factors such as quality of infrastructure, access to skilled personnel or preferential policies, but these are still indirectly explaining their localization choices. These contrasted local developments are reflected in the way Western imaginations perceive Beijing as a high-tech and modern metropolis, the Chinese centre of software production but also of media and cultural industries. It is therefore seen as the nation's political and cultural centre, suitable for knowledge-based service industries. Shanghai is seen as a major industrial centre in Asia, suitable for manufacturing oriented R&D and offering a market in which new products and processes can be successfully experimented and adapted. Managers interviewed insist that the main reason for choosing either city for their investments in R&D is the localization of their local partners, and therefore indirectly acknowledge that the two cities have experienced different sectoral developments.

The economic and social transformations of both Beijing and Shanghai that we have analysed in this chapter also open new perspectives for the future. An important conclusion from our interviews is the increasing 'clustering' of foreign investments, especially in R&D activities. Clusters, such as IT sectors in Beijing or pharmaceuticals in Shanghai, facilitate mobilization and distribution of resources (Webster and Muller, 2000).

Shanghai should continue to attract manufacturing-oriented research, as well as investments in manufacturing facilities. Beijing, whose main competitive advantage has been the presence of the central government and its different bureaus, is increasingly becoming the main domestic IT centre of China. In 2004, the city already generated 35 per cent of Chinese software exports, and hosted a quarter of all Chinese internet domains (Yu, 2005). Therefore, the 'path dependency' of the national capital is slowly changing trajectory, transforming Beijing's advantages from political ones to industrial ones, at least for IT and other culture oriented and creative sectors; at the same time, Shanghai is strengthening its comparative advantages in a diversity of manufacturing sectors.

ACKNOWLEDGEMENT

The first author is grateful for financial support provided by the National Science Foundation of China (Project #40871067).

PART III

Complementarity and rivalry among Asian trading and finance centres

10. The global economic crisis: opportunities for major cities in East and Southeast Asia?

Peter W. Daniels

INTRODUCTION

The global economic crisis of 2007–2009 was essentially a global financial crisis. The financial sector is the 'central nervous system of modern market economies',[1] distributing liquidity and mobilizing capital to finance large investment projects; allocating funds to the most dynamic sectors of the economy; and providing households with the necessary funds to smooth consumption over time.[2] Financial crises have happened before, but the events of 2007–2009 are often described as 'unprecedented'. This crisis is notable for the way in which national and international financial authorities have adopted a range of interventions that are new and unusual. The key, however, is that in contrast to many of the earlier financial crisis that had their origins in the emerging economies and then spread globally, the recent crisis emanated from the US which is the core of the global financial and economic system. This was new territory and in view of the deeply embedded financial links spanning the Atlantic the banks, insurance companies and investment managers in Western Europe were quickly exposed to diminishing liquidity and disappearing credit. This has provoked questions about the scope for re-regulation of financial markets, the paring down of high reward remuneration cultures and other interventions that may have the effect of corralling the apparently inexorable ability of London, Paris, New York or Frankfurt to retain, attract and control the lion's share of international financial activities and flows.

This is the context for questions about what this might mean for ambitious international financial centres in regions such as East and Southeast Asia. This chapter explores what they need to do to improve their position

---

[1] UNCTAD (2009b), p. 11.
[2] See also Clark and Wojcik (2006); O'Brien (1992); Porteous (1995).

in the ranking of global financial centres and what they can learn from their leading competitors in Western Europe and North America, both before and since the onset of the 2007–2009 financial crisis.

FINANCIAL CENTRES IN EAST AND SOUTHEAST ASIA IN A GLOBAL CONTEXT

Globalization and urbanization have driven the development of Asian cities and given added impetus to the rise of East and Southeast Asia region as a whole.[3] More than 60 per cent of the region's population will be urbanized by 2020. While this is a significant opportunity it also presents the major regional cities with big challenges which, until the 2007–2009 financial crisis, had been dominated by social and environmental issues; but there is no doubt that economic challenges are now also in the mix. It is an opportunity because 'this is the first major international crisis where Asian markets have been relatively stable and the difficulties and losses have been concentrated in the West. As such, this may be "a tipping point" in the emergence of Asia as a dominant force in the global economy'.[4] In late 2008, one survey identified Shanghai, Singapore, Mumbai and Beijing (in that order) amongst the top six financial centres most likely to become significant in the next few years and Singapore, Shanghai, Hong Kong[5] and Beijing amongst the top five centres where new corporate offices were likely to be opened (see Table 10.1).[6] In the good times these cities have benefited most from the positive externalities associated with financial globalization but now, in the bad times, they have also borne the brunt of the negative externalities.[7] For example, during 2008 the office vacancy level in Shanghai increased by 770 basis points to average 10.2 per cent, vacancy levels in Tokyo and Singapore increased 150 and 280 basis points to 4 per cent and 8.9 per cent, respectively. In the second half of 2008 alone the office vacancy rate in Hong King increased 2.5 per cent to finish the year at 4 per cent. Not surprisingly, the cost of leasing office space in these cities fell during the second half of 2008 with Singapore rents down 22.4 per cent to $97, Hong Kong down 16.8 per cent to $178, and Shanghai down 2.1 per cent to $53.

---

[3] Douglass (2002), pp. 131–151; Hutton (2004), pp. 1–74; Daniels (2005), pp. 21–51; Zhao (2003), pp. 535–571.
[4] City of London Corporation (2008), pp. 1–2.
[5] Hong Kong Special Administrative Region.
[6] City of London Corporation (2009).
[7] Moore (2009).

Table 10.1   Global ranks and changes 2006, 2008: East and Southeast Asia financial centres

City	Global Financial Centres Index 2006[1]	Global Financial Centres Index 2008[2]	Change	Centres of Commerce Index 2007[3]	Centres of Commerce Index 2008[4]	Change	GAWC 2008[5]
Hong Kong	3	3	=	5	6	–	4
Singapore	4	4	=	6	4	+	7
Tokyo	9	15	–	3	3	=	5
Shanghai	24	35	–	32	24	+	45
Beijing	36	51	–	46	57	–	35
Mumbai	39	49	–	45	48	–	*
Seoul	43	53	–	9	9	+	27
Taipei	*	41		*	22		21
Kuala Lumpur	*	45		38	50	–	37
Bangkok	*	50		36	42	–	22
Osaka	*	52		*	19		54
Shenzhen	*	*		*	60		*
New Delhi	*	*		*	61		*
Bangalore	*	*		*	66		*
Jakarta	*	*		*	68		24
Manila	*	*		*	71		39
Chengdu	*	*		*	72		
Chongqing	*	*		*	73		

Sources:
1. City of London Corporation (2007)
2. City of London Corporation (2009)
3. MasterCard Worldwide (2007)
4. MasterCard Worldwide (2008)
5. Aggregate scores for presence of offices of leading global service firms, from: Taylor and Walker (2009).

The combination of rapid urbanization and globalization does seem to have caused a shift of the world's economic centre of gravity towards East and South Asia.[8] The larger Asian financial centres, such as Hong Kong

[8]   The GFCI financial centres index, for example, uses objective evidence of competitiveness compiled from a wide variety of comparable sources and financial centre assessments via an online questionnaire that has been running continuously since 2007, see City of London Corporation (2009). The WCCI is compiled from research by a panel of eight independent economic, urban development and social science experts. The 75 cities in the 2008 list are rated according to the six dimensions: legal and political framework; economic stability; ease

and Singapore, are playing a more and more important role in both the economic development of their home regions as well as internationally. They have mushroomed not just as major agglomerations of financial services and the headquarters of major global corporations but also of political administration, scientific innovation (including leading universities), cultural creativity and economic dynamism more generally, especially but exclusively within their individual national contexts (see Table 10.2).

The East and South Asia region already hosts at least three well-established financial centres: Hong Kong, Singapore and Tokyo. A number of emerging regional financial centres such as Shanghai, Mumbai and Beijing have the potential to grow rapidly if the conditions are right. As to whether these aspirations can be fulfilled, it is worth noting that the region is diverse, not just with respect to its economies but also its languages, cultures and political systems. The economies span the development range from developed (Japan), tigers (Hong Kong, Singapore, Taiwan), high growth emerging (China, India), and emerging (Cambodia, Laos, Vietnam). Thus, the existing and aspiring financial centres in the region are part of a fragmented financial infrastructure and diverse capital markets.[9] This is the context for a set of financial centres that, in spite of this fragmentation, have flourished during the last decade on the back of support for export trade to Europe and North America and a growing intra-regional demand for financial services that helps to underwrite domestic corporate investment and increases in consumer incomes. The active development of regional trade agreements (RTAs) means that intra-regional trade accounts for the vast majority of developing countries' South–South trade has been increasing. Almost 52 per cent of total trade in Asia was intra-regional in 2006, a difference of 9 per cent from the 1990 figure; the equivalent statistics for Emerging Asia are 41 per cent and 10 per cent respectively.[10] By extending their coverage to include services, RTAs are expected to generate increased intra-regional services trade with knock-on effects on the demand for trade credit and enabling financial instruments.

---

of doing business; financial flow; business centre; and knowledge creation and information flow, see MasterCard Worldwide (2007).

[9]   The role of the local state and the problems of overcoming embedded practices of doing business are illustrated by the efforts to establish futures trading platform in Taiwan (Chen and Hsu, 2007).

[10]   IMF (2008).

Table 10.2   Distribution of Fortune 500 global companies' headquarters by city, 2005, 2008

City†	No. of Fortune 500 HQs			Global 500 Rank (Mean)		
	2005	2008	Change (no)	2005	2008	Change (+/–)
Tokyo	55	46	–9	257	248	+
Beijing	12	21	+9	235	272	–
Seoul	10	13	+3	241	237	+
Osaka	9	7	–2	288	253	+
Mumbai	3	5	+2	427	296	+
Kariya	2	3	+1	279	357	–
Kobe	2	1	–1	365	451	–
Nagoya	2	1	–1	386	391	–
Taipei	2	4	+2	387	280	+
Bangkok	1	1		373	135	+
Changchun	1	1		448	303	+
Chiba	1	1		112	154	–
Dehradun	1	1		454	335	+
Fukuoka	1	*		473	*	–
Guangzhou	1	1		316	226	+
Hamamatsu	1	1		255	251	+
Hiroshima	1	1		211	255	–
Hong Kong	1	4	+3	347	393	–
Iwata	1	*		496	*	–
Kadoma	1	*		25	*	–
Moriguchi	1	1		237	459	–
New Delhi	1	1		170	116	+
Pohang City	1	*		276	*	–
Sendai	1	*		409	*	–
Seongnam	1	1		414	387	+
Shanghai	1	2	+1	309	290	+
Singapore	1	1		375	292	+
Suwa	1	*		453	*	–
Toyota	1	1		7	5	+
Kuala Lumpur	*	1			93	+
Kui Shan	*	1			344	+
Malilao	*	1			395	+
Ulsan	*	1			378	+

Note: †Ranked by number of Fortune Global 500 headquarters, 2005.

Source: Compiled from data at: http://money.cnn.com/magazines/fortune/global500/2005/countries/C.html (accessed April 2009).

DIMENSIONS OF COMPETITIVE SUCCESS FOR ASPIRING GLOBAL CITIES

While such trends are encouraging at the intra-regional level, it remains the case that the financial centres in East and Southeast Asia are competing on the global stage for a share of the benefits from trade and financial globalization. It is therefore useful to consider what constitutes 'competitiveness' in this context; the monitoring of financial centre success undertaken in recent years by the City of London Corporation and presented as the GFCI identifies a number of factors that are deemed to be influential.[11] *Human capital* is a key factor of production for financial services; the availability, quality, and skills of personnel, together with development and training opportunities via top ranked universities/ business schools is crucial. The *business environment*, especially its regulatory attributes, is an important influence on the way that global centres work and their ability to stimulate growth and to attract and retain new players. The ease of doing business, levels of corruption and tax regimes contribute to the level of freedom or otherwise for doing business. Agglomeration effects (*market access*) are a third key factor, including levels of trading in bonds and equities, levels of securitization and proximity to other international business and professional services. The availability and quality of office space, intra-city transport systems and international transport connectivity are some of the infrastructural factors involved. Finally, the GFCI identifies a wide range of variables such as the quality of life, cultural milieu, cost of living, reputation and perception of a city as a place to locate a business that comprise a measure of general *competitiveness.*

Only two centres from East and Southeast Asia are in the top five global financial centres ranked by these factors of competitiveness (see Table 10.3). Indeed there are no other centres from the region in the top ten although cities such as Shenzhen were given high average assessments but by an insufficient number of respondents to be included. However, several 'respondents did identify Shenzhen as both "likely to become more significant" and as a location where their firm is "likely to open an office in the next 2 to 3 years"'.[12] Singapore and Hong Kong occupy interchangeable positions at third and fourth in the rankings (see Table 10.3) with Singapore ahead in relation to the business environment, infrastructure and human resources, having improved its position for the latter since GFCI4. Hong Kong, on the other hand, is ahead of Singapore for market access and general competitiveness (see Table 10.1).

[11] City of London Corporation (2009), pp. 22–23.
[12] City of London Corporation (2009), p. 27.

Table 10.3   *Top five global financial centres ranked by factors of competitiveness, GFCI5, late 2008*

Rank	Factors of Competitiveness[1]				
	Business Environment	People	Infrastructure	Market Access	General Competitiveness
1	London (–)[2]	London (–)	London (–)	London (–)	London (–)
2	New York (–)	New York (–)	New York (–)	New York (–)	New York (–)
3	Singapore (–)	Singapore (+1)	Singapore (–)	Hong Kong (–)	Hong Kong (–)
4	Hong Kong (–)	Hong Kong (–1)	Singapore (–)	Singapore (–)	Singapore (–)
5	Zurich (+1)	Zurich (–)	Frankfurt (+3)	Chicago (+1)	Zurich (–)

Notes:
1. Ranked from left to right by number of times each mentioned by respondents to GFCI5;
2. Change against GFCI4 in brackets.

Source: City of London Corporation (2009), compiled from Table 12, p. 23.

The GFCI is however a rather narrow measure orientated towards cities as financial centres. It is therefore helpful to look at the ranks of East and Southeast Asian cities using the rather broader indices in the WCCI.[13] London, New York and Tokyo top the overall ranking with Singapore ranked fourth in 2008 compared with sixth in 2007. A closer look at the seven components incorporated into the WCCI (some are not dissimilar to those in the GFCI while others such as knowledge creation and information flow or liveability add breadth to the analysis) reveals results that in some respects mirror the GFCI in that Hong Kong and Singapore are highly rated as places to do business and as business centres with Hong Kong topping the list for the latter in 2007 and 2008 and both cities moving to the top for the former in 2008 (see Figure 10.1). Singapore has improved from third to second for the legal and political framework component but is the only city in the region in 2008 scoring on that component. The WCCI method has the effect of enabling the inclusion of more cities from the region in the top ten with an increase in the number of entries in 2008 compared with 2007, especially when using the financial flow and business

---

[13]   MasterCard (2007); MasterCard Worldwide (2008).

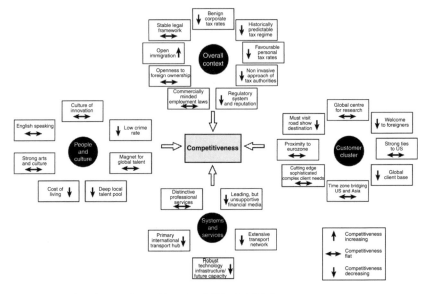

Source: Derived from Mayor of London (2008), Exhibit 8

*Figure 10.1   Four clusters that shape the competitiveness of financial
             centres*

centre components. Tokyo, Seoul and Mumbai are in the top ten for
financial flow in 2007 with Shanghai joining the list in 2008 and Mumbai
moving up from tenth to seventh. Only Tokyo and Seoul are rated as
significant centres for knowledge creation and information flow while the
only city rated in the top ten for liveability in 2008 is Tokyo. Overall, the
WCCI highlights two features; a wider cross section of East and Southeast
Asian cities in the top ten and an indication of upward movement in the
position of cities such as Mumbai, Shanghai and Seoul. Hong Kong and
Singapore tend to consistently occupy the highest positions.

CAN EAST AND SOUTHEAST ASIAN CITIES GRASP NEW OPPORTUNITIES?

Whether it will be possible for the region's cities to capitalize on this
potential will depend on numerous factors, ranging from the macro-
economic to local initiatives and policies adopted by individual cities.
The region was not well prepared when it was engulfed by the financial
crisis in 1997/98; the currency and banking crises that brought a number

of economies to their knees have since been addressed through the introduction of more careful fiscal management, reduced exposure to external debt, exchange rate regimes that are more flexible and the development of local currency bond markets. A number of the region's economies have accumulated sizable foreign currency reserves that provide greater protection against adverse changes to the balance of payments. Indeed, in 2009 China's foreign exchange reserves were US$2.4 trillion or about one-third of the world total.[14] The region cannot be totally isolated in circumstances where financial globalization means that risk is distributed widely amongst closely interlinked markets within which financial stress is transmitted rapidly. Thus, the effects of slowing growth and weakening business are now affecting emerging Asia's economic and financial systems. There are various steps that the region's policy makers can take to mitigate these effects such as: closely monitoring and adjusting where necessary the institutional arrangements for providing emergency liquidity and other support or the robustness of the frameworks for dealing with troubled institutions; ensuring that key financial institutions in the region can continue to provide credit to key economic activities, or by ensuring that the downward spiral associated with a broadening credit crunch that has greatly damaged the economies of Europe and North America, do not feed into the real economy. Inevitably, this turns attention to the financial and corporate centres in the region where many of the economic activities that shape its intra- and inter-regional performance are concentrated. What do they need to do to capitalise on the decline in confidence amongst the leading financial centres such as London or New York?

One approach to this question is to examine the response by London to the threats to the factors that have long shaped its international competitiveness as an international financial centre. Several of these strengths have been declining both before and during the most recent financial crisis as a consequence of prominent and successful strategies adopted by competitor cities to attract firms and investment away from London.[15] Indeed, in 2008 London was seen as decreasingly competitive in 15 factors and stable in 13 (see Figure 10.2). In only one factor, openness to immigration, was it considered that London's competitiveness is increasing. The systems and services cluster is especially vulnerable since the city's transport network, its status as a primary international transport hub, the robustness of the technology infrastructure (including future capacity) and an unsupportive financial media are all decreasingly competitive; only the distinctiveness of London's professional services activities has been holding steady. While the balance

[14]   Hu (2010).
[15]   Mayor of London (2008); see also Roxburgh on New York: Roxburgh (2008).

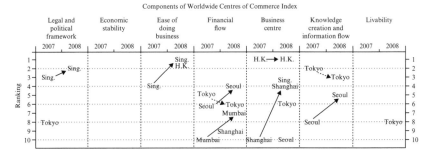

Source: Compiled from various tables in MasterCard Worldwide, 2007, 2008.

Figure 10.2   *Performance of leading trading centres in Asia, by WCCI*
components, 2007–2008

between decreasing competitiveness and steady state is more even for the customer cluster and the people and culture cluster there are some factors where competitor cities may see opportunities; on cost of living, depth of the local talent pool or the global client base (see Figure 10.2). In relation to the competitive strengths of three major regional financial centres in East and Southeast Asia, Hong Kong is notable for its potential to build on its historic ties to UK and its prominent role in international trade and Shanghai is regarded as working hard to position itself as the gateway to China.[16]

For the regional corporate and financial centres in East and South Asia to close the gap they need to address any competitive weaknesses of the kind highlighted for London. Yeandle and Mainelli have suggested an acronym, SPIN, to summarise what these cities need to do to improve their attractiveness.[17] The first focus for attention is *structure*. This is not just about the reliability and growth capacity of public transport or high speed computer and telecommunications services but also infrastructure such as housing, education, cultural or recreational facilities that influence what it is like to live as well as to work in a city. The second focus is *people* and regulation, especially the availability and enhancement (via appropriate education establishments) of a suitably qualified pool of professional workers and technicians with excellent IT skills. The third focus is *information* and knowledge exchange; this tends to be stimulated by the degree to which the economic activities found in a corporate/financial complex are diverse and dynamic and the way in which it is connected into international flows of companies, people and transactions. The final contribu-

---

[16]   Mayor of London (2008), p. 21.
[17]   Yeandle and Mainelli (2009).

tion to SPIN is the ability to engage in face-to-face contact, both for the conduct of formal business activity and also for the less formal *networking* through social and other activities that leads to collaborative work or the early identification of potential business opportunities.

The interventions that are needed to influence this mix of tangible and intangible factors that will avowedly impact on the competitiveness of East and Southeast Asian trading and financial hubs will vary according to the circumstances in each city but, amongst other things, the outcome may ultimately depend upon the evolving dynamics of the relationships between the region's largest economies: India, China and Japan.[18] Even if this obstacle can be overcome it remains the case that many of the elements of SPIN require time either to be introduced or for the effects of specific policies, such as those for boosting human resource capacities, to become evident on the ground. In the meantime, the established international financial hubs will be devising their responses to the new global economic and financial circumstances and will be able to draw upon the significant network and agglomeration advantages that they already possess and which have accumulated over a period of more than a century.

By this standard, the major regional centres in East and South Asia are 'teenagers' that have yet to accumulate the skill, knowledge and gravitas that accompany middle and old age. It has been noted, for example, that 'neither global financial institutions such as US money centre banks nor multilateral international financial institutions such as the IMF have their headquarters in Asia'.[19] This, in spite of the fact that evidence for the increasing global financial role of the region was evident when Nomura, the Japanese bank, purchased the European and Asian operations of Lehman Brothers, the US investment bank that went bankrupt in September 2008. At about the same time the value of initial public offerings (IPOs) launched on the Hong Kong stock exchange exceeded the value of those launched in New York for the first time. These are green shoots of encouragement but they do not disguise the reality that centres like Singapore, Hong Kong and Shanghai do not possess the attitude to risk taking (even if this is reined in by regulators in New York or London) found amongst managers at their European or North American rivals. The competitive advantage of the latter is also built upon a substantial track record of innovation and even though, for example, some of the resulting derivatives and hedge funds have not inspired confidence in the last few years it is unlikely that the propensity to innovate will transfer quickly enough to Asia centres to usurp the ingrained capacity present elsewhere.Perhaps the region's larger

18 City of London Corporation (2008), p. 62.
19 Yoshikuni (2008), p. 87.

role in the international financial system is solely dependent on the fact that, with its very large savings reserves, China can act as a major creditor. However, a large proportion of these savings is denominated in foreign currencies and is managed by intermediaries in financial centres elsewhere, notably London and New York (City of London Corporation, 2008). If the recent growth and diversification of the Chinese economy, which has relied heavily on exports to global markets, encourages a stronger orientation towards domestic demand this will have the potential to create significant opportunities for financial services.[20]

If market restrictions are relaxed by Chinese regulators, the demand for household, travel or health insurance will drive the development of consumer financial services alongside the needs of Chinese companies for markets in equities or corporate bonds. Should this happen at least one of the beneficiaries will be Shanghai. Hong Kong may also be able to further enhance its position as a leading regional hub but its aspirations to be an international financial centre will require a larger role in commodities, foreign exchange or bond trading; the success of New York is founded upon its major share of international trades in these categories. Another handicap for Hong Kong is that more than half of the market capitalization of the Hang Seng Index comprises Chinese companies on the mainland; this emphasizes its regional rather than global role. After Tokyo, the Shanghai stock exchange has the second largest market capitalization in Asia (and the sixth largest in the world) but this apparent advantage over Hong Kong, for example, will not be easy to feed in to its ambitions to become an international financial centre. There seems little prospect for some years of the Chinese currency (RMB) becoming fully convertible and inward flows of international capital are controlled by the government. Even though there is a commitment to loosening market regulation, political intervention remains important, and investors will be cautious about involvement in a stock market that is notable for its volatility even by the standards of other international exchanges; it rose by 80 per cent in 2007, fell by over 60 per cent in 2008, and rose by some 15 per cent in 2009. Perhaps the main difficulty for Singapore, which has worked tirelessly to create a business and living environment that is attractive to international financial services and other corporate activities, is that it does not offer sufficient critical mass. There are also challenges arising from its hinterland in that, apart from Thailand, most of its neighbours are at varying stages of post-colonial independence from the Netherlands, Britain, Japan, France and the US. This has created a variety of challenges including lower levels of achievement in economic growth that have provoked suspicions

[20]   Böhme et al. (2008).

about Singapore's motivations when it seeks to foster improved regional trade agreements or similar. Success has come in the form of prominence in international oil and currency trading but this niche will be hard to enhance in a regional market that is still small by comparison with Hong Kong and the constraints imposed by its geography (island city state) and population size (4.6 million).

ENHANCING REGULATION, SKILLS AND TAXATION: TOKYO, HONG KONG, SINGAPORE

Ultimately, the challenge is to enhance the competitiveness of the existing Asian regional centres on three fronts: regulation, skills, and taxation.[21] Japan and in particular Tokyo has, for example, recently embarked on a better markets initiative led by the Financial Supervisory Agency but it may be the case that the historical legacy of reluctance to actually carry out regulatory reforms that will make Tokyo a truly global financial centre will be an obstacle. There was an opportunity for Tokyo to assert its global position during the 1980s when the Japanese economy was at its strongest but while Japanese financial institutions were able to establish branches, for example, in New York or London it was very difficult for financial service firms from outside Japan to set up a business in Tokyo or elsewhere. As a UK banker put it, there is much said in Japan about:

> Tokyo as a global financial centre but actually to carry out the reforms that are needed seems to be very difficult for them. They suffer from a legal system which impedes innovation. Tokyo is up there in the top ten primarily because Japan is the second largest economy. What's so astonishing to me about Tokyo is that despite being in the capital of the world's second largest economy it is not a bigger global financial services market.[22]

Hong Kong does much better than Tokyo in relation to its approach to regulation. The financial markets benefit from a more open policy towards

---

[21]   City of London Corporation (2008). Using its Index of Economic Freedom the Heritage Foundation ranks Hong Kong and Singapore first and second respectively . They are also ranked first and second with the region . See: The Heritage Foundation (2009). The Foundation defines economic freedom as 'the fundamental right of every human to control his or her own labour and property. In an economically free society, individuals are free to work, produce, consume, and invest in any way they please, with that freedom both protected by the state and unconstrained by the state. In economically free societies, governments allow labour, capital and goods to move freely, and refrain from coercion or constraint of liberty beyond the extent necessary to protect and maintain liberty itself.' See: http://www.heritage.org/Index/ (accessed September 2009).
[22]   Cited in City of London Corporation (2008), p. 6.

the foreign ownership of shares and the SAR's close relationship with China.[23] But a lingering problem that has led to a recent tightening of the supervision of financial and other processes is the relative lack of transparency on the mainland. In the case of Singapore it is generally acknowledged that it has an effective supervisory system for its various markets but they are strongly based on rules that may be transparent but possibly not flexible enough for a timely response to market innovation or the pace of change in the business environment.

In relation to skills it was reported in 2008 that a large proportion of foreign service-sector firms operating in Japan found the availability of appropriately skilled employees the biggest challenge to operating there.[24] Another skills-related issue of major concern for Tokyo and its attraction for international financial and legal services is the limited pool of English-speaking professionals. In this regard, Tokyo clearly cannot compete with the significant bilingual labour markets in Singapore or Hong Kong. Some restrictions on supplementing the workforce with highly skilled foreign workers also limits Tokyo's potential as a global hub for trade and finance. In order to ameliorate skills and labour shortages that are holding it back, as well as to tackle the fiscal burdens associated with its aging population, the national government needs to do more to attract highly-skilled foreign workers.

Singapore is notable for the way in which it has endeavoured to open its markets to overseas workers; it now operates, for example, a very selective immigration policy targeted at skilled workers and it has some schemes for increasing the attractiveness of Singapore as a destination for financial services professionals. Hong Kong has the deepest and longest established pool of workers with advanced financial services and other professional skills but, as with other successful regional and financial centres around the world there is an ongoing need for continuous improvement to grow, attract and retain the talent that makes it competitive in the international rather than regional sphere.

The prospects for taxation reform in Japan that would contribute to the enhancement of Tokyo's competitiveness are limited as long as the country's public finances remain stretched. Singapore is highly interventionist on tax policy with targeted incentives for economic development, including a simplified tax system and reductions in tax rates for multinational service companies. Further tax incentives targeted at asset and wealth management, capital and treasury markets and captive insurance, have

---

[23]   For a useful historical perspective on the emergence of Hong Kong as a financial centre see Schenk (2001).
[24]   Japan External Trade Organization (2008a, 2008b).

been introduced more recently. This has spurred Hong Kong into further tax-based competition with Singapore that has involved various concessions and reductions but whether this tit-for-tat approach is sustainable against a background of its demographic structure and volatile revenue flows that will place an increasing burden on public finances remains to be seen.

CONCLUSION

Even though there have been various city-specific initiatives of the kind briefly outlined in this chapter, without more developed value-added financial services it is unlikely that East and Southeast Asia can fully integrate its financial architecture into the global economy. Meanwhile, and at the risk of oversimplifying real-world complexities, there have been suggestions that perhaps Asia and the Europe/North America economic systems could exist in complimentary roles: services expertise flowing into Asia, merchandise trade flowing into Europe/North America.[25] The idea of 'Asia as a production centre and the US/Europe as a financial centre' (Yoshikuni, 2008: 84) seems rather farfetched but the scale of the imbalance between 'East' and 'West', and therefore the size of the gap to be closed, is underlined when some information on capital inflows and outflows[26] for major world regions in 2007 is considered (see Figure 10.3). The UK and the Eurozone account for a major share of total global outflows; only China stands out in the 'East' with outflows exceeding those of the US. Inflows are even more concentrated in the 'West' and the scale of the imbalance, even allowing for the potential for a reconfiguration of the global financial system consequent upon the 2007–2009 crisis, suggests that any significant enhancements to the global standing of financial centres in East and Southeast Asia will be really difficult to achieve.

There is perhaps good reason therefore to focus on an inter-regional agenda: raising the status of financial centres through enhancing the local/regional added value of the services that they provide rather than seeking to compete directly with the leading global financial centres. The sheer weight of comparative advantage held by London or New York remains a powerful, even if somewhat weakened, counterweight to the ambitions of

---

[25] Daniels (2001), pp. 213–230; Daniels (2005), pp. 21–51.
[26] Capital inflows/outflows are defined as total monies invested into and out of a country during a given year in foreign direct investment (i.e. investment in more than 10 per cent of equity), equity, debt, currency and deposits, loans, other residual flows, foreign trade credits and foreign exchange reserve assets.

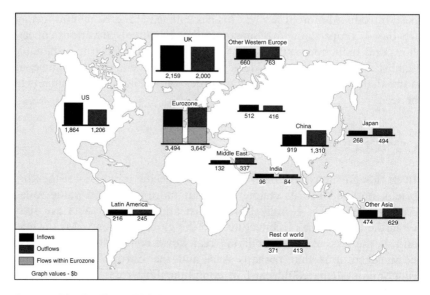

Source: After McKinsey Global Institute, in Mayor of London (2008), Exhibit 1

Figure 10.3   Inflows and outflows of capital, by major world region, 2007

trading centres in East and Southeast Asia (see Figure 10.4). An on-going focus on the region will ensure that it builds up its skills, knowledge and infrastructure to support its emerging economies but will also allow better local use of the large capital reserves that it possesses. On the assumption that the Asia will continue to be a provider of savings for many years ahead it should encourage private capital outflows by liberalizing capital account transactions and developing regional domestic financial markets, and national monetary authorities such as central banks should manage their international reserves more efficiently and/or diversify their investment policies

In circumstances where global services trade has held up much better than goods trade, the development of Asian trading hubs and financial centres will for foreseeable future probably rely on intra-regional competition.[27] But it will also be important not to lose sight of the potential for cities in contiguous regions to offer a challenge. In the case of Singapore, not the least of these is Mumbai with its advantages in the relative ubiquity of English as the business language and the use of Anglo-Saxon law as the foundation for mediating and closing business transactions. The challenge

[27]   Borchert and Mattoo (2009).

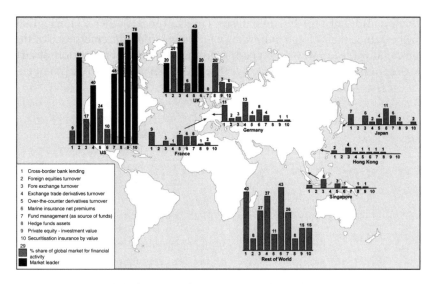

Source: Based on calculations and estimates by International Financial Services London, in Mayor of London (2008), derived from data in Exhibit 2

Figure 10.4   Global share of selected financial activities, by country, 2007–2008

nearer home for Hong Kong arises less from what is happening in Singapore than from Shanghai and Beijing; each is trying to assert its long term role as the premier regional centre meeting the very dynamic requirements of the Chinese economy. Hong Kong has had a head start and its strong legal, financial and trade services sector makes it the natural choice as an intermediary for Chinese investors looking abroad. The reality is that even though the Chinese mainland offers a large and liquid capital market there is a significant lag in the degree to which Shanghai and Beijing have been able to reform their fiscal, tax or skills regimes quickly enough to meet domestic expectations at the same time as those of the international financial community. Does this mean that in the short- to medium-term (five to ten years) the East and Southeast Asian region is more likely to achieve a strengthened network of regional trading and financial centres that reflect geopolitical, historical and cultural variations? There will be on-going 'loose' ties with financial centres elsewhere; the current global economic crisis has, if anything, simply magnified the need for the cities in the region to continue enhancing their human resources and technical capacities in readiness for the renewed competition that will surely reappear when the centres at the heart of the present crisis emerge from a temporary slowing of their activities. It is also worth reflecting upon whether there is also scope for East Asian cities to incorporate other strategies that will enhance their global ambitions by drawing upon the emergence of the new cultural economy to shape the production and reproduction of city spaces or human resources in ways that will underpin their global competitiveness as trading hubs.[28]

[28]   Daniels et al. (2011).

11. The eastward shift: rising role and new positioning of East Asian cities in the global economy

Alice Ekman

Tokyo is not the only global city of East Asia: Hong-Kong and Singapore are world trade and finance centres, and Beijing and Shanghai, with the opening and development of the Chinese market, now have new global ambitions. Most East Asian cities are eager to play a stronger role in international trade and finance. Local governments have to be even more imaginative than ever: foreign direct investment attraction and tourism are not the only fields of competition anymore; in order to gain 'global' status, cities have to find ways to attract entrepreneurs and creative companies, foreign students, a new generation of temporary but qualified workers, institutional investors, globally developing companies and develop university campuses, business schools, research centres, cultural facilities, among other infrastructures. Conscious of these necessities, East Asian cities such as Hong Kong, Singapore, Beijing, Shanghai, Tokyo or Seoul have managed, at different levels, to become more global than they used to be during the last decade. As a result, a significant phenomenon is currently taking place: the rising role of East Asian cities in the global economy. Such 'eastward shift' leads to a geographical reordering of global economic centres. In this context, East Asian cities have to adapt their development according to their new role in the global economy. Using both quantitative and qualitative perspectives, crossing available figures with interviews of economic actors conducted in late 2008 and 2009 in Shanghai and Tokyo, this chapter analyses the increasing role East Asian cities play in the global economy and the positioning challenge it generates at regional and global level.

THE INCREASING ROLE OF EAST ASIAN CITIES IN THE GLOBAL ECONOMY

East Asian cities do not all start from the same point in their race for global economic power. Hong Kong and Singapore have enjoyed international exposure for several decades now, thanks to their historical legacy. And Tokyo already ranks within the top three global cities, behind London and New York, according to Saskia Sassen.[1] But today, cities in emerging markets in Asia are rapidly acquiring influence in global commerce. Recent research pieces on the topic all converge on the same conclusion: Asian cities are gaining growing power in the global economy in comparison to their Western counterparts. This was already obvious before the global financial and economic crisis. For instance, a report issued in June 2008[2] on the top 75 worldwide centres of commerce (Table 11.1), showed that a stable legal framework, transparent business regulation and large financial flows contributed to top ranking for London, ahead of New York in second place, with Tokyo third and Singapore fourth. Most of all, the index ranking underlined the growing global importance of emerging Asian cities such as Shanghai and the relative decline of big cities in the US. In total, four out of the top ten centres of commerce in the world, according to this mid-2008 research, are located in East Asia. If the emergence of East Asian cities among the club of world trade centres is not a new phenomenon, the global financial and economic crisis has certainly accelerated it since autumn 2008. The strong resistance of the Chinese economy in comparison to most Western ones reinforced the position of several Chinese cities as world trade centres and thus the overall weight of East Asian cities in the global economy.

Regarding finance more specifically, recent figures are also outlining the increasing role of East Asian cities. Indeed, since the end of January 2009, total stock market capitalization of Asian stock exchanges rose twice as fast as Western ones, according to figures from the World Federation of Exchanges (WFE).[3] Moreover, for the first time since its creation, the Shanghai stock exchange (SSE) overtook the London Stock Exchange (LSE), regarding total market capitalization:[4] at the end of April 2009,

---

[1]   Sassen (1991).

[2]   The index combines seven measures of commercial power: legal and political framework, economic stability, ease of doing business, financial flow, business centre, knowledge creation, information flow and liveability. It was developed by a team of academics specializing in economics, business, urban studies and finance.

[3]   Les Echos (14 May 2009).

[4]   *Ibid.*

Table 11.1   Top ten centres of commerce in the world

Top ten centres of commerce in the world (2008)	Index (max = 100)	Rank
London	79,17	1
New York	72,77	2
Tokyo	66,60	3
Singapore	66,16	4
Chicago	65,24	5
Hong Kong	63,94	6
Paris	63,87	7
Frankfurt	62,34	8
Seoul	61,83	9
Amsterdam	60,06	10

Source: MasterCard Worldwide Centres of Commerce Index (2008).

the SSE had a total market cap of about US$1,949 billion, whilst the LSE amounted to US$1,946 billion. The gap between both capitalizations, though small, has remained constant: at the end of June 2009, the SSE still ranked before the LSE (total market capitalization of US$2,329 billion for the SSE, US$2,198 billion for the LSE – according to the World Federation of Exchanges, July 2009).[5]

In mid-2009, the ranking of global market place according to total market capitalization is as follows (top ten):[6] Nyse Euronext (US), Tokyo Stock Exchange, Nasdaq OMX, Shanghai Stock Exchange, London Stock Exchange, Nyse Euronext (Europe), Hong Kong Exchanges, TSX Group, BME Spanish Exchanges, Deutsche Börse. In total, among the top five global stock exchanges, two are East Asian. Such evolutions within the stock exchanges ranking are highly symbolic: a small revolution that confirms the rising financial role of East Asian cities within the global economy. There is a general movement of trade and finance agents towards Asian markets. Such phenomenon is not only about trade but growingly concerns finance, as the above figures show. Hong Kong and Singapore remain the leading global node of the region.[7] Singapore performs well in national foreign exchange and derivative markets, almost

---

[5]   Les Echos (28 July 2009).
[6]   World Federation of Exchange, July 2009.
[7]   Probably due to the fact that Singapore established the Asian dollar market in 1968, and also to the rather successful Singaporean Government's 'dual industrial strategy of becoming both an important hub of business as well as a site for up-market manufacturing', according to Hills and Mee (2003), pp. 151–165.

on a par with Tokyo,[8] and Hong Kong has a high number of offices of international banks, followed by Singapore and Tokyo.[9]

However, several regional financial centres need to conduct improvements in order to gain global status. The Chinese case is particularly relevant: although the volume of Chinese stock exchanges is increasing sharply, their products remain fairly basic because of the highly restrictive regulation of the People's Republic of China. The variety of financial instruments available is far inferior to those of American and European markets. The SSE still has a long way to go to become a global financial centre. It would have to face major current issues such as the lack of transparency and information, and even diffusion of unreliable information. The most significant indication that Shanghai is not an international financial centre at the moment is that no foreign companies are listed at the SSE. Nonetheless, most national and local governments show deep ambition and commitment to convert their city into an international financial centre, especially Chinese cities – they are certainly the most eager to gain worldwide 'face'. PRC's central government said it would support Shanghai's long-held ambition of becoming a global financial centre, setting a goal of 2020. As part of a dedicated plan 'to turn the city into a global financial centre', the government intends to allow foreign companies to list on the Shanghai stock exchange.[10] In late April 2009, China's State Council mapped out a cautious plan to increase foreign investor participation in the mainland market and to allow foreign companies to issue A shares. The goal is to allow 'qualified foreign firms' to issue A shares 'at an appropriate time', gradually to increase renminbi-denominated bond issues by multilateral development agencies, and gradually to increase the participation of foreign investors in the city's financial markets, said the statement.[11] New regulations issued a year later, in April 2010, confirmed the initial plan of the State Council. The 2010 regulations also encourage multinationals 'to set up regional headquarters, research and development centers, procurement hubs, financial management and other functional offices in China'.[12]

The authorities' will is clear, but there are still many obstacles to Shanghai and other Chinese cities achieving their goal of becoming global financial centres: non-convertibility of the currency, their still developing legal system, lack of experienced personnel in the financial services sector and, most of all, a lack of transparency and sophistication in the financial system. Nonetheless, the global ambition of Shanghai is fuelled

[8]   Baum (1999), pp. 1095–1117, p. 1114.
[9]   Hills and Mee (2003), pp. 151–165.
[10] *Financial Times* (30 April 2009).
[11] *Ibid.*
[12] *Xinhua* (13 April 2010).

by many development projects, and it can be argued that such combined improvement and projects, together with the recognition of its own limits and strong desire to gain global recognition, will progressively confirm Shanghai's position in international finance.

BECOMING A 'GLOBAL CITY'

With or without considering the specific case of Shanghai, all the above indicators lead to the same conclusion: the club of global trade and finance centres is shifting eastward – the power of East Asian trade and finance centres is significantly increasing within the global economy. The 'eastward shift' phenomenon is still observed from a broader perspective: global city mapping. A global city – terminology developed by Saskia Sassen in reference to London, New York and Tokyo in 1991[13] – is an important node point in the global economic system. The internationalization process of a city goes beyond the mere promotion of value-added service: global cities possess extra-economic characteristics that facilitate flows of good, services and labour on a global scale. The characteristics of a global or world city are numerous, and they may vary according to the definition taken into account, but they usually have the following specificities and infrastructures:[14]

- international financial institutions, law firms, corporate headquarters, international conglomerates and stock exchanges that have influence over the world economy;
- international, first-name familiarity, whereby a city is recognized without the need for a political subdivision;
- active influence on and participation in international events and world affairs;
- a large population;
- a major international airport (hub for several international airlines);
- advanced transportation system that includes several highways and/or a large mass transit network offering multiple modes of transportation;
- large foreign businesses and related expatriate communities;
- advanced communications infrastructure on which modern multinational entreprises rely (wi-fi networks, cell phone services, etc);
- world-renowned cultural institutions/lively cultural scene;

---

[13] Sassen (1991).
[14] Doel and Hubbard (2002), pp. 351–368; GaWC Research Bulletin 5 (28 July 1999), GaWC, Loughborough University online publication, available at http://www.lboro.ac.uk/gawc/publicat.html (accessed May 2011).

- powerful and influential media outlets with an international reach;
- strong sporting community, including major sports facilities, the ability and historical experience to host international sporting events.

The vast majority of the East Asian trade and finance centres have understood the importance of promoting communication, technology, culture, sports at global level. For instance, in Shanghai's search for global recognition, economic related plans are topped up with cultural projects, such as the participation and organization of events with strong international exposure (World Expo, etc). Tokyo, Hong Kong, Singapore, Shanghai, Beijing and Seoul all possess the majority of the above characteristics, although some are doing better in some areas than others: Hong Kong has better incentives to attract foreigners and foreign direct investments than mainland Chinese cities, for instance. From a basic observer's viewpoint, most of the East Asian cities above seem to possess the characteristics and infrastructures of a global city. It is hard to measure the 'global status' of a city as the criteria used may vary from one definition to another. However, the few existing rankings confirm the observer's viewpoint: the club of global cities is shifting eastward.

An interesting attempt to define, categorize and rank global cities was made in 2008 by the Globalization and World Cities Study Group and Network (GaWC) based at the Geography department of Loughborough University. It took into account several indicators[15] but ranked economics ahead of political or cultural importance: it ranked cities based on their provision of 'advanced producer services' such as accountancy, advertising, finance and law. The GaWC inventory identifies three levels of global cities and several sub-ranks: 'Alpha' world cities (four categories), 'Beta' world cities (three categories), 'Gamma' world cities (three categories) and cities with 'High sufficiency' and 'Sufficiency' world cities presence. Tables 11.2 and 11.3 represent the top world cities ranking according to the GaWC ('Beta' and 'Gamma' world cities are not shown).[16] Comparing the 2008 ranking with the 2000 one clearly shows the emergence of East

---

[15]   In 2000, the data collection and analysis exercise was carried out using 100 office networks of 'global service firms' in accountancy, advertising, banking/finance, insurance, law and management consultancy. Such firms were defined by having offices in 15 different cities or more including at least one office in each of the three main globalization arenas – northern America (USA plus Canada), Western Europe and Asia Pacific. Offices were traced across 315 cities worldwide. The task was repeated in 2004 and 2008, with larger data collection (175 firms collected by their size, between January and May 2008; new cities from emerging markets were added to create a list of 526). Taylor and Walker (2009).

[16]   *Globalization and World Cities Study Group and Network – GaWC* (7 May 2008), 'The World According to GaWC 2008', Loughborough University online publication, available at http://www.lboro.ac.uk/gawc/world2008.html (accessed May 2011).

Table 11.2   GaWC 2008 roster

Alpha World Cities ++	London, New York
Alpha World Cities +	**Hong Kong,** Paris, **Singapore,** Sydney, **Tokyo, Shanghai, Beijing**
Alpha World Cities	Milan, Madrid, **Seoul,** Moscow, Brussels, Toronto, Mumbai, Buenos Aires, Kuala Lumpur
Alpha World Cities –	Warsaw, Jakarta, Sao Paulo, Zurich, Mexico City, Dublin, Amsterdam, Bangkok, **Taipei,** Rome, Istanbul, Lisbon, Chicago, Frankfurt, Stockholm, Vienna, Budapest, Athens, Prague, Caracas, Auckland, Santiago

Source: 'The World According to GaWC 2008', Globalization and World Cities Study Group and Network (GaWC), Loughborough University.

Table 11.3   GaWC 2000 roster

Alpha World Cities ++	London, New York
Alpha World Cities +	**Hong Kong,** Paris, **Tokyo, Singapore**
Alpha World Cities	Chicago, Milan, Los Angeles, Toronto, Madrid, Amsterdam, Sydney, Frankfurt, Brussels, Sao Paulo, San Francisco
Alpha World Cities –	Mexico City, Zurich, **Taipei,** Mumbai, Jakarta, Buenos Aires, Melbourne, Miami, Kuala Lumpur, Stockholm, Bangkok, Prague, Dublin, **Shanghai,** Barcelona, Atlanta

Source: 'The World According to GaWC 2000', Globalization and World Cities Study Group and Network (GaWC), Loughborough University.

Asian cities in global economic order. The contrast between 2000 and 2008 is striking: top world cities ('Alpha' category) in Asia in the 2000 ranking were five in total, and are seven in the 2008 ranking, with Beijing and Seoul entering the group. Chinese cities bypassed whole steps on the ranking: Shanghai and Beijing are now both considered by the 2008 ranking 'Alpha World Cities +', along with Hong Kong, Singapore and Tokyo, but in 2000 Beijing was a second class world city (Beta World Cities +) and Shanghai was one of the 'Alpha World Cities –' along with cities such as Barcelona or Dublin. As a result, in the 2008 GaWC Roster, five of the nine top world cities are located in East Asia, whereas there were only three in the 2000 GaWC Roster.

The GaWC roster mainly took into account trade and finance related characteristics, and many different criteria could have been used to classify

Table 11.4   The 2010 Global Cities index

Ranking (2010)	City
1	New York
2	London
3	Tokyo
4	Paris
5	Hong Kong
6	Chicago
7	Los Angeles
8	Singapore
9	Sydney
10	Seoul
11	Brussels
12	San Francisco
13	Washington
14	Toronto
15	Beijing
16	Berlin
17	Madrid
18	Vienna
19	Boston
20	Frankfurt

Source: Foreign Policy/A.T. Kearney/Chicago Council on Global Affairs,
The 2010 Global cities index, August 2010, www.foreignpolicy.com (accessed May 2011).

world cities. But crossing the GaWC roster with other types of ranking led to the same result: for instance, the Global Cities indexes 2008 and 2010 (Table 11.4), conducted by Foreign Policy/ A.T. Kearney/Chicago Council on Global Affairs, also show that Asian cities are on the move.

The methodology[17] used for this Global Cities index is different from

[17] Methodology: the index ranks 60 cities on five dimensions:

1 Business activity – including Fortune Global 500 headquarters and Top 40 business service firms, size of stock and commodities markets, flow of goods, industry conferences;
2 Human capital – including data on top universities, international students, inhabitants with university degrees, size of foreign-born population, primary and secondary international schools;
3 Information exchange – including bureaus of global publications, coverage of international news, broadband penetration;
4 Cultural experience –including international visitors, performing arts venues, international shows and sporting events, diversity and quality of culinary scene;

Table 11.5   The 2008 and 2010 Global Cities index (top 10) (business activity dimension only)

Ranking (2010)	Ranking (2008)	City
1	1	New York
2	2	Tokyo
3	3	Paris
4	5	Hong Kong
5	4	London
6	9	Beijing
7	6	Singapore
8	8	Shanghai
9	7	Seoul
10	12	Chicago

Note: The business activity dimension considers the value of a city's capital markets, the number of Fortune Global 500 headquarters there, the number of international conferences held, the flow of goods (via airports and ports) and the volume of goods that pass through the city.

Source: Foreign Policy/A.T. Kearney/Chicago Council on Global Affairs, The 2008 and 2010 Global cities index, October 2008 and August 2010, www.foreignpolicy. com (accessed May 2010).

the one used for the GaWC roster, as it considers, in addition to business activity, other areas of influence such as human capital, information exchange, cultural experience and political engagement. And the business activity is measured in a very different, more pragmatic, way: consideration of the Fortune Global 500 headquarters and top 40 business service firms, size of stock and commodities markets, flow of goods and industry conferences. But the index leads to a similar conclusion to the GaWC ranking: a significant proportion of global cities are now located in East Asia. Of the top ten cities, four are in the East Asian region – Tokyo, Hong Kong, Singapore, and Seoul – according to both the 2008 and 2010 indexes. Many others, especially in China, are knocking at the door: traditional top-ranking cities face strong competition from emerging cities, including Beijing and Shanghai. In 2008, Shanghai ranks eighth and Beijing ranks ninth in the 'Business Activity' dimension of the index; in 2010, Shanghai still ranks eighth but Beijing jumped to sixth position (Table 11.5).

Independently of the ranking used and the criteria considered, the

----

5   Political engagement – including embassies, consulates, international organizations, think tanks, international policy conferences and sister-city arrangements, investment promotion agencies and NGOs.

various observations all underline the same phenomenon: East Asian cities are becoming more important trade and finance nodes within the global economy. Beyond pure economic criteria, they possess characteristics that enable them to convert into true global cities, with strong international recognition and power of global attraction.

THE INCREASING ROLE OF EAST ASIAN CITIES IN THE GLOBAL ECONOMY: NEW POSITION, NEW VISION

The 'eastward shift' is a long-term, well-established, phenomenon. Indeed, the increasing role of East Asian cities in the global economy is the result of multiple structural and contextual causes: globalization, urbanization, opening up and liberalization of the economy (Chinese case), overall economic development of the region. The development of Beijing and Shanghai directly results from such a combination. With the Chinese economy becoming market-based, increasingly integrated into the global economic system, Shanghai and Beijing became the symbolic portals to a very large emerging market.

In addition to structural causes, the economic context is facilitating the eastward shift. Indeed, the global economic crisis can be seen as an opportunity for East Asian cities[18] to gain comparative power vis-à-vis Western cities. East Asian markets have been comparatively less impacted by the crisis than American markets and most Western European markets. Such difference of impact represents an opportunity for East Asian cities' markets to partly catch up with those of Western cities. For instance, the recent rise of the Shanghai Stock Exchange is related to the very high activity from the first months of 2009, which is an indirect consequence of the credit crunch. From a global and comparative perspective, there is no doubt that the increasing role of East Asian cities is a significant, on-going process, supported by strong structural, and, from autumn 2008, contextual causes.

Strategic Positioning of East Asian Cities in the Global Economy

The 'eastward shift' is obviously positive for the cities concerned, but it also generates a new challenge: now that East Asian trade and finance centres occupy a different position in the global economy, they should adapt to the new economic order, adopt a development strategy in accordance to their new position.

---

[18]   For further developments on the topic, see Chapter 10, this volume.

Theoretical debates on global cities among economists and urban specialists show that policymaking of megacities from semi-peripheral and peripheral zones is confronted by a major dilemma: how to integrate in a network when such configuration is not inherently stable. Allen and his colleagues note the vulnerability of such cities: any policy of exclusion from global connexions will probably 'stultify economic growth and exacerbate economic polarization'; being within the networks allows at least the possibility to negotiate inclusion.[19] But then a major issue arises: how to become part of this world city network? Categorization may have side effects, as the city labelled 'world city' or 'global city' can be viewed by local policymakers as models to imitate or copy, as they are comparatively more advanced and successful. That is what seems to be happening in several East Asian cities: emerging global cities such as Shanghai or Beijing tend to imitate extensively traditional global powers such as London or New York, they tend to follow a single model, copying the largest global financial centres. Government aims at developing similar economic functions (strong emphasis on financial services), geographical structure of the city (replication of Central Business District), economic hierarchy/prioritization of specific industries, and so on.

Such 'replication' phenomenon is highly problematic for the East Asian cities' global sustainability, as although it may have a short-run positive acceleration effect on the global economic integration of the city, it is not the best way to establish the solid positioning necessary to gain long-run global recognition. As Taylor points out, 'the future urban world will not consist of many "little New Yorks" and "mini-Londons"'.[20] He argues, along with other observers, that 'instead of pursuing policies to improve a city's ranking by adding to their stock of functions and practices, cities need to attend to their position within a network of cities',[21] insisting on the relevance of policies that focus upon connections and linkages within an overall framework of many networks.

Global cities tend to present similar characteristics (advanced transport and accommodation facilities, cosmopolitan population, international and highly qualified labour force, high level of communication flows, etc), but it does not imply that they share similar economic functions. Such assumption – global cities are similar – is a result of confusions between economic characteristics and functions, and may lead to wrong policy planning. London is a global financial centre, but Beijing can become a real global city without becoming so, or rather, trying to become so could

[19]   Allen (1999); Taylor et al. (2002a).
[20]   Taylor et al. (2002b).
[21]   Beaverstock et al. (2001), Taylor et al. (2002b).

prevent the city from gaining global status, as the London trend may not suit the history and geography of Beijing, and the political and economic context in which it is inserted (risk of regional redundancy for instance).

Many different factors have to be taken into account in order to design a sustainable economic strategy for a city with global ambitions. In the case of East Asia, the geographic factor is one of the most important: with economic development, the region possesses several potential global financial centres, but how many such financial centres does the region, and the world, really need? Economic needs have to be assessed in a geographical perspective that goes beyond national borders. Differences of economic functions among East Asian cities can naturally increase trade and finance exchanges in the region, and global attractiveness as a result.

In this context, rival strategies purely aimed at overtaking one city or another is counterproductive. It can be argued on that basis that, for example, Shanghai, Beijing and Hong Kong should be viewed as complementary economic centres of greater China rather than rivals in the global city ranking – because the Shanghai/Hong Kong and Shanghai/Beijing rivalries are economic non-sense from a regional perspective. Both Shanghai and Hong Kong have advantages: Hong Kong has the advantage of a stronger legal system, international market integration, superior economic freedom, greater banking and service expertise. Shanghai has stronger links to both the Chinese interior and the central government, in addition to a stronger base in manufacturing and technology, and high development potential (the city has recorded a double-digit growth for 14 consecutive years since 1992). In practice, Shanghai's aim to become China's financial capital seems more an individual struggle for dominance with Hong Kong than a cooperative process. Moreover, with the progressive development of Japan, South Korea and now China, new global economic centres have emerged in the region, competing with traditional international economic players such as Hong Kong and Singapore. The fast and significant remapping of economic powers may contribute to exacerbate competition rather than cooperation among cities.

The general issue most East Asian cities have to address, by considering different economic realms, is to conduct a thorough assessment of the underexploited potential within the region and to design a regional and global economic long-run strategy accordingly. The vast majority of cities have already developed comprehensive strategies for their global development. For instance, Shanghai had set out a forward looking agenda in its 11th five-year plan for 2006–2011 that embraced economic, social and environmental goals, with ambitious targets (to raise the role of the service sector in the economy, to increase spending on research and development to 2.8 per cent of the city's GDP, to reach an internet penetration rate of

68 per cent, etc). Such strategy is a necessity for a city such as Shanghai, and the initiatives of local and national government and its determination for fast implementation is exceptional. However, Shanghai will need to implement new investment, and most of all to develop more stringent regulations and stronger environmental commitments.[22] Transparency, good public management, sound taxation and regulation system, market access . . . these are basic conditions for any city wanting to develop as a regional/international economic centre in the short run.

In the long run, sustainability but also identity – having internationally recognized characteristics and comparative advantages – matter. Creativity is one of the many tools that can be more efficiently used by East Asian cities for the promotion of their identity, and thus, to an extent, for the enforcement of their long-term strategic global positioning. It is often recognized that global cities are special places of knowledge and learning in competitive global markets.[23] Cities are the engines of national economies and crucial nodes of innovation and competitiveness. Most East Asian cities have launched good initiatives for the promotion of innovation,[24] such as clusters linking actors in the same industry. But in general terms, East Asian cities should, on the innovation front, occupy more accurately the different ranks, roles, niches and positions within the network of global cities. Many of them are developing significant innovation-related policies, but more could be done to underline local economic assets. In the case of Shanghai, good strategy already exists, but it could be argued that emphasis on sustainability and identity development is lacking. Some cities' specificities are globally recognized. Beijing, Shanghai, Seoul, Hong Kong and Tokyo have developed regional and global exposure during the last decades, as shown earlier, but to become more than an international portal to their growing domestic market, valuing diversity and building a strong identity would be an investment with precious returns.

CONCLUSION

East Asian trade and finance centres are gaining global recognition. Tokyo, Hong Kong, Singapore, but also Shanghai, Beijing and Seoul are all actively engaged in the global economy: they attract foreign direct investment and represent significant international trade and finance nodes with growing concentration of value-added services. Comparative data all

[22] Gurria (2006).
[23] Taylor et al. (2002b).
[24] Gurria (2006).

indicate that the power of East Asian cities in the global economy is significantly increasing. A combination of factors – globalization, urbanization, opening up of the Chinese economy – is at the origin of the phenomenon, and the economic context – the global economic crisis in particular – is amplifying it. East Asian cities are becoming essential portals for international trade and finance flows. But to remain so, they need to adapt their development strategy according to their new position in the global economy. In order to ensure long-term global recognition, a more specific and strategic urban planning is essential, taking into account the locations and functions of existing regional and global trade and finance centres. A wide strategic and geographic vision of the global economy can help cities adjust to a fast changing world and promote cities' economic identity and innovation. In fact, the best way to gain global status seems to be developing a 'world city' niche rather than copying or following existing global cities characteristics, not an easy task for late comers, especially when long-lasting successful examples such as London or New York prevail.

12. Can Shanghai become the new Hong Kong of China?

Yuan Zhigang

On March 25, 2009, the Chinese State Council gave the green light to speed up the process of turning Shanghai into a major international financial and shipping center by 2020. It urged Shanghai to develop into a multi-function financial center to keep up with China's economic influence and the Renminbi (RMB)'s international position, as well as an international shipping hub which can take advantage of the global shipping resources.

Although the goal of building Shanghai into an international financial center has long been established as the national strategy, this is the first time for the country has set up a coordination mechanism at the national level, and given equal strategic importance to the global shipping and financial center building. This shows that the speed of turning Shanghai into an international financial and shipping center has been accelerated. Can Shanghai then become the new Hong Kong of China?

SHANGHAI VERSUS HONG KONG

As China's economic center, Shanghai's development has been affected by the national strategy. Before 1949, Shanghai was once the most important metropolis in the Far East, as well as a financial and trading center with a relatively developed service sector. This was clearly indicated by the city's industrial structure. In 1952, the primary, secondary and tertiary industry accounted for 5.9 percent, 52.4 percent and 41.7 percent of Shanghai's GDP respectively. However, with the advance of socialist transformation during the first five-year plan period (1953–1957), the financial market in the city disappeared as 648 financial institutions in 1949 were reduced to four in 1957, with the remaining ones only serving as the state financial treasury. Meanwhile, 376 foreign firms went out of business and 1,629 private import and export companies were reduced and merged. In fact, all private trading agencies were incorporated into one state-owned foreign trade company by 1957 and Shanghai was no longer the trading center in

Table 12.1   Transition of the industry structure in Shanghai

Year	Primary Industry		Secondary Industry		Tertiary Industry	
	Value Added	Employment	Value Added	Employment	Value Added	Employment
1952	5.9	42.6	52.4	29.6	41.7	27.8
1978	4.0	34.4	77.4	44.0	18.6	21.6
1992	3.1	9.6	60.8	58.3	36.1	32.1
2009	0.7	4.6	39.9	39.7	59.4	55.7

Source: Statistic Yearbook of Shanghai 2010.

the Far East. At the same time, with the new strategy of giving priority to heavy industry, Shanghai was turned into an industrial center with a single manufacturing function. Since then, the city's economic structure has been manufacturing-based until the reform and opening up, with the secondary industry creating 80 percent of the local GDP and providing 40 percent of the job opportunities. In contrast, the service sector accounted for just 20 percent of local employment and GDP.

After the reform in 1978, the added value and employment proportion of the tertiary industry gradually began to increase. However, it was the development and opening up of Pudong in 1990 that started a new chapter for the city. The development of the tertiary industry in Shanghai moved into the fast lane after Deng Xiaoping's 1992 southern tour, which promoted the establishment of a '321' strategy that gave priority to the service sector.[1] From 1992 to 2009, the service sector in Shanghai achieved an annual growth of 12.4 percent, with its added value and employment proportions increasing by 16.5 and 24.3 percentage points respectively. In 2009, the added value in Shanghai's tertiary industry reached 893.1 billion Yuan. Table 12.1 shows the added value and employment proportion of the three industries in Shanghai from 1952 to 2009.

Relying on the nation's support and its own advantages, Shanghai has preliminarily established its position as the financial centre of the mainland in the course of the last 30 years of reform and opening up. In 1990, the first stock exchange in the country came into existence in Shanghai. In 1991, for the first time after the reforms, six foreign banks entered the Chinese market and set up branches in Shanghai. Then, China Foreign

---

[1]   '321' refers to the third, second and first industry respectively. This strategy means the service sector is given the most importance in development, followed by the manufacturing and agricultural sectors.

Exchange Trade Center (1994), Shanghai Futures Exchange (1999), China's Gold Exchange (2002), the second Central Bank headquarters (2005) and China Financial Futures Exchange (2006) were established in Shanghai one after another. By 2009, the number of financial institutions in Shanghai reached 787, among which 170 are foreign-owned. By the end of 2009, there were 20 foreign-funded institutions with legal person status in Shanghai, accounting for more than two-thirds of the total in the whole nation.

Shanghai's status as the mainland's financial center is also indicated by its great economic influence. In 2009, the transaction volume of Shanghai's financial market (excluding the foreign echange market) reached 251 trillion, with the stock turnover ranking third in the world, second only to the NASDAQ Stock Exchange and New York Stock Exchange. Meanwhile, the turnover of Shanghai Futures Exchange amounted to 73.8 trillion, 57 percent of the total futures market turnover in the country. The volume of gold spot trading ranked first in the world. In the same year, direct financing in the financial market of Shanghai accounted for 25 percent of the nation's total financing volume. All these demonstrate the radiation power of Shanghai's financial market in China.

Although Shanghai is reshaping its status as China's financial center, there is still a long way to go to achieve the goal of becoming an international financial center. We can see this by using Hong Kong, the international financial center in the Asia-Pacific region, as an example. In 2009, the per capita GDP in Hong Kong was about US$30,000, with the service sector contributing 92.1 percent of the total added value, among which 18 percent was created by the financial sector, accounting for 16 percent of the local GDP. In contrast, the per capita GDP in Shanghai in the same year was about US$11,320, with the service sector contributing only 59.4 percent of the total added value, among which 20.2 percent was created by the financial sector, accounting for 12 percent of the local GDP.

With its participants and capital coming from various countries in the world, the financial market in Hong Kong provides services to the whole world. Currently, Hong Kong is the seventh largest trading center and fourth largest gold market, as well as the fifth largest foreign exchange and financial derivatives trading center, with daily average trading volume of foreign exchange and financial derivatives accounting for 5 percent and 6 percent of the global market respectively. In fact, Hong Kong obviously has greater competitive strength as an international financial center than other markets in Asia. In the 'index of global financial center', Hong Kong ranks third in the whole world, behind London and New York.

Table 12.2   Hong Kong versus Shanghai (2009)

	Hong Kong	Shanghai
GDP (US$ Billion)	224	199
Per capita GDP (US$ Billion)	30,006	11,320
Added value of the service sector (US$ Billion	206	118
Added value of the financial sector (US$ Billion)	37	24

Source: China Statistical Yearbook 2010, China Statistics Press, Beijing, China.

Hong Kong became an international center not only because it is the main channel for capital coming in and going out of the Chinese mainland, but because it has its own advantages.

Hong Kong has always attached great importance to the regulation of its financial market. A relatively complete, effective and transparent financial regulation system has been established, in line with international standards. Major regulatory institutions such as the Monetary Authority and Securities and Futures Commission are very professional, can adapt well to changes in the market and constantly revise and improve relevant rules and regulations.

A sound legal system and free market environment then ensure fair competition, which attracts a large number of foreign financial institutions. Low tax rates and a simple tax regime provide greater autonomy and innovation opportunity, so that Hong Kong's financial industry can remain vibrant and progressive.

Finally, Hong Kong has a wealth of qualified professionals. For example, it has 3,000 chartered financial analysts, second only to the US, Canada and UK in the world and ranking the first in Asia, along with 25,000 certified public accountants and more than 6,000 lawyers; Hong Kong has a large contingent of financial talents.

OPPORTUNITIES FOR SHANGHAI

At present, Shanghai is facing rare historical opportunities which are based not only on policy support at the national level, but also on China's economic status and development strategy.

The Chinese economy, with its broad scale, rapid development and great vitality, is now more and more closely linked with the global market, which lays the foundation for upgrading Shanghai's position in the international financial market. Since the reform and opening up in 1978, the share of China's economy in the world has risen from 1.8 percent to

8.0 percent (2009), and China's GDP in 2010 ranks second in the global market, second only to the US. In 2007, China's industrial added value and import and export trading volume accounted for 10 percent and 8 percent of the world's total respectively, both ranking third in the world. Meanwhile, with China's economy more and more integrated into the globalization process, the total import and export trading volume accounted for more than 60 percent of the country's GDP. FDI (Foreign Direct Investment) reached approximately 1 trillion, which played an important role in China's foreign trade. In fact, of all developing countries, China has the largest amount of FDI. From 1979 to 2007, China achieved an annual real GDP growth rate of 9.8 percent, which is not only far above the contemporary world average economic growth rate (3 percent), but also higher than than in Japan's taking-off stage (9.2 percent). China's economic growth rate for the year 2008 still reached 9 percent even under the influence of current financial crisis, which was a bright spot in the global economy. In 2009, the GDP growth rate of China reached 8.7 percent, which took the lead in the world's economic recovery.

At the same time, China's future economic development is also promising. Demographic dividend will continue to play a role in the years to come. Industrialization and urbanization are also rapidly advancing. Ongoing agricultural modernization will further improve agricultural efficiency, while the reform of the household register system and land system can promote the transfer of the agricultural labor force into non-agriculture industries. As more and more people gather in China's Eastern coastal areas, the urbanization process will provide greater space for the development of the service sector. China's economy will probably continue to grow at an annual growth rate of 10 percent in the next decade or two, because a population of 1.3 billion constitutes a large market in terms of both supply and demand.

The Yangtze River Delta, where Shanghai is located, has the best economic foundation and the highest level of opening up in China. The market-oriented economic system in this area has taken shape, and is increasingly well connected with the international market under the WTO rules. This region contributes 25 percent of the nation's GDP and 38 percent of the foreign trade volume, and attracts 40 percent of the total foreign direct investment. Located at the center of the Yangtze River Delta, Shanghai is endowed with a huge space – adjoining the mainland – for the development of its financial industry.

The promotion of free convertibility of RMB will serve as a catalyst in the transition of Shanghai from 'Chinese financial center' to 'international financial center'. RMB internationalization being a national strategy, RMB will have free convertibility and become an important international currency in the future. Building Shanghai into an international financial center is one of the key strategies in advancing the free convertibility of RMB, while the latter will also play an important role in promoting the former. Therefore, China has connected the goal of building Shanghai into an international financial center and the goal of RMB internationalization, which is illustrated by the recent approval of RMB settlement for foreign trade in Shanghai. This is an important step as free convertibility of the RMB is conducive to building Shanghai into an RMB-dominated financial center. Meanwhile, as international capital is seeking investment opportunities in the Asia-Pacific area, free convertibility of RMB will also help Shanghai to take advantage of this opportunity, so that it can accelerate the construction of an innovation and trading center for financial products, and serve as an intermediary for guiding global capital into the Chinese market. In addition, free convertibility of the RMB can assist Shanghai to develop its financial market by taking advantage of both domestic and foreign resources, to expand the participating proportion and scale of offshore investors and to introduce advanced foreign institutions and regulations, in order to accelerate the internationalization of Shanghai.

The global financial crisis which started in 2008 is also promoting the status of and the free convertibility of RMB. The position of the US dollar as the international reserve currency is bound to be shaken, which leaves room for upgrading the RMB. By virtue of the existing international monetary system, the US dollar still retains the status of international reserve currency, and the US also retains its position as the global financial center. However, the origination of the current financial crisis in America shocked the international status of the US economy and the US dollar assets, as well as having a major impact on the US-dominated currency system. Although the US dollar cannot be replaced in the short term, it is bound to decline in the long term. Moreover, the Chinese financial system and its generally healthy economy are less affected by the current crisis, which lays a solid foundation for enhancing the status of the RMB. The currency swap with central banks of other nations, along with the increasing use of the RMB as the valuation and settlement currency in the neighboring countries, expands the impact of the RMB. Finally, the inherent defects of the current international monetary system have been fully exposed in the crisis, propelling the decision-makers to make up their mind to promote the internationalization of the RMB.

Finally, the recent financial crisis has provided Shanghai with rare historical opportunities. Although the financial market in Shanghai has also been affected, with the index of the security market falling more than two-thirds, the financial system is still very safe as the direct impact is relatively small. Except for the improved assets quality resulting from the recent reform, one of the key reasons for this is China's low level of development and opening up in the financial sector. However, this should not lead to the conclusion that China will slow its financial development. On the contrary, developing countries are expected to receive more attention since the crisis will exert great impact on the global financial market structure, and impel international capital to flow to emerging market economies which are safer and have better growth prospects. After the crisis, in seeking new investment opportunities, global capital will surely gather in countries like China, which enjoys a soundly-functioning real economy and whose financial system is less affected by outside factors. All these create huge potential for accelerating the building of Shanghai into an international financial center.

CHALLENGES FOR SHANGHAI

Compared with other mature international financial centers, Shanghai's challenges are mainly institutional. This is because Shanghai's development is subject to the overall pace of the economic reform in China.

First, China has a shortage of laws and supporting measures which are in line with the international practice in the financial sector. According to the 'Financial Service Agreement' of WTO, there is a large legal gap in China. Many laws and regulations need to be modified or abolished, while others need to be added, such as setting up offshore financial centers, the forms and standards of financial regulation, the regulation covering financial innovation, risk control, foreign exchange trading, market access and national treatment, etc. All these legal gaps also cause problems for Shanghai as it does not have independent legislative power. As a result, administrative intervention dominates government regulation, while supervision in accordance with the law is still relatively weak. However, a sound legal system which can protect market competition and investors is the key to the construction of an international financial center. Only efficient and fair regulations can guarantee the stable development of an international financial center.

Second, the formation of interest rate and exchange rate mechanisms have not been completely market-oriented. The non-flexible exchange rate system and non-market-oriented interest rate is a major obstacle to Shanghai becoming an international financial center. One important function of the financial market is the transaction of financial derivatives, which is closely linked to the risk of changes in exchange rate and interest rate, as the main goal of derivatives is to resolve and spread risk.

Therefore, a market regulation mechanism is a necessary condition for the development of financial derivatives, and the non-market-oriented interest rate and exchange rate will directly restrict the perfection of the financial system, as well as the financial-product innovation.

Third, the RMB is not freely convertible. Owing to the constraint of capital account management and the non-free convertibility of Yuan, there has been no major breakthrough in the internationalization of Shanghai's financial sector. Currently, capital account transactions and non-residential RMB business is under severe restrictions imposed by the government. However, controls on capital account have been loosened in recent years. For example, the Qualified Foreign Institutional Investors quota was increased from 10 billion to 30 billion in May, 2007. However, this volume is still very limited when taking into account the scale of China's financial market. On the other hand, from the perspective of RMB internationalization, the use of the Chinese currency in the offshore area is restricted to limited border trade transactions. With these institutional restrictions, participation by non-residents is still at a very low level. As long as the free convertibility of the RMB is not fully realized, Shanghai will not be able to complete its transition from China's financial center to an international financial center.

Fourth, there is a great lack of financial professionals in Shanghai. The enhancement of financial service needs professional skills. However, although Shanghai is a metropolis with nearly 20 million people, there are fewer than 200,000 financial professionals. In comparison, there are 770,000 financial professionals in New York, 240,000 in Tokyo and 350,000 in Hong Kong. This shortage of highly qualified professionals is mainly due to the high level of personal income tax in China. In fact, the personal income tax rate can reach 45 percent if one's monthly income is higher than 100,000 RMB, while the corresponding rate in Hong Kong is only 20 percent.

CONCLUSION

Shanghai has the potential to become an international financial center. However, whether this can be realized depends primarily on institutional reform. As Shanghai's reform is part of the overall economic reform in China, it must abide by existing laws and regulations. But the future is promising if Shanghai can consolidate its financial sector in the following ways. First, by developing electronic transactions, the interconnection of various financial information system and market transaction systems can be promoted, so that a unified and efficient modern financial supporting system can be formed to upgrade the financial market in Shanghai. Second, by making full use of the comprehensive integrated reform in Pudong, Shanghai can design policies to promote financial innovation. Third, a fair and just financial dispute arbitration mechanism can be established by accelerating the formulation of financial taxation and legal system that are in line with international common practice. Finally, a sound financial regulation system and high professional quality of the supervisory team are important to the construction of Shanghai as an international financial center.

13. China's emerging financial centers: Shanghai, Beijing and Hong Kong[1]

Simon X.B. Zhao, Zhang Li and Christopher J. Smith

INTRODUCTION

China's development in the past two decades has demonstrated a growing interaction with the global economy and the transformation of its spatial economy. At the regional level, there is a polarizing tendency of the national economy in certain city-regions along the Pacific coast, notably the Pearl River Delta region (PRD) in southern China, the Yangtze River Delta region (YRD) in southeastern China and the Bohai Rim region (BRR) in northern China. By 2009, these three regions accounted for 41.5 percent of the national gross domestic product (GDP), 76.7 percent of the country's foreign trade, and 90.5 percent of China's total inward foreign direct investment (FDI).[2] At the city level, several mega-cities, especially Hong Kong, Beijing and Shanghai, are globalizing, undergoing gradual but significant functional transformation from a manufacturing-based economy to a service-based economy. This trend has been supported by the increasing weight of tertiary industry in those regions' GDP composition.

Associated with the making of Chinese global cities is the competition for the status of a national financial center. The cities that are top in the Chinese roster of urban competitiveness like Hong Kong, Beijing, Shanghai, Guangzhou and Shenzhen have sought such status as one of their developmental goals.[3] With the end of the grace period it was given on WTO entry, China's banking and financial industry reached a new

[1] The authors wish to acknowledge the financial support for this study from the Mrs. Li Ka Shing Fund, Hui Oi Chow Trust Fund and Strategic Research Theme in Contemporary China Studies at the University of Hong Kong under the sub-themes of 'China Business and Economics' and 'Hong Kong and Greater PRD'.
[2] National Development and Reform Commission, Department of Regional Economy, 2010, Beijing, People's Republic of China.
[3] Yu Ke, 2003.

era in 2007 with the full opening-up for foreign financial firms of market access and the geographic coverage of their business; China's financial sector also became increasingly market-driven. Taking into consideration that China's economic development has been spatially polarized in several city-regions and China's WTO membership has changed the 'rules of the game' for the previously state-monopolized financial sector, one could anticipate the inevitable spatial restructuring of financial centers with the entry of foreign financial firms. Exploring the prospect of certain metropolises as major financial centers is an important issue which this chapter attempts to address.

Adopting the perspective of financial geography into the Chinese context, this chapter aims to examine the spatial restructuring of financial centers, against the background of China's political economy and financial market opening up following the entry into WTO. The development in this century of the financial services sector, like all other sectors, relies heavily on the flow of information. Accordingly, we will examine the role of information in influencing the location of financial activities and the formation of financial centers in China.

THE ROLE OF INFORMATION FOR THE DEVELOPMENT OF FINANCIAL CENTERS

A financial center is conventionally regarded as a geographical location with a collection of financial institutions providing high-level banking and financial services. There exists a hierarchical structure of financial centers which can be classified, in terms of geographic significance, as national, regional, or global.[4] While the accumulation of financial institutions is practically an indicator of a financial center, its importance is rated by the nature of its function: the leadership in strategic planning or concentration in operational management.

Conceptualizing about financial centers is easy but finding determining forces is difficult. A number of studies have focused on factors that determine changes in the preeminence of a financial center.[5] Among various factors, both centrifugal and centripetal, the information factor has been singled out as the key for influencing the location of financial activities even in the time when electronic communications are effectively shrinking space-time and making the financial market almost 'virtual'. Financial services rely on the huge flow of information as an input and produce it as

[4]   Kindleberger, 1974; Reed, 1981; Daly, 1984.
[5]   Reed, 1981; Ohmae, 1995; Porteous, 1995, 1999; Yamori, 1998; Martin, 1999.

an output.[6] The way in which information has been generated, transmitted and interpreted is significant to the viability of financial institutions. Functionally, one role of financial centers is to act as the site of information aggregation and value-added exploitation. Financial centers tend to primarily host information-sensitive activities.[7] The ability to collect, exchange, rearrange and interpret information is the most persistent characteristic of an international financial center.[8]

Following Porteous' influential work,[9] the theoretical framework of financial geography has incorporated several attributes of information, including information externalities, information heartland and hinterland and information asymmetry, into the analysis of the rise and fall of financial centers. Such a framework, taking into account information accessibility and reliability, has undermined the power of traditional forces, such as path-dependency and local preferential/discriminatory policies, in influencing the location of financial activities. Information externalities generally refer to the effects of information on the profit prospect of financial institutions that are generated during the process of information spillover. Such externalities are localized in their impact, with a distance-decaying effect in their extent and intensity. Financial institutions tend to be located near the source of positive externalities in order to grab the value of information. The information hinterland refers to a region that can, with low cost, profitably exploit information flows generated by a particular core city, that is information heartland.[10] These previous studies interpreted that the 'information hinterland' has critical influence in the financial centre development in China. They refer 'information hinterland' to an area or region of enduring focus, attention or publicity, particularly an area/region of global investment, business, commerce, trade and FDI. The information hinterland is often the accumulation of diverse activities of productions of many Multinational Corporations (MNCs) and FDIs and is therefore an active region of enduring international production, manufacturing, trade and commerce. Technological and policy changes are constantly reshaping the information hinterland. In terms of the previous findings, the information hinterland could act as a intangible framework with super powerful forces that could determine the rise and downfall of a financial center within the hinterland. A financial center emerges, grows and moves as its hinterland grows, changes and moves.

The information heartland is the best access point for information

---

[6]   Thrift, 1994; Dicken, 1998; Martin, 1999; Porteous, 1999.
[7]   Kindleberger, 1974; Laulajainen, 2003.
[8]   Laulajainen, 2003, p. 332.
[9]   Porteous, 1995.
[10] *Ibid.*

generated from that information hinterland.[11] It can be referred to as an information center that generates and disseminates a variety of information (trading, financing and regulatory) for controlling the operation of productive and financial activities within the information hinterland.[12] It can be also referred to as a business deal-making place, transaction center of business, service and trading hub and a place for strategic policy-making and financial settlements for the very large information hinterland. Over time, a financial center emerges and grows from the information heartland and its dominance can be reinforced or undermined with changes in the development landscape of its information hinterland. As financial institutions are increasingly mobile, the geographical significance of a financial center can be sustained or promoted only by securing and enlarging its information hinterland.[13]

We use the concept of information asymmetry to refer to the problem in assessing the value of information coming from remote sources. Depending on the types and complexities of information, there are many different cases of information asymmetry. Gaspar and Glaeser[14] have classified information as straightforward or complex. Straightforward information can be easily communicated via means of modern information technology. Complex information, however, requires face-to-face contact, especially when the interpretation of the information is highly contingent on many variables. The difference between the two categories of information is that straightforward information, usually published in an open and standardized format, can be easily interpreted, while complex information, often appearing in a non-transparent and non-standardized style and hard to be communicated readily by means of standardized communication facilities, may involve face-to-face manipulation and clarifications. The quality of non-standardized information may decline sharply over the distance between generators and users.[15] The effect of information asymmetry would push financial institutions closer to the information heartland in order to collect and interpret non-standardized information that financial institution can use to make profits.

Overall, the 'distance-decaying' nature of information externalities, the information heartland, and information asymmetry powerfully limit the footloose distribution of financial institutions even in today's cyberspace era. Therefore, the characteristics of local information are in fact a decisive determinant for the accumulation of financial activities and, consequently,

[11] *Ibid.*
[12] Zhao, 2003; Zhao et al., 2004.
[13] *Ibid.*
[14] Gaspar and Glaeser, 1996.
[15] *Ibid.*; Porteous, 1999.

the prospect of a locality to become a premier financial center. To a certain extent, it is the ranking in the hierarchy of China's cities that determines what kinds and levels of information can be produced in a city.

CHINA'S ADMINISTRATIVE SYSTEM AND THE HIERARCHY OF ECONOMIC CENTERS

The economic elements of the economic system in pre-reform China, such as public ownership of the means of production, planning mechanisms of resource mobilization and distribution and policy-making and institutional arrangements of bureaucratic control, were organized in a multi-tier hierarchy of administrative/spatial units with which the upper level of the hierarchy always possessed more political and economic powers than the lower level. While the absolute control powers were concentrated at the top, each geographic unit (city, urban district or county) was designated as a specific administrative rank with corresponding political and fiscal powers to retain and utilize resources. Notably, the ranks of cities did not fall under one particular administrative category but were commensurate with the various administrative levels, in descending order of administrative status, of the province (centrally administered cities), sub-province (provincial capital cities), prefecture (prefecture-level cities) and county (county-level cities). This unitary and centralized power structure therefore defined the role, and conditioned the relations, of different-level cities in development with the upper-level cities in a favorable and leading position.[16] As more powers and resources were concentrated in the upper-level cities, they functioned especially as political and economic heartlands and the spatial foci for regional development. Lower-level units with little decision-making power for their own local development functioned as economic hinterlands and executors of the orders emanating from higher-level units. The hierarchy of economic centers, including financial centers, was basically in parallel with the hierarchy of administrative centers.

With the introduction of market forces in shaping the Chinese economy and society under the reforms, the highly centralized power structure has experienced a transformation along with a significant devolution of certain administrative and economic powers to lower-level governments. This transformation has involved a reshuffling of power among administrative/spatial units and the functional transition of local governments from order executors of the upper-level government to financially more independent entities. Sub-national administrative/spatial units such

---

[16]   Chan, 2010.

as provinces and cities are empowered to play a more active role in driving local economic growth. However, the political structure, the national development strategy, and key economic enterprises and projects remain centrally controlled. The decentralization of powers to the local level are embedded in and accomplished through the long-existing hierarchical structure of administrative and spatial systems.[17] Though the urban system has been substantially reorganized vertically and horizontally through the scheme of 'city administering county', the scheme of 'converting county into city' and the annexation of suburban counties,[18] the nature of hierarchical control remains. Local governments still supervise and directly participate in the economy. The improved chance to be 'centers' is continuously highly skewed to those administratively high-ranking cities. This is why the higher the administrative hierarchy position of the city, the better its economic and social performance will be.[19]

The hierarchical system of the power structure in China also means the hierarchy of regulatory information centers with the most authoritative information and the power to release information is concentrated at the top. This highlights the significance of upper-level administrative cities, which are hosts to high-level governments, as the heartlands of regulatory information. Proximity to the source of regulatory information is important for the survival of any business sector as such information is often very abstract for implementation and clarification and detailed articulation is required from time to time. One can observe that, despite the relatively high costs, many MNCs would like to locate their headquarters into the upper-level cities. In other words, the physical accumulation of high-level information is an important factor in defining a city as a financial center in China.

SPATIAL RESTRUCTURING OF MAJOR FINANCIAL CENTERS IN CHINA

There are few empirical assessments to rank China's financial centers in terms of their national importance. Many qualitative studies have generally accepted that China as a geographically sizable country should have several financial centers, but the taxonomy of China's financial centers is hardly identified. One assessment, published in one of the most popular Chinese websites in 2003 (http://business.sohu.com/84/07/column212820784.shtml, accessed December 2010), has tried to quantify

[17] Ma, 2005.
[18] *Ibid.*
[19] Zhao and Zhang, 1995; Chan and Zhao, 2002.

Table 13.1   *Comparison of key financial indexes among three Chinese cities*

	Hong Kong	Shanghai	Beijing
Rating on direct and financial infrastructural factors			
International reputation	7	6	7
Financial institutions and supporting agents	7	5	6
Degree of internationalization	7	7	7
Global influence of financial prices	6	8	9
Freedom in market access	9	8	8
Effectiveness of the financial monitoring system	7	6	6
Quality of financial professionals	7	5	6
Financial infrastructure	7	8	6
Transparency of financial information	8	6	6
Score in the category	7	6	6
Rating on macro environmental factors			
Economic capacity	6	6	6
Economic growth	6	9	9
Legal environment	8	7	7
Fiscal and policy environment	8	7	7
International economic status	6	5	5
Transparency of information	8	6	6
Quality of manpower	8	8	9
Social and political risks	8	7	7
Urban infrastructure	9	9	9
Urban human environment	7	8	9
Score in the category	7	6	6

Note: Items are rated on a nine-point scale, with a maximum value of nine.

Source: Yu Ke, 2003.

the relative importance of Chinese financial centers by rating financial indexes of given cities.[20] Judging from its scores of different indexes, this assessment seems to acknowledge Hong Kong's leading position. Nonetheless, this study recognizes that different cities have their own comparative advantages as a national financial center. It is hard to have a conclusive view on the premier financial center in China. In fact, owing to the different kinds, tiers and sources of financial institutions, Hong Kong, Shanghai and Beijing perform distinct roles in China's financial market.

[20]   See Table 13.1.

INFORMATION HEARTLANDS AND THE HIERARCHY OF FINANCIAL CENTERS

The information hinterland is made up of three coastal city-regions along the Pacific Coast, namely, from south to north, the PRD, the YRD and the BRR. These three city-regions are the major recipients of global capital in the country and have become China's economic spearheads. Within this information hinterland, Hong Kong, Beijing and Shanghai are the information heartlands at different levels, with Hong Kong at an international level, Beijing at a national level and Shanghai at a sub-national level. Compared with Hong Kong and Beijing, Shanghai is a secondary center in terms of the importance of information. The cities of Guangzhou and Shenzhen are further down in the hierarchy, although they are an important part of the information hinterland. With reference to the relative nature and importance of specific cities, namely Hong Kong, Beijing and Shanghai, as the information heartlands, the implications on the spatial restructuring of financial centers are discussed.

Hong Kong

For the past several decades, Hong Kong's status as an international financial center has given it a position as the most important heartland of standardized business and financial information in China. Hong Kong is one of the largest 'foreign' investors in mainland China. As a free trade region with the free flow of capital and information, Hong Kong is home to some 70 of the world's 100 largest banks. Hong Kong has the largest number of financial-related news agencies and media in the Asia Pacific area. The world's most renowned financial news corporations, Economist, Business Week, Financial Times, the Wall Street Journal Asia and International Herald Tribune selected Hong Kong as the regional base for their Asian edition, and are printed in Hong Kong. Hong Kong has numerous 24-hour connection with worldwide financial news radio and television channels, instead of publishing media. A study conducted by Oxford University reveals that out of the 72 countries and 239 cities surveyed, Hong Kong ranks second in global broadband leadership.[21] To support the effective operation of the financial market, Hong Kong has transparent and reliable legal and accounting systems, world-class transport and IT infrastructures, as well as an

---

[21] The study was conducted by a team of MBA students from the Saïd Business School at Oxford University, and sponsored by Cisco, see http://www.sbs.ox.ac.uk/newsandevents/news/Pages/globalbroadbandquality.aspx (accessed December 2010).

advanced exchange and clearing system, which can reduce investment uncertainties.

After reunification, the governance model of 'one country, two systems' has maintained and strengthened Hong Kong's role and advantage as a global financial center. The 'one country, two systems' model places Hong Kong in a unique position in global finance to serve both the outflow of funds from, and the inflow to, China. Hong Kong can take the opportunity from the mainland's fast economic growth by pushing deeper into the mainland's financial market and, at the same time, by maintaining its own capitalist, liberal financial system.

While the Chinese economy has experienced fast growth and penetrated more deeply into international business, there is a growing number of enterprises in the mainland with an appetite for seeking opportunities to make their next investment in Hong Kong. The gradual liberalization of the mainland's closed capital account will allow enterprises there to access investment opportunities overseas. Hong Kong has become the most important stock market of Chinese enterprises outside of China.[22] Table 13.2 indicates that many mainland enterprises have tapped the international stock market for capital and know-how. By the end of November 2010, Chinese enterprises raised nearly US$126 billion through the Initial Public Offering (IPO) of 'H-shares' and 'Red-chips' listed on the Hong Kong Stock Exchange (HKEx) since 1993. The share of Chinese enterprises in the market capitalization of HKEx increased from 27 percent in 2000 to 46 percent in 2010.[23] While the HKEx housed only 221 listings, a number much smaller than the 890 on the Shanghai Stock Exchange (SSE) and 1,136 on the Shenzhen Stock Exchange (SZSE), the apparently higher degree of liquidity of the HKEx indicates that, compared with the SSE and the SZSE, the HKEx has become a favorable listing choice for Chinese large and internationally-oriented state-owned enterprises. Another example is the Qualified Domestic Institutional Investor Scheme, or QDII, which enables eligible mainland banks, securities and insurance companies to invest in Hong Kong and overseas. Hong Kong's access to international finance, coupled with its highly developed professional services, has provided useful facilities for mainland Chinese enterprises to enter the world market. Being the largest fund-raising stock market in China, Hong Kong has gradually performed domestic financial service functions in the outward mobility of funds from the mainland.

While the 'one country, two systems' model has formed the basis for Hong Kong as an international financial center serving the interests of the

[22] See Table 13.2.
[23] See Table 13.2.

*Table 13.2   Market capitalization of Chinese enterprises by places,
November 2010*

Place	Number of listed Chinese enterprises	Market capitalization	
		Amount (US$ billion)	% of domestic market capitalization
Mainland China (SZSE & SSE)[1]	2,026	3,964	100
Hong Kong[2]	221	1,231	46
New York	66	998	7
NASDAQ	186	97	2
London (including AIM)[3]	50	30	1
Total	2,549	6,320	–

Notes:
1. Figures of mainland China include the Shenzhen Stock Exchange (SZSE) and the Shanghai Stock Exchange (SSE).
2. The Hong Kong figures include Red-chip companies (mainland China companies which have operations in Hong Kong) and the Chinese state-owned enterprises.
3. Figures of London Stock Exchange include the Alternative Investment Market (AIM).

Sources:
The Hong Kong Stock Exchange and Clearing Ltd, China Dimension, http://www. hkex.com.hk/eng/stat/smstat/chidimen/chidimen.htm; The New York Stock Exchange web page, http://www.nyse.com/about/listed/lc_ny_region_7.html?country=2; NASDAQ web page, http://www.nasdaq.com/screening/companies-by-region. aspx?region=Asia&country=China; The London Stock Exchange web page, http://www. londonstockexchange.com/statistics/companies-and-issuers/companies-and-issuers.htm (all accessed December 2010).

mainland, certain institutional arrangements allow Hong Kong to enjoy the openness of the Chinese financial market beyond China's WTO commitments. One remarkable example is the Closer Economic Partnership Arrangement between Hong Kong and mainland China (CEPA), which is more or less equivalent to a free trade pact and provides Hong Kong companies with preferential and WTO-plus access to the mainland market in 42 service sectors. These service sectors include banking, insurance and securities and futures, among others. For example, Hong Kong's financial firms have been allowed to provide financial services in mainland China a few years ahead of other foreign firms. Also, the asset threshold for Hong Kong incorporated banks has been substantially lowered from US$20 billion to US$6 billion. Because of the size, vibrancy and promising future of the Chinese economy and market that it is serving, Hong Kong has great potential and is a strong competitor for being an Asian world-class financial center with far-reaching global influence. We anticipated that Hong Kong, with its increasing insertion into both Chinese and southeast Asian economies, will grow into Asia's No.1 and the world's No.3 international financial center, overtaking Tokyo and resembling London.

Beijing

Studies by several authors have shown that Beijing has the potential to become a global financial center according to its number one status in financial competitiveness supported by effective communication between the government agencies and foreign financial institutions.[24] 'Financial competitiveness' refers to the ability and potential to develop the capital market and financial industries. Beijing as the national capital possesses many advantages for internationalization and infrastructure development. At the national level, Beijing's overall economic power is next only to Shanghai. Beijing has the largest accumulation of MNCs' regional headquarters on the mainland. Beijing is also the country's largest science and technology hub with more than 70 universities and 400 research institutes, which means that the city has developed strong high-tech industries too.[25] Additional evidence of the importance of Beijing in the information sector is the preponderance of representative offices of various provincial and city governments.[26] The decision to hold the 2008 Olympics Games in Beijing created many investment opportunities, further increasing demands for the development of finance-related services. Beijing's potential to be a financial center is evidenced by the emergence of two financial streets with concentration of tall and state-of-the-art retail and commercial buildings in the CBD (Central Business District) of the city, that is, Central Business District in Chaoyang District and Jinrong Street in Xicheng District.

Information asymmetry between market regulators and market participants provides a rationale for an MNC regional headquarters, in general, and high-level financial activities, in particular, to be located in Beijing. Information asymmetry exists between market regulators and market participants when market regulations are subject to various interpretations. Even after China's accession to the WTO, industries, especially the strategic ones, are still ministry-led in administration and operation. Financial operations are heavily regulated by various central government departments. In order to reduce the negative effect of information asymmetry, market participants must find ways to learn policy details and to

[24]　Zhao, 2006.
[25]　See Chapter 9, this volume.
[26]　We would like to thank Professor Gipouloux for raising this point.

verify policy interpretations as soon as possible, and, finally, to anticipate the trade-offs of any alternative options. One effective way to do so is to keep close face-to-face contact with relevant government authorities, the source of policy information. Obviously, the friction of distance necessarily limits the frequency of contact by making it costly in terms of time and travel expenditure. This is the major reason why the MNCs' regional headquarters and financial institutions tend to be highly concentrated in the center of economic control and the heartland of policy information.

As the capital of China, Beijing is the financial policy-making center. It is in Beijing that the central government and all ministries enforce their administrative power. China's centralized administrative bodies in the financial sector, including the China Securities Regulatory Commission and the China Stock Clearing Center and the China Insurances Regulatory Commission, are all located in Beijing. Due to the need for quick access to the central government's policy, all Chinese banks have their national headquarters in Beijing. Many global financial giants have also established their regional headquarters there.

The conglomeration effect of information asymmetry is intensified by certain information externalities, which are known as the 'risk of politics' and the 'risk of polity' in business administration. The 'risk of politics' refers to frequent changes in regulatory policies among the functional departments involved, creating inconsistencies from one department to another and from one time to another at the level of implementation. The 'risk of polity' refers to frequent shifts of authoritative control over a particular sector from one government department to another, which introduces a redistribution of interests among different government departments and often creates a conflict of interests. Regulations for the financial services of foreign firms are formulated by a number of governmental departments, each of them administering one or more aspects of foreign financial services. Implementation of the regulations is subject to the interpretation articulated by the departments in charge. Because of the 'risk of politics' and the 'risk of polity', it can be expected that the interpretations from different departments are different and even contradict each other. The final version of a specific financial policy is usually the outcome of the cross-ministerial negotiation on a deal-by-deal basis. This has created an effect of intervention on business and the financial market in an unpredictable manner and underlines the importance of the geographical proximity of the financial headquarters to regulatory departments.

Given that the MNCs' regional headquarters and financial institutions need to be close to the center of policy information in order to reduce information asymmetry and externalities, Beijing's strength as an international financial metropolis rests on its national significance for administration and its uniqueness as the major source for non-standardized information. Beijing plays an irreplaceable role in the formulation and implementation of the country's macro-economic and financial policies. There is no other comparable competitor in this respect. This is not to say other cities, such as Hong Kong and Shanghai, are not important for the Chinese financial market. Nor is it correct to underestimate Hong Kong and Shanghai's international significance. Rather, we argue that different cities have different comparative characteristics and as a result different functional roles in China's financial market. The effect of information asymmetry and externalities are crucial in the case of Beijing which is the national heartland of non-standardized regulatory information. Beijing could take its innate advantage over information asymmetry and become China's strategic control center, complete with the regional headquarters of MNCs and high-end and top-ranked financial services. In short, Beijing has supreme and unique advantages for being China's top tier financial centre for strategic control and high-end corporate financial services. It could function as the role of Tokyo in China.

Shanghai

Benefiting from central government's policy support and having an advantageous location, Shanghai has become the most important manufacturing and commercial hub in mainland China for the past one and half decades. In the mid-to-late 1990s, central government explicitly shifted the focus of regional development from the Pearl River Delta (PRD) to the Yangtze River Delta (YRD), with the implementation of the 'T-Shaped Development Strategy'. The 'T-Shaped Development Strategy' proposed that national development would spread along two axes centered in Shanghai, one south-north axis along the coastline of the YRD and the other east-west axis following the Yangtze River transport corridor. With the designation of the Pudong New District as a state key development zone, Shanghai has become the national core of development. After China's accession to the WTO, the nature of FDI has changed from production relocation to market penetration. Foreign investors have repositioned their investment strategies and production base. Initially, the MNCs invested in China for their export-orientated productions with more focus on the PRD. Now their investment is more China market-orientated. Situated in a more central location of China, Shanghai has become a new strategic magnet for the MNCs' regional offices which provide the management of day-to-day operations of the enterprises, which are clustering in the YRD – the hinterland of Shanghai. Shanghai is now China's largest global operation center and is packed with the operational offices/branches of the MNCs.

Shanghai also holds a very important position in China's financial market. Shanghai was the premier financial center of the Far East prior to World War II. Since the late 1990s central government has prioritized Shanghai to be the number one financial center of the country. Many incentive policies have been introduced to promote the financial sector there. The central government has announced a plan to build Shanghai into an International Financial Centre that will match the country's economic strength and the international status of its currency RMB by 2020. Many world-class banks have also established their regional offices in Shanghai and the Pudong Lujiazui Financial and Trade Zone is being developed. The Shanghai Stock Exchange is one of only two stock markets in mainland China. One assessment, mentioned earlier, indicated that in terms of the development of the international financial industry Shanghai was not behind Hong Kong and Beijing in many aspects (Table 13.1). Taking into account Shanghai's economic power and the staunch support from central government, there is frequent media speculation that Shanghai will replace Hong Kong as China's, or even Asia's, financial center.

Nonetheless, a manufacturing and commercial hub is not necessarily the proxy of China's primary financial center. Nor is the presence of a stock exchange. A stock exchange is normally made up of three functions: a listing approval and monitoring, stock trading/transactions and the central registry of stock. Whilst these three functions can be housed in one site (one building physically) in many market economies, in China they are actually located separately. The Shanghai Stock Exchange only holds the function of stock trading/transactions. The other two regulatory functions are held in Beijing by the China Securities Regulatory Commission, which is the Central Government's ultimate governing body. It is widely recognized that the function of stock trading/transactions can go 'virtual' through modern IT technology (as we have already seen the case of the NASDAQ).[27] Therefore, the location of a stock exchange is not a critical condition for the formation of a primary financial center.

From the point of view of financial geography, Shanghai's prospect of being the leading national financial center is by and large overshadowed by one grave weakness: it does not hold any unique position in China's information heartland. Shanghai falls behind Hong Kong as the heartland of standardized information. Its significance as the heartland of regulatory information is also less marked compared with Beijing. Under state-led

---

[27]   Korbin, 1997; Budd, 1999; Warf, 1999.

economic liberalization, there is no simple policy measure that can mobilize the central source of non-standardized information from Beijing to Shanghai. In fact, the importance of Shanghai as an information heartland can be shared by many domestic regional centers such as Guangzhou.

Besides, there is another great obstacle to Shanghai becoming the top-notch financial centre in China: the RMB is not fully convertible, and there are restrictions on capital account activities. Overall, the amount of currency circulation is an obvious indicator which reveals a financial centre that provides a meeting place for people with surplus money to make deals with those in need of funds. Given the increasing use of the RMB in the world for dealing business with China, Shanghai's competitiveness is unclear. On the one hand, Shanghai is not the central source of monetary policy information as mentioned above, the demand for RMB currency is low in Shanghai compared to other cities such as Shenzhen. From 2001, cash demand in Shenzhen has made it the highest ranking city in China, with more than 50 percent of total national cash injection.

Shanghai's position appears to be undermined by Beijing. This is consistent with the results of one widely publicized study, conducted by Chinese scholars, on the development of 'headquarters economy' in China.[28] Although Shanghai has been heavily publicized and promoted as China's number one financial center, the basic function of Shanghai as a financial center is mainly operational rather than strategic. There is little doubt, however, that Shanghai will become China's largest financial center for manufacturing, trade and producer services. Its role seems similar to that of Chicago and Frankfurt. The difference between Beijing and Shanghai is, in terms of financial centers, the former is strong in strategic controls, policy-making and supervision, while the latter is strong in production services and operations.

CONCLUSION

China's landmark WTO accession has generated a profound impact on its economic landscape and financial market. Applying the perspective of financial geography to China's situation and taking into consideration the hierarchical nature of China's power structure, this chapter has examined the role of information in the spatial restructuring of China's financial centers against the general background of a financial market fully opening-up in the post-WTO entry period. We have incorporated the concepts of information heartland/hinterland, information externalities

[28]   Zhao, 2010.

and information asymmetry into the analysis of the relative importance of a given city as a financial center. Our approach is consistent not only with the information requirements highlighted in the literature of financial centers, but also with the characteristics of the Chinese financial market which remains basically a policy-regulated market. We have used the listing place of Chinese enterprises as a reflective measurement of the ranking of the financial center hierarchy, since the spatial concentrations of corporate regional headquarters in Chinese globalizing cities constitute strategic control points and correspond to the upper tier of the financial center system and the functional division of information heartlands in China. In the current situation, we anticipate that the pattern of China's financial centers will remain dominated by Hong Kong, Beijing and Shanghai according to their different comparative advantages. Hong Kong will act as a springboard and international fund-raising platform continually for mainland enterprises seeking to explore global market through excellent linkages with the world's economy. A favorable geographical position, bridging the time gap between North America and Europe; a sound regulatory regime on a par with international standards and the free flow of information and the rule of law have all have helped Hong Kong develop into an important financial center in the Asia-Pacific region and an important node in the international financial landscape. Beijing will become the most strategic financial center in the mainland with its dominant policy-making and regulatory roles. Shanghai will be the most important industrial and commercial hub as well as the leading domestic capital formation centre for mainland enterprises because it possesses a pool of national financial services and capital but is not the paramount financial center in China because the Renminbi is not yet fully convertible.

In contrast to central government's aspiration that Shanghai will be China's main financial center, we have argued that Shanghai's chance to unseat Beijing is downgraded by its relative insignificance as an information heartland. Although many 'technical' or policy measures can be adopted to upgrade the competitiveness of Shanghai as a financial center – including deregulation, transparency and technological infrastructure – Shanghai is unlikely to replace Beijing as the national regulatory and non-standardized information heartland. In the competition for financial supremacy in China as well as having a status comparable to New York, Shanghai does not have all the necessary attributes of a national financial center and is restricted by the country's state-led economic development. In other words, the Central Government has the final power to decide where the national financial center will be or whether the status quo will be maintained. Beijing, Hong Kong, and Shanghai could pro-actively complement each other and work cooperatively to promote balanced regional development.

Theoretically, this chapter suggests that developments in communication and information technology are unlikely to completely upset the role of the financial centers as sites for evaluating local information under the state-led developmental model. As financial centers need to aggregate complex information, face-to-face communication can hardly be supplanted by online communication. Information externalities reinforce the benefits of spatial concentration for users of high-value information. Overall, geographical location remains important to the formation of financial centers in China and its restructuring in the future.

14. Evaluating Beijing and Shanghai as global financial centers[1]

Xu Xun and Meng Jianjun

After China's entry into the WTO, one of the most frequently asked questions is whether Beijing or Shanghai will become a global financial center (GFC). In this chapter we attempt to answer this question. A GFC is often backed by a robust and vibrant domestic economy. It occupies a central and dominant position in the international network of financial centers. By examining the current place of Beijing and Shanghai in China's economic development and in the world financial system, we try to evaluate their roles as GFCs.

Our conclusion is that Beijing and Shanghai are not qualified as GFCs at present and are unlikely to be in the near future. This is based on two reasons. First, although both cities are well-established national financial centers, they have been inefficient in fueling domestic economic growth. Without further reform, China's financial system is likely to undermine the country's future economic development. Second, compared with the world's major financial centers, Beijing and Shanghai so far have very limited participation in the global financial businesses. Their further internationalization requires the liberalization of China's capital account. This, however, is not plausible in the short run, given that China's financial sector is still at an early stage of development.

This chapter is ordered as follows: the following section provides an overview of China's economic and financial development. Then we examine the position of Beijing and Shanghai in the overall economy, and assess how they contribute to China's economic growth. The next section briefly examines the roles of the two metropolises in the global financial network and discusses issues with the opening up of the financial sector. The last section concludes this chapter.

[1] We thank François Gipouloux and seminar participants at Tsinghua University for helpful comments and suggestions. We are also grateful to William du Pont IV of University of Hawaii for his work in correcting and improving this chapter.

OVERVIEW OF CHINA'S ECONOMIC AND FINANCIAL DEVELOPMENT

After 30 years of economic reform and development, the Chinese economy has grown significantly. Calculated in real terms, in 2009 China's GDP was more than 18 times larger than the 1978 level, and per capita GDP grew around 12 times more than the initial level. In 2009, China overtook Germany as the world's largest exporter. During the first half of 2010, China overtook Japan to become the world's second largest economy.[2]

The Chinese financial sector also underwent substantial changes over the past three decades.[3] Prior to 1978, there were no financial intermediaries or financial markets in China. The People's Bank of China served as a subsidiary to the Treasury Department and allocated resources to various levels of state-owned production units according to central economic plans.

Since the beginning of China's economic reform, banks and other financial intermediaries have been established. Four big state-owned commercial banks (SOCBs) were founded between 1979 and 1984 to take over most of the banking business from the People's Bank of China. Several commercial banks and three policy banks were also formed. At the provincial and municipal level, regional banks, Urban Credit Cooperatives and Rural Credit Cooperatives were set up. Postal Savings (renamed Postal Savings Bank of China in 2006), trust and investment corporations, foreign banks, insurance companies, mutual funds and security firms also emerged during this period. The financial intermediary sector has become a significant component of the national economy. From 1978 to 2009, the share of value-added of financial intermediation in tertiary industry grew from 7.81 per cent to 12 per cent. Its share in GDP rose from 1.87 per cent to 5.21 per cent, which almost tripled in 30 years.

Among all financial intermediaries, the depository institutions achieved the largest growth. The total assets of all depository institutions grew more than 16 times since 1978, amounting to 80,923 billion RMB in 2009. In comparison, assets held by insurance companies and security firms are small. The assets of insurance companies reached 4,063 billion RMB at the end of 2009. The assets of security firms are highly influenced by the volatility of the stock market. After the stock indexes fell from the peak,

---

[2]   Unless otherwise noted, all data in this chapter are from *China Statistical Yearbook*, *Almanac of China's Finance and Banking*, *China Compendium of Statistics 1949-2008*, *China Securities and Futures Statistical Yearbook*, *Beijing Statistical Yearbook*, and *Shanghai Statistical Yearbook*.

[3]   For a comprehensive review of China's financial development, see Allen, Qian and Qian (2008).

assets held by security firms decreased from 1,731 billion in 2007 to 1,191 billion RMB in 2008.

The second major component of China's financial sector is the financial market. Since the establishment of the Shanghai Stock Exchange and Shenzhen Stock Exchange, the Chinese stock market has grown quickly. From 1992 to 2009, the market capitalization grew at an annual rate of 37.78 per cent. Meanwhile, the ratio of market capitalization to GDP rose from 3.93 per cent to 71.64 per cent.

The bond market was developed earlier than the stock market but it did not start to grow until after 1990. At the end of 2008, the total outstanding balance of bonds reached 9,930.4 billion RMB, of which 50 per cent were Treasury bonds, 37 per cent were financial bonds and the remaining 13 per cent were enterprise bonds.

Financial derivatives made up another important part of the financial market. As this market is strictly regulated by the government, only futures and a few other derivatives are traded in China. Similar to the bond market, the growth of the market for financial derivatives was at first very slow. After 2002, it grew rapidly with an average annual rate of 64.8 per cent.

BEIJING AND SHANGHAI IN CHINA'S ECONOMY AND FINANCIAL SYSTEM

In this section we first examine the position of the two metropolises in the overall economy. Beijing and Shanghai are each located in one of China's economic areas: the Bohai Economic Rim (BER) and the Yangtze River Delta (YRD).[4] These two regions are among the three largest and fastest-growing economic zones in China. From 1997 to 2009, the combined share of BER and YRD in China's GDP steadily increased from 44 per cent to 50 per cent.

The two cities each serve the central position in the hierarchical production network that connects all cities in their economic zones. Home to the headquarters of many multinational corporations, domestic businesses and financial institutions, both cities have accumulated enormous economic resources and business opportunities. Over the years, Shanghai has played a leading role in boosting regional economic development. Industrial production and foreign investment has spilled over to

---

[4]   BER includes Beijing, Tianjin and major cities from Hebei, Liaoning and Shandong provinces. YRD includes Shanghai and major cities from Jiangsu, Zhejiang. In 2008, two cities from Anhui Province (Hefei and Maanshan) are administratively added into YRD.

surrounding cities and areas. As a result, Shanghai's GDP share in the YRD gradually decreased after 2000. In comparison, Beijing assumed an increasingly important role in the BER. As the economic reform deepens many firms have moved their management, financial and research departments to the city. From 1997 to 2009, Beijing's GDP share in the BER rises from 10 per cent to around 15 per cent.

From the perspective of economic structure, both cities are developing a more service-based economy. Reaching 76 per cent in 2009, the share of Beijing's tertiary sector is higher than most cities in China. Shanghai used to be an industry-intensive city, but its tertiary sector has also been growing steadily since 2003.

In 2009, the share of financial sector in GDP averaged 5.21 per cent at the national level. For Beijing and Shanghai, this ratio was 13 per cent and 12 per cent respectively. Combined deposits of the two cities constituted 16 per cent of China's total deposits, and combined bank credits accounted for 20 per cent of total bank credits. Home to China's largest stock exchange, Shanghai occupied 65 per cent of total stock trading and 99 per cent of total bond trading. Though Beijing does not house any major financial market, its role in equity trading is still significant. From 2003 to 2009, turnover of stock trading in Beijing averaged 24.7 per cent of total turnover in China.

After China's entry into the WTO in 2001, the increasing engagement of the Chinese economy in the world substantially accelerated the internationalization of China's financial centers. In the *Global financial center Index 8* (Z/Yen 2010), Beijing and Shanghai are ranked the second and third most promising financial centers in Asia. Two decades ago, when the Japanese economy was at its peak, Tokyo was also considered Asia's leading financial center. However, the economic stagnation of Japan severely impacted Tokyo's position and prevented its further development to become a global financial center.

Tokyo's experience undoubtedly demonstrated the importance of a sustainable economic development, which is a precondition for the sustainment of a global financial center. Hence, we next examine whether Beijing and Shanghai as national financial centers have been efficient in supporting China's growth.

China's economic development since 1978 is marked by the decreasing role of the state sector and increasing influence of non-state sector in the economy. For example, in 1998, the industrial output of the SOEs was twice the level of the foreign sector and more than 16 times that of the private sector. Total employment in the state sector amounted to four times the combined employment of the private and foreign sectors. By the end of 2009, both the private and foreign sectors outperformed the SOEs

Table 14.1   Comparison of bank credit and capital raised from the equity market

Year	Raised Capital/ Bank Loans (%)	Raised Capital/ Fixed Asset Investment (%)	Enterprise Bond/GDP (%)	Bank Credit/ GDP (%)
1993	4.96	2.41	2.32	93.23
1994	1.91	0.81	1.46	84.67
1995	1.27	0.59	1.11	83.13
1996	3.20	1.49	0.88	85.92
1997	8.72	3.74	0.70	94.86
1998	6.99	2.83	0.85	102.51
1999	8.27	3.04	0.95	104.52
2000	11.55	4.68	0.96	100.16
2001	9.50	4.25	NA	102.43
2002	4.11	2.37	NA	109.11
2003	2.97	1.49	NA	117.06
2004	4.49	1.55	0.77	111.46
2005	2.05	0.38	1.76	105.27
2006	8.05	2.24	2.63	104.18
2007	21.21	5.63	3.12	98.45
2008	8.48	2.05	4.27	96.61

Source: China Securities Regulatory Commission (2009); China Society for Finance and Banking (2009).

in terms of industrial output and employment. From 1998 to 2009, total employment in the state sector fell from 37.5 million to 18 million, while those employed in private and foreign industries increased at an annual rate of 30.37 per cent and 11 per cent respectively.[5]

According to an alternative measure of total industrial output of sectors by status of registration, enterprises registered as 'state-owned' accounted for 30.5 per cent of total domestic output in 1999. Private enterprises only accounted for 4.5 per cent. By 2009, private enterprises reached 29.6 per cent of the national total, while the fraction of SOE dropped to 8.3 per cent.

For the newly emerged non-state sector, bank loans and capital raised from the financial market are two formal sources of funds.[6] Table 14.1 explores the size of each financial sub-sector and their ability to meet firms'

[5]   Data is for enterprises whose annual revenues are more than 5 million RMB.
[6]   Compared to informal sources such as borrowings from family and friends and loans from underground banks.

Table 14.2   Fixed asset investment by ownership and financing source

2003	State Budget	Domestic Loans	Foreign Investment	Self Fundraising and Others	Total
Total	2687.82	12044.36	2599.35	41284.76	58616.29
State-owned	2248.30	5547.35	338.72	13472.63	21607.00
collective-owned	337.89	927.10	402.14	6455.70	8122.84
Individual and Private	1.74	895.04	20.49	7387.13	8304.39
Joint Ownership	0.95	22.57	1.87	181.20	206.59
Share Holding Co. Ltd.	89.97	3526.99	183.49	10591.07	14391.51
Foreign Funded	3.37	490.08	989.64	1280.51	2763.59
HK, Taiwan, Macao	1.00	596.03	656.51	1613.11	2866.65
Others	4.60	39.04	6.49	303.58	353.70

Note: Values are in 100 million RMB.

Source: China Statistical Yearbook 2004.

financing needs. From 1993 to 2008, the average ratio of capital raised in the stock market to bank loans is 6.73 per cent (the first column). Its share in fixed asset investment is even smaller, with an average ratio of 2.47 per cent (the second column). In the bond market, the issuance of enterprise bonds started to grow quickly after 2005. Its ratio to GDP reached 4.27 per cent in 2008. Though both the stock and bond markets are expected to have higher growth in the future, their size is not yet comparable to the banking sector. Banks remain the most important formal source of funds for Chinese firms.

Within the banking sector, the state-owned commercial banks have maintained a dominant position. Although other types of depository institutions have been growing at tremendous speed, their total assets are smaller than those of the state banks. In 2004, combined assets of SOCBs and policy banks accounted for 64.5 per cent of the total assets of the banking sector, among which the SOCBs alone had a share of 56.9 per cent. In 2008, its share remained 51 per cent of national total, despite rapid growth of other financial institutions.

Table 14.2 provides detailed information of financial sources for fixed asset investment of different types of firms.[7] For each category, 'Self

[7]   Data is not available after 2003.

Fundraising and Others' is the largest source of funds.[8] Bank loans are the second largest source, though their size is much smaller than 'Self Fundraising'.

One key point from this table is that funds from formal sources (the banking industry and the financial market) are not distributed equally across all sectors. In 2003, SOEs and share holding companies together received three-quarters of total domestic loans. Moreover, financial markets are only accessible to share holding companies, most of which were transformed from former SOEs. In contrast, the 'Individual and Private' sector's use of bank loans only accounted for 7.4 per cent of national total, while 89 per cent of their funds for fixed asset investment came from 'self fundraising'.

This indicates continued government intervention of the economy, since the domestic financial sector is still dominated by the SOCBs and the majority of the financial resources are allocated to former and present SOEs. The non-state sector is poorly supported, despite their increasing contribution to aggregate output and employment opportunities. During the period of 'Central Economic Planning', the state financial sector served as a core component of the economic system in directing funds to SOEs, for the purpose of fueling industrial development and creating employment opportunities. The maintenance of this policy at the current stage is consistent with China's incremental reform: to introduce changes from the outside while gradually reforming from the inside.

As the non-state sector has little access to bank lending and the equity market, most firms have to rely on retained earnings, or informal sources such as family and friends or underground banks (Gregory et al., 2000). The lending rate in the informal financial market provides a good measure of the difficulty for the private sector to obtain external capital. In Zhejiang province where private enterprises have the most vibrant presence, informal sources of financing are very important to their growth. During the fourth quarter of 2008, the average lending rate in the city of Wenzhou was about 15.88 per cent. In contrast, the official bank lending rate for short term loans was 5.31 per cent. Although private firms might have a higher default risk, the lending rate difference of more than 10 per cent nevertheless indicates a much higher costs of external financing for the private sector.

The inefficiency in resource allocation is a result of China's unfinished economic and financial reform. As the national capital, Beijing assumes a critical role in designing and implementing economic policies. It houses

---

[8] According to Allen, Qian and Qian (2009) these include retained earnings, funds from local government and other investors, as well as raised funds from stock and bond issuance.

the headquarters of a number of the state's largest SOEs and most of its financial institutions. Many government regulatory agencies, including the China Securities Regulatory Commission (CSRC) and China Banking Regulatory Commission (CBRC), are also located there.

During the waves of SOE reform in the late 1990s, most small and medium sized SOEs were privatized or shut down, while the government retained control over some of the most strategic and competitive SOEs. The state banking sector was reformed to encourage competition and improve efficiency. As the remaining SOEs were mostly industry giants or monopolies in highly-regulated fields, banks and other financial institutions continued to allocate most funds to the SOEs at favorable terms, despite the considerable growth of the non-state sector.

As future reform unfolds, this situation is subject to change. Policies to further develop the non-state financial sector will reduce the role of the SOCBs and improve the efficiency of China's financial system. This will accelerate the growth of various types of non-state firms, as their financial needs are better served. As a result, the role of SOEs will be reduced. However, these steps will not be accomplished within a short period. Home to headquarters of SOCBs and most SOEs, Beijing will remain a key figure.

As the second major financial center, Shanghai will assume a more important role for the Chinese economy. Though Shanghai has China's largest equity market, its role in fueling the domestic economic growth is limited, since the financial market is still at an early stage of development. The total market capitalization amounts to 71.64 per cent of GDP in 2009. Negotiable market capitalization, which is a better measure of stock value, is only 44.42 per cent of GDP, much lower than the ratio of bank credit over GDP. In addition, the equity market is highly regulated by the government, which grants few opportunities for non-state firms to be publicly listed.

Compared to Beijing, Shanghai has developed a more diversified economy and has a smaller state sector. For example, in 2009, state-controlled firms accounted for about half of total value of industrial output in Beijing, while in Shanghai this ratio was 37.3 per cent.[9] In the banking industry, around half of foreign banks are based in Shanghai, their assets accounted for 56.57 per cent of total assets of foreign banks in China. As foreign banks have been allowed to lend RMB-denominated loans, they will become an important financing source for SMEs.

The priority of future financial reform will be to improve the equity market and direct more resources to SMEs.[10] This will include enlarging

[9]   Data is for industrial enterprises whose annual revenues are more than 5 million RMB.
[10]   China Securities Regulatory Commission (2008).

the stock and corporate bond market, and making them more accessible to non-state firms. Another focal point will be to develop the financial derivative market. These reforms will improve Shanghai's position as a national financial center.

BEIJING AND SHANGHAI UNDER THE GLOBAL FRAMEWORK

Sassen (1999) points out that one of the extraordinary features of a global financial center is that it provides a great variety of financial products and services to international clients and customers. For cities like London and New York, exports of financial services constitute a significant part of their GDP.

Compared to Europe and America, China's financial centers are still at an early stage of development, not only because their contribution to the domestic economy has been small, as shown in the previous section, but also due to their very limited involvement in the international financial network. Figure 14.1 compares the ratio of financial service export over total service export between China and the four leading financial service

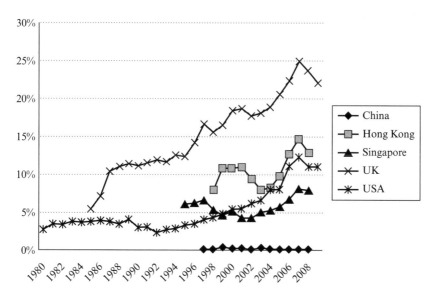

Source: UNCTAD (2009a).

Figure 14.1   Comparison of export of financial services

providers in the world. In 2009, among all five countries/regions, the
United Kingdom had the highest share of financial service exports, which
amounted to 22 per cent. This is consistent with the fact that London,
together with New York, has long been considered the world's leading
financial center.[11] Hong Kong, the United States and Singapore each had
a share of around 10 per cent.

In contrast, China's financial service exports only accounted for 0.21
per cent of total service exports in 2008. Though Beijing is the largest
financial center of China at present, it remains a net importer of financial services. Its total trade of financial service in 2008 was US$193
million, of which exports were US$53 million and imports were US$140
million.[12]

A precondition for the internationalization of China's financial centers
is capital account liberalization. However, without a well-developed
domestic financial system, a large scale of capital inflow and outflow will
possibly result in a national economic crisis.[13]

China's entry into the WTO substantially facilitated foreign trade with
other parts of the world. From 2001 to 2008, China's trade surplus grew
at an annual rate of nearly 40 per cent. Despite the impact of the world
financial crisis, in 2009 China managed to secure a trade surplus of 1503.33
billion RMB. Since 2001, China's currency RMB has appreciated by more
than 20 per cent.

The constant current account surplus and the anticipation of the
further appreciation of RMB have induced a large scale inflow of speculative foreign capital, despite strict capital account regulation. By the end
of first quarter in 2008, accumulated inflow of speculative fund since 2003
had reached US$1203.2 billion , which amounted to roughly two-thirds
of China's total foreign reserve (Zhang and Xu, 2008). This amount of
capital seems to have caused bubbles in the asset and equity market.
According to Wu et al. (2010), from 2000 to the first quarter of 2010,
housing prices in 35 major Chinese cities rose by more than 200 per cent
(see Figure 14.2). If not regulated properly, a quick outflow of speculative
money will result in the collapse of the asset market, which will directly
lead to a massive banking crisis and an economic recession.[14] Hence,
without a fully developed financial system, China is unlikely to liberalize
its capital account.

---

[11]   See Z/Yen Group (2010).
[12]   Although data about Shanghai is not available, similar conclusions can be inferred from
considering aggregate data of China.
[13]   For example, Kaminsky and Reinhart (1999) discussed the relationship between financial liberalization and banking crisis.
[14]   Such as those that happened during the Asian financial crisis in 1997.

2000Q1 = 100

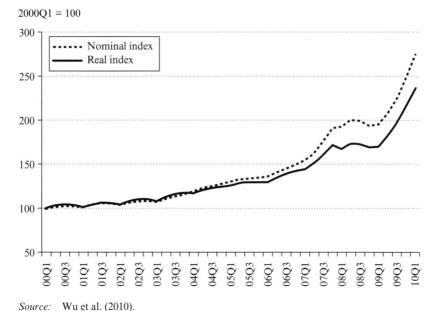

Source: Wu et al. (2010).

Figure 14.2   Housing prices in China 2000–2010

CONCLUSION

One of the most debated topics in China after 2000 has been whether Beijing or Shanghai will become the next global financial center. To answer this question, one needs to have a comprehensive understanding of its implication. In our opinion, a global financial center should first be a national financial center that fuels domestic economic development. Its second role is to provide financial services to international clients.

Our conclusion is as follows. First, although both cities are national economic and financial centers, they are part of a financial system that is not efficient in allocating financial resources. The Chinese economy has changed substantially after 30 years of reform and development. The non-state sector has replaced state-owned enterprises to become the driving force of the Chinese economy. The financial sector, however, largely maintained policies that dated back to the 'Central Planning' period to support the SOEs. As China's center for policy-making and headquarters of both SOEs and SOCBs, Beijing's role in the current financial system is significant yet ineffective. In comparison, though Shanghai is the other major financial center of China, its role is very limited.

Second, compared with the world's major financial centers, both Beijing and Shanghai have little participation in the international financial market. At present, neither is close to being a qualified global financial center.

As China's reform proceeds, the non-state sector will eventually become dominant in the national economy, while the roles of SOEs and SOCBs will diminish. The financial market will be further developed and be more accessible to all types of firms. Home to China's largest equity market, Shanghai is expected to become China's leading economic and financial center in the future. Beijing is more likely to maintain its place as a financial center for the state sector, as well as a regional center serving northern China.

From the international perspective, our best guess is that Shanghai, rather than Beijing, is more likely to become a global financial center. Whether it happens, however, still hinges on China's economic development and financial reform. Without a well-developed market economy and a full-fledged financial system, financial liberalization will only result in economic crisis and social instability, which is the largest obstacle to China's growth.

Bibliography

Aguilar, F. (1979) *Scanning the Business Environment*, New York: Macmillan

Allen, F., J. Qian and M. Qian (2008) 'China's Financial System: Past, Present and Future', in Loren Brandt and Thomas G. Rawski (eds) *China's Great Economic Transformation*, New York: Cambridge University Press, pp. 506–568

Allen, J. (1999) 'Cities of Power and Influence: Settled Formations', in J. Allen, D. Massey and M. Pryke (eds) *Unsettling Cities*, London: Routledge, pp. 181–228

Allen, J., D. Massey and M. Pryke (eds) (1999) *Unsettling Cities*, London: Routledge

Aminian, N., K.-C. Fung and H. Iizaka (2007) 'Foreign Direct Investment, Intra-Regional Trade and Production Sharing in East Asia', *REITI Discussion Paper Series 07-E-064*, Research Institute of Economy, Trade & Industry, Tōkyō, Japan

Arvanitis, R. and E. Jastrabsky (2006) 'A Regional Innovation System in Gestation: Guangdong', *China Perspectives*, **63**, 13–26

Arvanitis, R., W. Zhao, H. Qiu and J. Xu Jian-niu (2006) 'Technological Learning in Six Firms in Southern China: Success and Limits of an Industrialisation Model', *International Journal of Technology Management,* **36** (1/2/3), 108–125

Ash, A. and N. Thrift (2007) 'Cultural-economy and Cities', *Progress in Human Geography*, **31** (2), 143–161

Asian Development Bank (2008) *Managing Asian Cities*, Manila: ADB Publishing

Athukorala, P.-C. (2006) 'Multinational Enterprises and Manufacturing for Export in Developing Asian Countries: Emerging Patterns and Opportunities for Latecomers', *Hi-Stat Discussion Paper Series d06-193*, Institute of Economic Research, Hitotsubashi University

Athukorala, P.-C. (2008) 'Singapore and Asean in the New Regional Division of Labor', *The Singapore Economic Review*, **53** (3), 479–508

Bank for International Settlements (2001) *Triennial Central Bank Survey of Foreign Exchange and Derivatives Market Activity in March 2001 – Final Results*, Bank for International Settlements, Basel

Bank for International Settlements (2007a) *BIS Quarterly Review*, Bank for International Settlements, Basel, September

Bank for International Settlements (2007b) *Exchange and Derivatives Market Activity in April 2007*, Bank for International Settlements, Basel

Bank for International Settlements (2007c) *Triennial Central Bank Survey of Foreign Exchange and Derivatives Market Activity in April 2007*, Bank for International Settlements, Basel

Bank of East Asia (2009) *Economic Analysis*, Hong Kong, May

Barlett, C.A. and S. Ghoshal (1991) 'Global Strategic Management: Impact on the New Frontiers of Strategy Research', *Strategic Management Journal*, **12**, Special Issue, 5–16

Baum, S. (1999) 'Social Transformations in the Global City: Singapore', *Urban Studies*, **36** (7), 1095–1117

Beaverstock, J.V., R.G. Smith and P.J. Taylor (1999) 'A Roster of World Cities', *Cities*, **16**

Beaverstock, J.V., M.A. Doel, P.J. Hubbard and P.J. Taylor (2002) 'Attending to the World: Competition/Co-operation and Co-efficiency in the World City Network', *Global Networks*, **2** (2), 111–132

Beijing Central Business District Administrative Commission (2005) 'Headquarter Economy in Beijing'

Beijing Municipal Bureau of Statistics and NBS Survey Office in Beijing (2010) *Beijing Statistical Yearbook 2000–2010*, Beijing: China Statistics Press

Bernauer, K. (1983) 'Asian Dollar Market', *Economic Review* (Winter), Federal Reserve Bank of San Fransisco, pp. 47–63

Blackwell, N., J.P. Bizet, P. Child and D. Hensley (1992) 'Creating European Organizations that Work', *Mckinsey Quarterly*, **2**, 31–43

Blomqvist, Hans C. (2000) 'Development Policies of Singapore: Dynamics of Internationalisation versus Regionalisation', Discussion Paper 275, Finland: University of Vaasa

Blussé, Leonard (1981) 'The VOC as Sorcerer's Apprentice: Stereotypes and Social Engineering on the China Coast', in W.L. Idema (ed.) *Leiden Studies in Sinology*, Leiden: Leiden University Press, pp. 87–105

Blussé, Leonard (1990) 'Minnan-jen or Cosmopolitan? The Rise of Cheng Chih-lung alias Nicolas Iquan', in E.B.Vermeer (ed.) *Development and Decline of Fukien Province in the 17th and 18th Centuries (Sinica Leidensia XXII)*, Leiden–New York–København–Köln: Brill

Blussé, Leonard (2000) *Canton, Nagasaki and Batavia, and the Coming of the Americans*, Cambridge, MA: Harvard University Press

Böhme, M., D. Chiarella and M. Lemerle (2008) 'The Growing Opportunity for Investment Banks in Emerging Markets', *The McKinsey Quarterly*, August

Booth, A. (2008) 'The Economic Development of Southeast Asia in the Colonial Era: c.1870–1942', *History Compass*, **6** (1), 25–53.

Borchert, I. and A. Mattoo (2009) 'The Crisis-Resilience of Services Trade', *Policy Research Working Paper No. 4917*, Washington, DC: The World Bank

Breslin, S. (2005) 'Power and Production: Rethinking China's Global Economic Role', *Review of International Studies*, **31**, 735–753

Brotchie, J., M. Batty, E. Blakely, R. Hall and R. Newton (eds) (1995) *Cities in Competition*, Melbourne: Longman

Budd, L. (1999) 'Globalization and the Crisis of Territorial Embeddedness of International Financial Markets', in Ron Martin (ed.) *Money and the Space Economy*, Chichester: John Wiley & Sons, pp. 115–137

Bugge, H. (1989) 'Silk to Japan. Sino Dutch Competition in the Silk Trade to Japan, 1633–1685', *Itinerario*, **XIII** (2)

Bulcke, V.D.D., C.D.M. Esteves and H.Y. Zhang (2003) *European Union Direct Investment in China – Characteristics, Challenges and Perspectives*, Abingdon, UK and New York, NY: Routledge

Burgardt, A.F. (1971) 'A Hypothesis of Gateway City', *Annals of the Association of American Geographers*, **61** (2), 269–285

Burger, M., R. Wall and B. Van der Knapp (2008) 'Measuring Urban Competition on the Basis of Flows between Cities: Some Evidence from the World City Network', *GaWC Research Bulletin*, **273**, http://www.lboro.ac.uk/gawc/rb/rb273.html (accessed February 2009)

Cai, R.W. (2003) 'Shanghai Bound: New Regulations Seek to Attract Regional HQs', Davis Wright Tremaine LLP, Seattle, 1–4

Cantwell, J. (1994) 'The Relationship between International Trade and International Production', in D. Greenaway and A.L. Winters (eds) *Surveys in International Trade*, Oxford: Blackwell, pp. 303–328

Carioti, P. (1996) 'The Zheng's Maritime Power in the International Context of the 17th Century Far Eastern Seas: The Rise of a "Centralised Piratical Organization and Its Gradual Development into an Informal State"', in Paolo Santangelo (ed.) *Ming Qing Yanjiu,* Naples-Rome: Dipartimento di Studi Asiatici, Istituto Universitario Orientale-Istituto Italiano per l'Africa e l'Oriente, pp. 29–67

Carioti, P. (1998) 'Il cosiddetto *sakoku*: nuove linee interpretative della storiografia giapponese circa la politica di "chiusura" varata dal *bakufu* Tokugawa nel secolo XVII' (The So-called *Sakoku*: New Interpretative Lines of the Japanese Historiography concerning the 'Closed Country' Policy Pursued by the Tokugawa *Bakufu* during the XVII Century), *Giappone. Il futuro del passato* (*Atti del XXI Convegno di Studi sul Giappone,* Roma, 17–20 September 1997), Venezia, pp. 89–106

Carioti, P. (2000) 'The International Role of the Overseas Chinese in Hirado (Nagasaki), during the First Decades of the 17th Century', in Cen Huang and Zhuang Guotu (eds) *New Studies on Chinese Overseas and China (International Conference for Qiaoxiang Studies)*, Xiamen, Leiden, pp. 31–45

Carioti, P. (2003) 'The Portuguese Settlement at Macao: The Portuguese Policy of Expansion in the Far East in Light of the History of Chinese and Japanese Intercourse and Maritime Activities', *Revista de Cultura (Rewiev of Culture)*, **6**, 24–39

Carioti, P. (2006a) *Cina e Giappone sui mari nei secoli XVI–XVII*, Napoli: Edizioni Scientifiche Italiane

Carioti, P. (2006b) 'Hirado during the First Half of the 17th Century: From a Commercial Outpost for Sino-Japanese Maritime Activities to an International Crossroads of Far Eastern Routes', in Chiu Ling-yeong, with Donatella Guida (eds) *A Passion for China, Essays in Honour of Paolo Santangelo, for his 60th Birthday*, Leiden-Boston: Brill, pp. 1–32

Carioti, P. (2006c) 'The Origins of the Chinese Community of Nagasaki, 1571–1635', *Ming Qing Yanjiu*, Naples-Rome: Dipartimento di Studi Asiatici, Istituto Universitario Orientale-Istituto Italiano per l'Africa e l'Oriente, pp. 1–34

Carioti, P. (2010) 'Focusing on the Overseas Chinese in Nagasaki: The Role of the *Tōtsūji*', in Nagazumi Yōko (ed.) *Large and Broad. The Dutch Impact on Early Modern Asia. Essays in Honor of Leonard Blussé*, Tōkyō: Tōyō Bunkō, pp. 62–75

Carioti, P. (forthcoming) 'Japan Behind the Curtains: The Matsuura Clan of Hirado among *wokou*, *haikou* and Europeans', in Paola Calanca (ed.), Paris (forthcoming)

Cassis, Y. (2006) *Capitals of Capital: A History of International Financial Centres, 1780–2005*, Cambridge: Cambridge University Press

Castells, M. (1992) 'Four Asian Tigers with a Dragon Head: A Comparative Analysis of the State, Economy and Society', in Jeffrey Henderson and Richard P. Appelbaum (eds) *State and Development in the Asian Pacific Rim*, London: Sage, pp. 33–70

Castells, M. (1996) *The Rise of the Network Society*, Oxford: Blackwell

Chan, K.W. (2010) 'Fundamentals of China's Urbanization and Policy', *The China Review*, **10** (1), 63–94

Chan, K.W. and W. Buckingham (2008) 'Is China Abolishing the Hukou System?', *The China Quarterly*, **195**, 582–606

Chan, R. (1996) 'Urban Development Strategy in an Era of Global Competition: The Case of South China', *Habitat international*, **20** (4), 509–530

Chan, R.C.K. and X.B. Zhao (2002) 'The Relationship Between the Administrative Hierarchy Position and City-size Development in China', *GeoJournal*, **56** (2), 97–112

Chang, A. (1972) 'The Nagasaki Office of the Chinese Interpreters in the Seventeenth Century', *Chinese Culture*, **XIII** (3), 3–19

Cheng K'o-ch'eng (1990) 'Cheng Ch'eng-kung Maritime Expansion and Early Ch'ing Coastal Prohibition', in E.B. Vermeer (ed.) *Development and Decline of Fukien Province in the 17th and 18th Centuries (Sinica Leidensia*, XXII), Leiden–New York–København–Köln: Brill, pp. 217–244

Chia, Siow Yue (1997) 'Singapore: Advanced Production Base and Smart Hub of the Electronics Industry', in Wendy Dobson and Siow-Y. Chia (eds) *Multinationals and East Asian Integration*, Canada: IDRC, pp. 31–61

China Daily (2007) 'GE to Launch 5 Regional Headquarters in China', 8 November

China Daily (2008) 'Regional Reward', edited by *China Law & Practice*, 'Competition for Regional Headquarters Heats up for PRC', 12 February

China Daily (2009) 'Benefits of a Leaner Government', 10 January

China Securities Regulatory Commission (2008) *China Capital Market Development Report*, Beijing: China Financial Publishing House

China Securities Regulatory Commission (2009) *China Securities and Futures Statistical Yearbook 2001–2009*, Beijing: Academia Press

China Society for Finance and Banking (2009) *Almanac of China's Finance and Banking 1995–2009*, Beijing: Almanac of China's Finance and Banking Editorial Board

China State Statistical Bureau (2007) *2006 Zhongguo tongji nianjian* (China Statistical Yearbook, 2006), Beijing: Zhongguo tongji chubanshe

China State Statistical Bureau (2008) *2007 Zhongguo tongji nianjian* (China Statistical Yearbook, 2007), Beijing: Zhongguo tongji chubanshe

China State Statistical Bureau (2009) *2008 Zhongguo tongji nianjian* (China Statistical Yearbook, 2008), Beijing: Zhongguo tongji chubanshe

China Statistical Bureau and Ministry of Science and Technology (2009) *2008 nian Zhongguo keji tongji nianjian* (Chinese Statistical Yearbook on Science and Technology, 2008), Beijing: Zhongguo tongji chubanshe

City of London (2004) *Sizing Up the City – London's Ranking as a Financial Centre*, City of London Corporation

City of London (2007) *Global Financial Centres Index 2007*, City of London, March

City of London Corporation (2008) *The Future of Asian Financial Centres: Challenges and Opportunities for the City of London*, London: City of London Corporation, pp. 1–2

City of London Corporation (2009) *The Global Financial Centres Index 5*, London: City of London Corporation

Clark, D. (1998) 'Interdependent Urbanization in an Urban World: An Historical Overview', *The Geographical Journal*, **164** (1), 85–95

Clark, G.L. and D. Wojcik (2006) *The Geography of Finance: Corporate Governance in the Global Marketplace*, New York: Oxford University Press

Cohen, R. (1981) 'The New International Division of Labour, Multinational Corporations and the Urban Hierarchy', in M. Dear and A. Scott (eds) *Urbanisation and Urban Planning in Capitalist Societies*, London: Methuen, pp. 287–318

Cong, C. (2004) 'Zhongguancun and China's High-Tech Parks in Transition', *Asian Survey*, **44** (5), 647–668

Daly, M.T. (1984) 'The Revolution in International Capital Markets: Urban Growth and Australian Cities', *Environment and Planning A*, **16** (8), 1003–1020

Daniels, P.W. (1993) *Service Industries in the World Economy*, Oxford: Blackwell

Daniels, P.W. (2001) 'Globalisation, Producer Services and the City: Is Asia a Special Case?', in R.M. Stern (ed.) *Services in the International Economy*, Ann Arbor: University of Michigan Press, pp. 213–230

Daniels, P.W. (2005) 'Services, Globalization, and the Asia-Pacific Region', in P.W. Daniels, K.C. Ho and T.A. Hutton (eds) *Service Industries and Asia-Pacific Cities: New Development Trajectories*, London: RoutledgeCurzon, pp. 21–51

Daniels, P.W. and James W. Harrington (eds) (2007) *Services and Economic Development in the Asia-Pacific*, Aldershot: Ashgate

Daniels, P.W., K.C. Ho and T.A. Hutton (eds) (2011) *New Economic Spaces in Asian Cities: From Industrial Restructuring to the Cultural Turn*, London: Routledge (in press)

D'Cruz, J., M.A. Rugman and A. Verbeke (2005[1995]) 'Internalization and De-internalization: Will Business Networks Replace Multinationals?', in Alan M. Rugman and Alain Verbeke, *Analysis of Multinational Strategic Management: The Selected Scientific Papers of Rugman M.A. and Verbeke A.*, Cheltenham, UK and Northampton, MA: Edward Elgar Publishing, pp. 27–48

Dent, C.M. (2003) 'Transnational Capital, the State and Foreign Economic Policy: Singapore, South Korea and Taiwan', *Review of International Political Economy*, **10** (2), 246–277

Dicken, P. (1998) *Global Shift: Transforming the World Economy*, 3rd edition, New York: Guilford Press

Doel, M. and P. Hubbard (2002) 'Taking World Cities Literally: Marketing the City in a Global Space of Flows', *City*, **6** (3), 351–368

Dos Santos Alves, Jorges (1990) 'Aceh, une ville inquiète et un Sultan barricadé, Aceh vers 1588, d'après le Roteiro das cousas do Achem de l'archevêque de Melaka', Archipel, **39**, 102

Douglas, S. and M.A. Rugman (1986) 'The Strategic Management of Multinationals and World Product Mandating', in Hamid Etemad and Louise Seguin Dulude (eds) *Managing the Multinational Subsidiary*, Kent: Croom Helm, pp. 90–101

Douglass, M. (2002) 'Globalization, Inter-city Competition and the Rise of Civil Society: Towards Liveable Cities in Pacific Asia', *Asian Journal of Social Sciences*, **3** (1), 131–151

Doz, Y. and C.K. Prahalad (1987) *The Multinational Mission: Balancing Local Demands and Global Vision*, New York: The Free Press

Drennan, M.R. (1996) 'The Dominance of International Finance by London, New York and Tokyo', in P.W. Daniels and W.F. Lever (eds) *The Global Economy in Transition*, London: Addison Wesley Longman, pp. 352–371

Du, D. (2003) 'Zai Hu kuaguo gongsi yanjiu jigou de tedian yu zuoyong (Characteristics and utility of research organisations of foreign multinational companies in Shanghai)', *Research on Scientific and Technological Development*, **8**

Du, D. (2009) *Kuaguo gongsi zai hua yanfa: fazhan, yingxiang ji duice yanjiu* (R&D in China by Foreign Multinationals: Development, Influence and Chinese Strategy), Beijing: Kexue chubanshe

Dunning, H.J. (1992) *Multinational Enterprises and the Global Economy*, Wokingham: Addison-Wesley

Dunning, H.J. (1998) 'Multinational Enterprises and Public Policy', *Journal of International Business Studies*, **29** (1), 115–136

Eliana, C.R. and P.J. Taylor (2006) '"Gateway Cities" in Economic Globalisation: How Banks are Using Brazilian Cities', *Tijdschrift voor Economische en Sociale Geografie*, **97** (5), 515–534

Elmhorn, C. (2001) *Brussels: A Reflexive World City*, Stockholm: Almqvist & Wiksell International

Enright, M., Edith E. Scott and David Dodwell (1997) 'Hong Kong: The Interconnected Economy', University of Hong Kong working paper

Enright, M. et al. (2005) *Regional Powerhouse: The Greater Pearl River Delta and the Rise of China*, John Wiley & Sons (Asia) Pte Ltd

Fang Youyi (1982) *Zheng Chenggong shiliao xuanbian*, Fuzhou: Fujian Renmin Chubanshe

Fang Youyi (1985) *Zheng Chenggong dang'an shiliao xuanji*, Fuzhou: Fujian Renmin Chubanshe

Fang Youyi (1987) *Zheng Chenggong Manwen dang'an shiliao xuanze*, Fuzhou: Fujian Renmin Chubanshe

Fang Youyi (1994) *Zheng Chenggong yanjiu*, Xiamen: Fujian Renmin Chubanshe

Farrell, D. and A. Grant (2005) 'China's looming talent shortage', *The McKinsey Quarterly*, **4**, 70–79

Financial Times (2009) 'Shanghai v Beijing: A City's Appearance can be Deceptive', 29 April

Financial Times (2009a) 'Shanghai Set to Allow Listings of Foreign Groups', 30 April

Financial Times (2009b) 'Emerging-market Cities Climb World Rankings', 8 June

Findlay, A.M., F. Li, A. Jowett and R. Skeldon (1996) 'Skilled International Migration and the Global City: A Study of Expatriates in Hong Kong', *Transactions of the Institute of British Geographers, New Series*, **21** (1), 49–61

Fleming, D.K. and Y. Hayuth (1994) 'Spatial Characteristics of Transportation Hubs: Centrality and Intermediacy', *Journal of Transport Geography*, **2** (1), 3–18

Florida, R. and M. Kenney (1994) 'The Globalization of Japanese R&D: The Economic Geography of Japanese R&D Investment in the United States', *Economic Geography*, **70** (4), 344–369

Frankel, J.A., Ernesto Stein and Shang-Jin Wei (1997) *Regional Trading Blocs in the World Economic System*, Washington, DC: Institute of International Economics

Friedmann, J. (1986) 'The World City Hypothesis', *Development and Change*, **17** (1), 69–84

Friedmann, J. (1995) 'Where we Stand: A Decade of World City Research', in R L. Knox and R.J. Taylor (eds) *World Cities in a World System*, Cambridge: Cambridge University Press, pp. 21–47

Friedmann, J. (1998) 'World City Futures: The Role of Regional and Urban Policies in the Asia Pacific Region', in Yeung Yue-man, *Urban Development in Asia, Retrospect and Prospect*, Hong Kong, The Chinese University of Hong Kong

Friedmann, J. (2006) 'Four Theses in the Study of China's Urbanization', *International Journal of Urban and Regional Research*, **30** (2), 440–451

Friedmann, J. and G. Wolff (1982) 'World City Formation: An Agenda for Research and Action', *International Journal of Urban and Regional Research*, **3**, 309–344

Fröbel, Folker, Jürgen Heinrichs, Otto Kreye and Pete Burgess (1980) *The New International Division of Labour: Structural Unemployment in*

Industrialised Countries and Industrialisation in Developing Countries, Cambridge, UK and New York, USA: Cambridge University Press

Frost, M.R. (2004) 'Asia's maritime networks and the colonial public sphere, 1840–1920', *New Zealand Journal of Asian Studies*, **6** (2), 63–94

Fu Chonglan, Bai Zhenyi, Cao Wenming and alii (2009) *Zhongguo Chengshi fazhanshi* (The Urban History of China), Shehui Xexue wenxian chubanshe, Beijing

Fu Lo-Shu (1966) *A Documentary Chronicle of Sino-Western Relation, 1644–1820*, 2 vols, Tucson: Arizona University Press

Fujian Shifan Daxue Lishixi (1982) *Zheng Chenggong shiliao xuanbian*, Fujian: Zheng Chenggong Yanjiuhui

Fujita, K. (1991) 'A World City and Flexible Specialization: Restructuring of the Tokyo Metropolis', *International Journal of Urban and Regional Research*, **15**, 269–284

Fujita, K. (2000) 'Asian Crisis, Financial Systems and Urban Development', *Urban Studies*, **37** (12), 2197–2216

Fulton T., Li Jinyan and Xu Dianqing (1998) *China's Tax Reform Options*, Singapore: World Scientific

Gaspar, J. and E.L. Glaeser (1996) 'Information Technology and the Future of Cities', *NBER-Working Paper 5562*, Cambridge, MA: National Bureau of Economic Research

Gipouloux, F. (2011) *The Asian Mediterranean: Port-cities and Trading Networks in China, Japan and Southeast Asia, 13th–21st Century*, Cheltenham, UK and Northampton, MA: Edward Elgar Publishing

Gordon, I. (2003) 'Compétitivité des villes: quelle importance au XXIème siècle, comment la mesurer?', *Cahiers de l'IAURIF*, **135**, 33–41

Gregory, N.F., S. Tenev and D.M. Wagle (2000) *China's Emerging Private Enterprises: Prospects for the New Century*, Washington, DC: International Finance Corporation

Grundy-Warr, C., K. Peachey and M. Perry (1999) 'Fragmented Integration in the Singapore-Indonesian Border Zone: Southeast Asia's "Growth Triangle" against the Global Economy', *International Journal of Urban and Regional Research*, **23** (2), 304–328

Guo, Z.H. (2008) 'HQ Economy Boosts Chaoyang's Growth', *China Daily*, 15–16 November, p. 10

Gurría , A. (2006) 'Building an Innovative City: The Macro Perspective', OECD Secretary-General's speech, 18th International Business Leaders Advisory Council (IBLAC) Annual Meeting Promotion of an Innovative Environment, Shanghai's Future

Gurría, A. (2007) 'Globalising Cities and Regions – Rethinking the Urban and Regional Policy Agenda', Speech as OECD Secretary-General, Danish Growth Council, Copenhagen

Hall, P. (1966) *The World Cities*, London: Heinemann

Hamashita, Takeshi (2003) 'Tribute and Treaties. Maritime Asia and Treaty Port Networks in the Era of Negotiation, 1800–1900', in Giovanni Arrighi, Takeshi Hamashita and Mark Selden (eds) *The Resurgence of East Asia: 500, 150 and 50 Year Perspectives*, New York: Routledge, pp. 17–50

Han, L., Y. Pang and R. Tian (2007) 'Research of the Development Model of the Headquarter Economy in Beijing', **3**, *Research of City Development*

Hanawa, T. (2001) 'Nihonban Kinyu Big Bang Saiko' (Reconsidering of the Japanese Big Bang), *The Journal of Commerce*, **42** (5), Tōkyō, Chuo University, 129–149

Haneda, Masashi (ed.) (2009) *Asian Port Cities, 1600–1800, Local and Foreign Cultural Interactions*, Singapore and Kyoto University: NUS Press

Hang Seng Bank (2009) *Economic Focus*, 24 June

Hayashi Fukusai (ed.) (1912–1913) *Tsūkō ichiran*, 8 vols, Tōkyō: Kokusho Kankōkai

Heck, V.N. and P. Verdin (2001) *From Local Champions to Global Masters: A Strategic Perspective on Managing Internationalization*, Basingstoke: Palgrave, pp. 133–134

Hennart, J.F. (1986) 'What is Internalization?', *Weltwirtschaftliches Archiv*, **122** (4)

Henriot, C. (1995) 'Mise en perspective historique', in Christian Henriot and Alain Delissen (eds) *Les métropoles chinoises au XXème siècle*, Paris: Editions Arguments, pp. 191–208

Hill, R.C. and J. Kim (2000) 'Global Cities and Developmental States: New York, Tokyo and Seoul', *Urban Studies*, **37** (12), 2167–2195

Hills, P. and Ng Mee Kam (2003) 'World Cities or Great Cities? A Comparative Study of Five Asian Metropolises', *Cities*, **20** (3), 151–165

Hiradohan (1973) 'Hiradohan no seiritsu to hatten', in *Nagasaki kenshi (Hanseihen)*, Tōkyō, Yoshikawa Kōbunkan

Historiographical Institute (1955–1968) *Tōtsūji Kaisho Nichiroku* (Official Diaries of Chinese Interpreters at Nagasaki), 7 vols, in *Dai Nihon Kinsei shiryō*, Tōkyō: University of Tōkyō Press

Ho, K.C. (2000) 'Competing to be Regional Centres: A Multi-agency, Multi-locational Perspective', *Urban Studies*, **37** (12), 2337–2356

Hong, Mark (2007) 'Overview of Singapore's Energy Situations', in Mark Hong and Teo Kah Beng (eds) *Energy Perspectives on Singapore and the Region*, Institute of Southeast Asian Studies, pp. 1–22

Hong Kong Securities and Futures Commission (2010) 'Fund Mangement Activities Survey 2009', July

Hong Kong Stock Exchange (2007) 'Equity Funds Raised by China-related Companies (Main Board and GEM)', Hong Kong Stock Exchange, September

Hsu, J.-Y. and P.-H. Chen (2007) 'From financial depression to financial deregulation? The construction of futures trading industry in Taiwan', in P.W. Daniels and J.W. Harrington (eds) *Perspectives on Services and Development in the Asia-Pacific*, Farnham: Ashgate, pp. 173–191

Hu, Y.-W. (2010) *Management of China's Foreign Exchange Reserves: A Case Study of the State Administration of Foreign Exchange*, Brussels: European Commission DG for Economic and Financial Affairs

Huff, W.G. (1987) 'Patterns in the Economic Development of Singapore', *The Journal of Developing Areas*, **21** (3), 305–326

Huff, W.G. (1995) 'The developmental state, government, and Singapore's economic development since 1960', *World Development*, **23**(8), 1421–1438

Huff, W.G. (1997) *The Economic Growth of Singapore: Trade and Development in the Twentieth Century*, Cambridge, UK and New York, USA: Cambridge University Press

Hutton, T.A. (2004) 'Service industries, globalization, and urban restructuring within the Asia-Pacific: new development trajectories and planning responses', *Progress in Planning*, **61** (1), 1–74

IMF (2008) http://www.imf.org/external/pubs/ft/survey/so/2008/CAR026 08A.htm (accessed April 2009)

Ishihara Michihiro (1945) *Minmatsu Shinsho Nihon kisshi no kenkyū*, Tōkyō: Naigai Shoseki

Ishii, K. (2007) *Keizai Hatten to Ryogaesho Kinyu* (Economic Development and the Finance of Moneychangers), Tōkyō: Yuhikaku

Ito, K. (2005) 'Higashi Ajiya ni okeru Kokusai Kinyu Center no Kyosoyuui (Competitive Supremacy of the Financial Center in East Asia), *Kokusai Boueki to oushi*, **60**, Tōkyō, Institute for International Trade and Investment, pp. 44–60

Ito, M. (1989) *Nihon no Taigaikinyu to Kinyuseisaku 1914–1936* (Japanese External Finance and Financial Policy 1914–1936), Nagoya: Nagoya University Press

Iwao Seiichi (1936) 'Minmatsu Nihon kyogu Shinajin Kapitan Li Tan-kō', *Tōyō gakuhō*, **XX** (3), 63–119

Iwao Seiichi (1958a) 'Li Tan, Chief of the Chinese Residents at Hirado, Japan in the Last Days of the Ming Dynasty', *Memoirs of the Research Department of the Toyo Bunko*, **XVII**, 27–83

Iwao Seiichi (1958b) *Shuinsen bōekishi no kenkyū*, Tōkyō: Kōbundō

Iwao Seiichi (1960) *Shuinsen to Nihonmachi*, Tōkyō: Yoshikawa Kōbunkan

Jao, Y. (1979) 'The Rise of Hong Kong as a Financial Center', *Asian Survey*, **19** (7), 674–694

Japan External Trade Organization (2008a) *Survey on Attitudes of Foreign-Affiliated Companies toward Direct Investment in Japan 2007*, Tokyo: JETRO

Japan External Trade Organization (2008b) *Japan Attractiveness Survey 2008*, Tōkyō: JETRO

Jin Banggui (2000) *La réforme des procédures fiscales en Chine*, Aix-en-Provence : Presses Universitaires d'Aix-Marseille

Jin Guoping – Zhang Zhengchun (1996) 'Liampó reexaminado à luz de fontes chinesas', in António Vasconcelos de Saldanha and Jorge Manuel dos Santos Alves, *Estudos de Hisória do relacionamento Luso-Chinês séculos XVI–XIX*, Macao-Lisbona, Instituto Português do Oriente, pp. 85–135

Jin Renqing (2007) 'Explanation on Draft Enterprise Income Tax Law', Minister of Finance, Fifth Session of the Tenth National People's Congress, 8 March

Jones, Geoffrey (2000) *Merchants to Multinationals: British Trading Companies in the Nineteenth and Twentieth Centurie*s, Oxford, UK and New York, NY: Oxford University Press

Jones, G. and J. Wale (1998) 'Merchants as Business Groups: British Trading Companies in Asia before 1945', *The Business History Review*, **72** (3), 367–408

Kamal-Chaoui, L., E. Leman and R. Zhang (2009) 'Urban Trends and Policy in China', *OECD Regional Development Working Papers*, New Milford: OECD Publishing

Kaminsky, Graciela L. and Sergio L. Schmukler (1999) 'The Twin Crises: The Causes of Banking and Balance-of-Payments Problems', *American Economic Review*, **89** (3), 473–500

Ken, W.L. (1978) 'Singapore: Its Growth as an Entrepôt Port, 1819–1941', *Journal of Southeast Asian Studies*, **9** (1), 50–84

Kim, Y.-W., I. Masser and J. Alden (1996) 'Urban and Regional Development Strategies in an Era of Global Competition', *Habitat International*, **20** (4), vii–viii

Kimiya Yasuhiko (1955) *Nikka bunka kōryūshi* (History of Cultural Exchange between Japan and China), Tōkyō: Fuzanbō

Kindleberger, C.P. (1974) *The Formation of Financial Centers: A Study of Comparative Economic History*, Princeton, NJ: International Finance Section, Princeton University

King, A. (1995) 'Re-presenting World Cities: Cultural Theory/Social Practice', in P. Knox and P. Taylor (eds) *World Cities in a World-System*, Cambridge: Cambridge University Press, pp. 215–231

Kirkulak, B. (2003) 'Realities in Tokyo Stock Exchange', *Economic Journal of Hokkaido University*, **32**, July, 151–159

Kobayashi, C. (1926) *Mitsui-Ginko Gojyunenshi* (History of 50 Years of the Mitsui Bank), Tōkyō: Mitsui Bank Kokusai Kinyu Jyohyo Center (2007) *Zainichi Gaikoku Kinyukikan no Tokyo Kinyu/Shihon Shijyo ni taisuru Hyoka to Snryaku* (Evaluation and Strategy for the Tokyo Financial and Capital Markets by Foreign Financial Institutions), Tōkyō: Japan Center for International Finance, September

Korbin, Stephen J. (1997) 'Electronic cash and the end of national markets', *Foreign Policy*, **107**, 65–77

Korff, R. (1987) 'The World City Hypothesis: A Critique', *Development and Change* **17**, 483–495

Kratoska, P.H. (2006) 'Singapore, Hong Kong and the End of Empire', *The International Journal of Asian Studies*, **3**, 1–19

Kroymann, B. (2005) 'Regional Headquarters Schemes by China's Ministry of Commerce and the Shanghai Municipal Government Differences, Limitations, and Possible Combinations', *Asia Pacific Law Review*, City University of Hong Kong, 67–94

Krugman, P. (1994) 'Competitiveness: A Dangerous Obsession', *Foreign Affairs*, **73** (2), 28–44

Lai-To, L. (2000) 'Singapore's Globalization Strategy', *East Asia*, **18** (2), 36–49

Landry, C. (2008) 'The Creative City', *China Review*, **42**, 6–7

Lasserre, P. (1996) 'Regional Headquarters: The Spear-Head for Asia Pacific Markets', *Long Range Planning*, **29** (1), February, 30–37

Latham, A. J. H. (1994) 'The Dynamics of Intra-Asian Trade, 1868–1913', in A.J.H. Latham and Heita Kawakatsu (eds) *Japanese Industrialization and the Asian Economy*, London, UK and New York, USA: Routledge, pp. 145–193

Laulajainen, R. (2003) *Financial Geography: A Banker's View*, London, UK and New York, NY: Routledge

Leadebeater, C. and J. Wilsdon (2007) *The Atlas of Ideas: How Asian Innovation Can Benefit Us All*, London: Demos

Lee, K.S. and M. Lim (2007) 'Foreign direct investment in Singapore, 1995–2005', *Statistics Singapore Newsletter*, September

Lee, T.K.Y. and Y.K. Tse (1991) 'Term Structure of Interest Rates in the Singapore Asian Dollar Market', *Journal of Applied Econometrics*, **6** (2), 143–152

Lefebvre, F. (2004) 'Chine: Juridique, fiscal', *Dossiers Internationaux*, 24 May, 125–145

Leong, S. (2008) 'New Provisions to Encourage the Establishment of Regional Headquarters', *China Business Success Stories*, 2 September

Les Echos (2009) 'La Bourse de Shanghai passe devant la City', 14 May

Les Echos (2009) 'Les Bourses asiatiques repartent plus vite que les occidentales', 14 May

Les Echos (2009) 'La Chine bouscule le classement des grandes places boursières', 14 May

Les Echos (2009) 'Shanghai au pied du podium des grandes places boursières', 28 July

Leung, A. (2002) 'Entrepôt No More? Why China's WTO Entry is Not a Zero Sum Game for Hong Kong', *Harvard Asia Pacific Review*, **2**, 33–36

Levinson, M. (2006) *The Box: How the Shipping Container Made the World Smaller and World Economy Bigger*, Oxford, UK, Princeton, NJ, USA: Princeton University Press

Li Jinyan (2007) 'Development and Tax Policy: Case Study of China', *CLPE Research Paper*, **27**, 25 September

Li Jinyan (2008) 'The Rise and Fall of Chinese Tax Incentives and Implications for International Tax Debates', *Florida Tax Review*; CLPE Research Paper No. 5

Li, Z. and F. Wu (2006) 'Socioeconomic Transformations in Shanghai (1990–2000): Policy Impacts in Global-National-Local Contexts', *Cities*, **23** (4), 250–268

Liu Mingxing and Ran Tao (2004) 'Regional Competition, Fiscal Reform and Local Governance in China', paper presented at the conference, 'Paying for Progress. Public Finance, Human Welfare, and Inequality in China', held at the Institute for Chinese Studies, 21–23 May, Oxford, UK

Liu Wujun and Huang Xiang (2007) *Shanghai Urban Planning*, Singapore: Cengage Learning

Liu Zuo (2005) *Tax System Overview of China*, Edition Economic Science Press

Lo, Fu-chen and Yeung, Yue-Man (eds) (1998) *Globalization and the World of Large Cities*, Tōkyō: United Nations University Press

Lou, Y. (2004) 'Development Research of the Headquarter Economy in Beijing', *Horizontal-Vertical Social Science*, **5**

Low, Linda (2001) 'The Singapore Developmental State in the New Economy and Polity', *The Pacific Review*, **14** (3), 411–441

Lu, D. (2009) 'Banking and Financial Sector Reform in China: Experience and Prospects for the Future', in Nazrul Islam (ed.) *Resurgent China: Issues for the Future*, London: Palgrave Macmillan, pp. 258–288

Lu, Dadao, Yao Shimou, Liu Hui, Gao Xiaolu, Li Guoping and Duan Jinjun (2006) *Zhongguo quyu fazhan baogao, Chengzhenhuo jincheng ji kongjian kuozhang* (2006 Report on China's Regional Development), Shangwu yinshuguan, Beijing

Luo Huangchao (1994) *Riben huaqiao shi*, Guangzhou: Guangdong gaodeng jiaoyu chubanshe

Lyons, D. and S. Salmon (1995) 'World Cities, Multinational Corporations, and Urban Hierarchy: The Case of the United States', in P. Knox and P. Taylor (eds) *World Cities in a World-system*, Cambridge: Cambridge University Press, pp. 98–114

Ma, L.J.C. (2005) 'Urban Administrative Restructuring, Changing Scale Relations and Local Economic Development in China', *Political Geography*, **24** (4), 477–497

Martin, R. (1999) 'The New Economic Geography of Money', in Ron Martin (ed.) *Money and the Space Economy*, Chichester: John Wiley & Sons, pp. 3–27

MasterCard Worldwide (2007) *Worldwide Centres of Commerce Index 2007*, available at http://www.mastercard.com/us/company/en/insights/studies/2008/wcoc/index.html (accessed April 2009)

MasterCard Worldwide (2008) *Worldwide Centres of Commerce Index 2008*, available at http://www.mastercard.com/us/company/en/insights/studies/2008/wcoc/index.html (accessed April 2009)

Matsumoto, I. (1952) 'Tōtsuji no kenkyū', *Hōsei shigaku*, **X**, 111–117

Mayor of London (2008) *London: Winning in a Changing World*, London: Office of the Mayor, available at http://www.london.gov.uk/mayor/economy/london-winning.jsp (accessed June 2009)

McGee, Terry (1967) *The Southeast Asian City: A Social Geography of the Primate Cities of Southeast Asia*, London: Bell

McKendrick, David G., Richard F. Doner and Stephan Haggard (2000) *From Silicon Valley to Singapore: Location and Competitive Advantage in the Hard Disk Drive Industry*, Stanford, CA: Stanford University Press

McKinsey & Company (2003) 'Strengthening Hong Kong's Port and Trade Sector, an Internal Report to Hong Kong SAR Government', 23 October

Meyer, D.R. (1998) 'World Cities as International Financial Centres', in Fu-Chen Lo and Yue-Man Yeung (eds) *Globalization and the World of Large Cities*, Tōkyō: United Nations University Press, pp. 410–432

Minami, S. (1989) 'Kokusai Kinyu Center wo meguru Ronten: Kokusai Kinyu Torihiki no Chukaku toshiteno Yakuwari' (The Point at Issue in the Matter of International Financial Center: The Core Role of International Financial Trading), *Kinyu Kenkyu*, **8** (3)

Ministry of Foreign Trade and Economic Cooperation (2001) *Zhongguo jiaru shijie maoyi zuzhi falu wenjian* (Compilation of the Legal Instruments on China's Accession to the World Trade Organization), Beijing: Law Press

Mirza, Hafiz (1986) *Multinationals and the Growth of the Singapore Economy*, London: Routledge

Mitsui-Ginko Chosabu (Research Department, Mitsui Bank) (1984) *Monogatari Mitsui-Ryogaeten* (The Story of Mitsui Exchange House), Tōkyō: Toyo Keizai Shinpo Sha

Miyamoto, M. (ed.) (1969) *Kinsei Osaka no Shogyo-shi/Keiei-shi teki Kenkyu* (A Study of the Commercial and Business History in Pre-modern Osaka), Osaka: Seibundo-Shuppan

Moore, R. (2008) 'Global Financial Centres take it on the Chin', available at http://www.commercialpropertynews.com/cpn/content_display/property-types/office/ (accessed April 2009)

Moore, T. (2008) 'China as an Economic Power in the Contemporary Era of Globalization', *Journal of Asian and African Studies*, **43**(5), 497–521

Morisset, J.P. and Nede Pirnia (1999) 'How Tax Policy and Incentives Affect Foreign Direct Investment: A Review', *World Bank Policy Research Working Paper No. 2509*, 30 November

Morrison, A.J., D.A. Ricks and K. Roth (1991) 'Globalization Versus Regionalization: Which Way for the Multinational?', *Organisational Dynamics*, Winter, 17–29

Nagasaki Kenshi Hensan Iinkai (1973) 'Hiradohan no seiritsu to hatten', *Nagasaki kenshi (Hanseihen)*, Tōkyō, Yoshikawa Kōbunkan

Nagazumi, Yōko (1987) *Tōsen yushutsunyūhin sūryō ichiran, 1637–1833-nen* (Summary of imports and exports for the years 1637–1833), Tōkyō: Sōbunsha

Nagazumi, Yōko (1998) 'From Company to Individual Company Servants: Dutch Trade in Eighteenth-century Japan', in Leonard Blussé and Femme S. Gaastra (eds) *On the Eighteenth Century as a Category of Asian History. Van Leur in Retrospect*, Aldershot: Ashgate, pp. 147–172

Nagazumi Yōko (ed.) (2010) *Large and Broad. The Dutch Impact on Early Modern Asia. Essays in Honor of Leonard Blussé*, Tōkyō: Tōyō Bunkō

Nakagawa, K., H. Morikawa and T. Yui (eds) (1997) *Kindai Nihon Keieishi no Kisochishiki* (Basic Knowledge of the Modern Japanese Business History), Tōkyō: Yuhikaku Publishing

Nakagawa, S. (2003) *Osaka Ryogaesho no Kinyu to Shakai* (Finance and Society of Osaka Moneychangers), Osaka: Seibundo Shuppan

Nakamura, T. (1952) 'Sakoku jidai no zai Nichi kakkyō-tōtsuji no kenkyū', *Shigaku kenkyū*, **XXX**, 1–20

National Bureau of Statistics (NBS) (2005) *Zhongguo tongji nianjian* (China Statistical Yearbook 2005), Beijing: China Statistics Press

National Bureau of Statistics of China (2010) *China Compendium of Statistics 1949–2008*, Beijing: China Statistics Press

National Bureau of Statistics of China (2010) *China Statistical Yearbook 1992–2010*, Beijing: China Statistics Press

Naughton, B. (2007) *The Chinese Economy: Transition and Growth*, Cambridge: The MIT Press

Ni Pengfei et al. (n.d.) 'Annual Report on Urban Competitiveness', No. 3, Li and Fung Research Centre, Social Sciences Academic Press

Ni, Pengfei (ed.) (2009) *2009 nian chengshi jingzhengli lanpishu* (2009 Blue Book of City Competitiveness in China), Beijing: Shehui kewue wenxian

Notteboom, T.E. and J.P. Rodrigue (2005) 'Port Regionalization: Towards a New Phase in Port Development', *Maritime Policy and Management*, **32** (3), 297–313

O'Brien, R. (1992) *Global Financial Integration: The End of Geography*, New York: The Royal Institute of International Affairs Council on Foreign Relations Press

OCDE (2004) 'Examens de l'OCDE des politiques de l'investissement – Chine: Progrès et enjeux de la réforme', Paris: OCDE

OECD (2006) *The Role of Advanced Nations in the Global Economy*, Speech by OECD Secretary General Angel Gurría, Tōkyō Policy Forum, Institute for International Studies and Training, United Nations University

OECD (2006) *Competitive Cities in the Global Economy, Territorial Reviews*, Paris: OECD

OECD (2006), *Seoul, Korea, Policy Brief*, Paris: OECD

Ohmae, K. (1995) *The End of the Nation State: The Rise of Regional Economies*, New York: Free Press

Okamoto, I. (2005) 'Kinyu Big Bang ha Naze Shippai Shitanoka: Kanryo-shudou-kaikaku to Seijika no Kainyu' (Failure of Japanese Financial 'Big Bang': Bureaucracy-led Reform and Political Intervention), *Journal of Social Science*, **56** (2), 109–139

Okazaki, T. (1999) *Edo no Shijyo Keizai: Rekishiseido Bunseki kara mita Kabunakama* (Market Economy in Edo: Guild Groups from the View of Historical SystemicAnalysis), Tōkyō: Kodansha

Okazaki, T. (2005) 'The Role of the Merchant Coalition in Pre-modern Japanese Economic Development: An Historical Institutional Analysis', *Explorations in Economic History*, **42** (2), 184–201

Olds, K. and H. Yeung (2004) 'Pathway to Global City Formation: A View from the Developmental City-state of Singapore', *Review of International Political Economy*, **11** (3), 489–521

Pereira, A. (2009a) 'State Entrepreneurship and Regional Development: Singapore's Industrial Parks in Batam and Suzhou', *Entrepreneurship & Regional Development*, **16** (2), 129–144

Pereira, A. (2009b) 'Singapore's Regionalization Strategy', *Journal of the Asia Pacific Economy*, **10** (3), 380–396

Perry, M. (1992) 'The Singapore Growth Triangle: "State, Capital and Labour at a New Frontier in the World Economy"', *Singapore Journal of Tropical Geography*, **12** (2), 138–151

Perry, Martin, Lily Kong and Brenda S.A. Yeoh (1997) *Singapore: A Developmental City State*, Chichester: Wiley

Phelps, N. (2007) 'Gaining from Globalization? State Extraterritoriality and Domestic Economic Impacts –The Case of Singapore', *Economic Geography*, **83** (4), 371–393

Pillai, J. (2006) 'Importance of Clusters in Industry Development: A Case of Singapore's Petrochemical Industry', *Asian Journal of Technology Innovation*, **14** (2), 1–27

Porteous, D.J. (1995) *Geography of Finance: Spatial Dimensions of Intermediary Behaviour*, Aldershot: Ashgate

Porteous, D. (1999) 'The Development of Financial Centers: Location, Information Externalities and Path Dependence', in Ron Martin (ed.) *Money and the Space Economy*, Chichester: John Wiley & Sons, pp. 95–114

Preston, Peter W. (2007) *Singapore in the Global System*, Abingdon, UK and New York, NY: Routledge

Ramasamy, Esa (2007) 'Singapore's Role as a Key Oil Trading Center in Asia', in Mark Hong and Teo Kah Beng (eds) *Energy Perspectives on Singapore and the Region*, Singapore: Institute of Southeast Asian Studies (ISEAS)

Reed, H.C. (1980) 'The Ascent of Tokyo as an International Financial Center', *Journal of International Business Studies*, **11** (3), 19–35

Reed, H.C. (1981) *The Preeminence of International Financial Centers*, New York: Praeger

Rimmer, P.J. (1998) 'Transport and Telecommunications among World Cities', in Fu-Chen Lo and Yue-Man Yeung (eds) *Globalization and the World of Large Cities*, Tōkyō: United Nations University Press, pp. 433–470

Robinson, J. (2002) 'Global and World Cities: A View from Off the Map', *International Journal of Urban and Regional Research*, **26** (3), 531–554

Rodan, G. (1989) *The Political Economy of Singapore's Industrialization: National State and International Capital*, Basingstoke: Palgrave Macmillan

Rodan, G. (2004) 'International Capital, Singapore's State Companies, and Security', *Critical Asian Studies*, **36** (3), 479–499

Roxburgh, C. (2008) 'New York's Future Competitiveness as a Global

Financial Centre. Presentation to the Council of Foreign Relations', May, New York: McKinsey

Ruane, F. and A. Ugur (2004) 'Export Platform FDI and Dualistic Development', *Institute for International Integration Studies (IIS) Discussion Papers No. 28*, Trinity College, Dublin

Rugman, A. and A. Verbeke (2005) 'Location Competitiveness, and the Multinational Enterprises', in Alan M. Rugman and Alain Verbeke, *Analysis of Multinational Strategic Management: The Selected Scientific Papers of Rugman M.A., and Verbeke A.*, Cheltenham, UK and Northampton, MA: Edward Elgar, pp. 223–250

Sadamune, K. (1959) 'Kinsei Chu-Nichi bōeki ni okeru tōtsuji', *Shigaku kenkyū*, **LXXV**, 51–66

Said Business School (2010) 'The Third Annual Study of the Quality of Broadband Connections around the Globe', Oxford University: CISCO

Sassen, S. (1988) *The Mobility of Labour and Capital*, Cambridge: Cambridge University Press

Sassen, S. (1991) *The Global City: New York, London, Tokyo*, Oxford, UK and Princeton, NJ, USA: Princeton University Press

Sassen, S. (1998) *Globalization and its Discontents*, New York: New Press

Sassen, S. (1999) 'Global Financial Centers', *Foreign Affairs*, **78** (1), 75–87

Sassen, S. (2006) *Territory, Authority, Rights: From Medieval to Global Assemblages*, Oxford, UK and Princeton, NJ, USA: Princeton University Press

Schenk, C.R. (2001) *Hong Kong as an International Financial Centre: Emergence and Development, 1945–65*, London: Routledge

Schenk, C. (2002) 'Banks and the Emergence of Hong Kong as an International Financial Center', *Journal of International Financial Markets, Institutions and Money*, **12** (4–5), 321–340

Schmitz, H. and K. Nadvi (1999) 'Clustering and Industrialization: Introduction', *World Development*, **27** (9), 1503–1514

Schoenberger, E. (1988) 'Multinational Corporations and the New International Division of Labour', *International Regional Science Review,* **11**, 105–119

Schütte, H. (1998) 'Between Headquarters and Subsidiaries: The RHQ Solution', in J. Birkinshaw and H. Hood (eds) *Multinational Corporate Evolution and Subsidiary Development*, London: Macmillan, pp. 102–137

SEDB (2009) 'Jurong Island Factsheet 2009', Singapore: Singapore Economic Development Board

Shahid, Yusuf and Kaoru Nabeshima (2006) *Post Industrial East Asian Cities: Innovation for Growth*, Washington, DC: The World Bank

Shanghai Development and Reform Commission and Shanghai Institute for Reform and Development (2010) *Development Report of Shanghai*

International Economic, Financial, Trading and Shipping Centers for Year 2009/2010, China: Shanghai People's Publishing House

Shanghai Municipal Bureau of Statistics (2010) *Shanghai Statistical Yearbook 2000–2010*, Beijing: China Statistics Press

Shanghai Statistical Bureau (2010) *Statistic Yearbook of Shanghai 2010*, China: China Statistics Press

Short, J.R. (2004), *Global Metropolitan: Globalizing Cities in a Capitalist World*, London: Routledge, pp. 21–46

Short, J.R., C. Breitbach, S. Buckman and J. Essex (2000) 'From world cities to gateway cities: extending the boundaries of globalization theory', *City*, **4** (3), 317–340

Singstat (2010) *Foreign Equity Investment in Singapore 2008*, Singapore: Singapore Department of Statistics

Siong, N. Boon and Geraldine Chen (2007) *Dynamic Governance: Embedding Culture, Capabilities and Change in Singapore*, Singapore: World Scientific

Sit, V.F.S. (1998) 'Hong Kong's "Transferred" Industrialization and Industrial Geography', *Asian Survey*, **38** (9), 880–904

Soon, T.-W. and W.A. Stoever (1996) 'Foreign Investment and Economic Development in Singapore: A Policy-Oriented Approach', *The Journal of Developing Areas*, **30** (3), 317–340

Stopford, J.M. and L.T. Wells (1972) *Managing the Multinational Enterprise*, New York: Basic Books

Storper, M. (1997) *The Regional World*, New York: Guilford Press

Sun, Y., D. Du and L. Huang (2006) 'Foreign R&D in Developing Countries: Empirical Evidence from Shanghai, China', *The China Review*, **6** (1), 67–91

Sung, Y.-W. (1996) 'Dragon Head of China's Economy?', in Y.M. Yeung and Yun-Wing Sung (eds) *Shanghai: Transformation and Modernization under China's Open Policy*, Hong Kong: The Chinese University Press, pp. 171–198

Sung, Y.-W. (1997) 'Hong Kong and the Economic Integration of the China Circle', in Barry Naughton (ed) *The China Circle*, Washington, DC: Brookings Institution Press

Sung, Y.-W. (1999) 'Shanghai and Hong Kong as Service Hubs', Occasional Paper No. 102, Hong Kong: Hong Kong Institute of Asia-Pacific Studies, Chinese University of Hong Kong

Sung, Y.-W. (2005) *The Emergence of Greater China: The Economic Integration of Mainland China, Taiwan and Hong Kong*, New York: Palgrave Macmillan

Sung, Y.-W. (2006) 'The Evolving Role of Hong Kong as China's Middleman', in Lok Sang Ho and Robert Ash (eds) *China,*

Hong Kong and the World Economy, New York: Palgrave Macmillan, pp. 152–169

Sung, Y.-W. (2011) 'Shanghai and Hong Kong as Global Service Hubs', *Occasional Paper,* Hong Kong: Hong Kong Institute of Asia-Pacific Studies, Chinese University of Hong Kong (in Chinese)

Tan, T.-Y. (2007) 'Port Cities and Hinterlands: A Comparative Study of Singapore and Calcutta', *Political Geography*, **26** (7), 851–865

Tan, T.-Y. (2008) 'Singapore's Story: A Port City in Search of Hinterlands', in Grad Arndt and Chua Beng Huat (eds) *Port Cities in Asia and Europe: Asian and European Transformations*, Abingdon, UK and New York, NY: Routledge

Taylor, P.J. (1997) 'Hierarchical Tendencies amongst World Cities: A Global Research Proposal', *Cities*, **14**, 323–332

Taylor, P.J. (1999) 'The So-Called World Cities: The Evidential Structure of a Literature', *Environment and Planning*, **A 31**, 1901–1904

Taylor, P.J. (2001) 'Specification of the World City Network', *Geographical Analysis*, **33** (2), 181–194

Taylor, P.J. and M. Hoyler (2000) 'The Spatial Order of European Cities under Conditions of Contemporary Globalization', *Tijdschrifte voor Economische en Sociale Geografie*, **91** (1), 76–89

Taylor, P.J. and D.R.F. Walker (2009) 'Globalization and World Cities Research Network', GaWC, Data Set 6: World Cities and Global Firms, available at www.lboro.ac.uk/gawc/data.html (accessed April 2009)

Taylor, P.J., M. Hoyler and David R. Walker (2001) 'A New Mapping of the World for the New Millenium', *The Geographical Journal*, **167** (3), 213–222

Taylor, P.J., D.R.F. Walker, G. Catalano and M. Hoyler (2002a) 'Diversity and Power in the World City Network', *Cities,* **19** (4), 231–241

Taylor, P.J., G. Catalano and D. Walker (2002b) 'Measurement of the world city network', *Urban Studies*, **39** (13), 2367–2376.

Teece, D.J. (1985) 'Transaction Cost Economics and the Multinational Enterprise: An Assessment', *Journal of Economic Behaviour and Organization*, **7**, 21–45

The China Review (2010) 'Urbanization in China: Processes and policies', edited by Gu Chaolin and Wu Fulong, **10** (1)

The Economist (1998) 'A Survey of International Financial Centres, Capitals of Capitals', 9 May, 3–46

The Heritage Foundation (2009) *2009 Index of Economic Freedom.* Washington, DC: The Heritage Foundation

Thrift, N. (1987) 'The Fixers? The Urban Geography of International Commercial Capital', in J. Henderson and M. Castells (eds) *Global*

Restructuring and Territorial Development, Beverly Hills, CA: Sage, pp. 203–233

Thrift, N. (1994) 'On the Social and Cultural Determinants of International Financial Centers: The Case of the City of London', in Stuart Corbridge, Nigel Thrift and Ron Martin (eds) *Money, Power, and Space*, Oxford: Blackwell, pp. 327–355

Thun, E. and A. Segal (2001) 'Thinking Globally, Acting Locally: Local Governments, Industrial Sectors, and Development in China', *Politics and Society*, **29** (4), 557–588

Tōkyō Ginko (The Bank of Tōkyō) (1984) *Yokohama-Shokin-Ginko Zenshi (The History of Yokohama Specie Bank)*, Tōkyō: The Bank of Tōkyō Ltd

Tong, Ong Eng (2007) 'The Singapore Oil Situation', in Mark Hong and Teo Kah Beng (eds) *Energy Perspectives on Singapore and the Region*, Institute of Southeast Asian Studies, pp. 91–97

Toya, T. (2003) *Kin'yu Bigguban no Seiji Keizaigaku* (The Political Economy of the Japanese Financial Big Bang), translated by M. Aoki and R. Toya, Tōkyō: Toyo Keizai Shinpo Sha

Toyama Mikio (1987) *Matsuurashi to Hirado bōeki*, Tōkyō, Kokushō Kangyōkai

Trace, K. (2002) 'Globalisation of Container Shipping: Implications for North-South Liner Shipping Trades', *Economic Papers: A Journal of Applied Economics and Policy*, **21** (4), 1–21

Trocki, C.A. (2005) *Singapore: Wealth, Power and the Culture of Control*, London, UK and New York, NY: Routledge

Tsai, J.-F., (1995) *Hong Kong in Chinese History: Community and Social Unrest in the British Colony, 1842–1913*, New York: Columbia University Press

Tsang, S. and Y. Cheng (1994) 'China's tax reforms of 1994: Breakthrough or Compromise?', *Asian Survey*, **34** (9), 769–788

Tse, K.L. (2009) 'Assessing the Prospects and Impacts of Hong Kong's RMB Trade Settlement Business', *Economic Review*, Hong Kong: Bank of China

Tsuji Zennosuke (1942) *Kaigai kōtsū shiwa*, Tōkyō: Nagai Shoseki

UNCTAD (2009a) *World Investment Report 2008*, Geneva: United Nations Conference on Trade and Development (UNCTAD)

UNCTAD (2009b) *The Global Economic Crisis: Systemic Failures and Multilateral Remedies*, New York and Geneva: UNCTAD

Utis, K. and D. Webster (2000) 'Globalization and Urbanization', in S. Yusuf, W. Wu and S. Evenett (eds) *Localization in an Era of Globalization*, Oxford: Oxford University Press

Van Heck, N. and P. Verdin (2001) *From Local Champions to Global*

Masters: A Strategic Perspective on Managing Internationalization, London, UK and New York, NY: Palgrave Macmillan, pp. 133–134

Vandermerwe, S. (1993) 'A Framework for Constructing Euro-Networks', *European Management Journal*, **11**, 55–61

Veltz, P. (1996) *Mondialisation, Villes et Territoires: L'économie d'archipel*, Paris: Presses Universitaires de France

Veltz, P. (1997) 'Une organisation géoéconomique à niveaux multiples', *Politique étrangère*, **62** (2), 265–276

Wagakuni Kinyu/Shihon Shijyo no Kokusaika no tame no Kenkyukai Zacho Torimatome (2003) (Report of the Study Group Working on Internationalization on the Japanese Financial and Capital Markets), Ministry of Finance, Tōkyō, Japan

Wakita, S. (2001) 'Efficiency of the Dojima Rice Futures Market in the Tokugawa-period Japan', *Journal of Banking and Finance*, **25** (3), 535–554

Walsh, K. (2003) 'Foreign High-tech R&D in China – Risks, Rewards, and Implications for US–China Relations', Final Report for The Henry L. Stimson Center, accessed from http://www.stimson.org/techtransfer/ pdf/FinalReport.pdf (accessed February 2009)

Wang, J.J. and M.C. Cheng (2009) 'From a Hub Port City to a Global Supply Chain Management Center: A Case Study of Hong Kong', *Journal of Transport Geography*, **18** (1), 104–115

Wang, J. and D. Olivier (2007) 'Shanghai and Ningbo: In search of an identity for the Changjiang Delta Region', in K. Cullinane and D.-W. Song (eds) *Asian Container Ports*, New York: Palgrave Macmillan, pp. 193–197

Wang, J. and X. Tong (2005) 'Sustaining Urban Growth through Innovative Capacity: Beijing and Shanghai in Comparison', *World Bank Policy Research Working Paper 3545*, Washington, DC

Wang, S.Y. and R.N. Wang (2008) 'Nianjing Regional Headquarters Economy of Advantage Analysis and Strategy Research', *Review of Economy Research*, **10**

Wang, Y.P. (2003) *New Regulations Make it Easier for Foreign Multinationals to Establish Regional Headquarters in Shanghai*, Davis Wright Tremaine LLP, Seattle, pp. 1–4

Wang, Z. and S.J. Wei (2007) 'The Rising Sophistication of China's Exports: Assessing the Roles of Processing Trade, Foreign Invested Firms, Human Capital, and Government Policies', paper prepared for the NBER Project on the Evolving Role of China in the World Trade directed by Robert Feenstra and Shang-Hin Wei, accessed from http://www.usitc.gov/ind_econ_ana/research_ana/seminars/documents/ Wang%20&%20Wei_Seminar.pdf (accessed February 2009)

Wanner, H. (2006) 'Global and Regional Corporate Headquarters', in H.

Christian (ed.) *Kählin, Switzerland Business & Investment Handbook*, Chichester: Orell Füssli and Wiley

Warf, B. (1999) 'The Hypermobility of Capital and the Collapse of the Keynesian State', in Ron Martin (ed.) *Money and the Space Economy*, Chichester: John Wiley & Sons, pp. 227–239

Webster, D. and L. Muller (2000) 'Urban Competitiveness Assessment in Developing Country Urban Regions: The Road Forward', initially presented at the World Bank Course, *Towards a Methodology for Conducting City Development Strategies*, Washington, DC

Wei, S. (1999) 'Does Corruption Relieve Foreign Investors of the Burden of Taxes and Capital Controls?', *World Bank, Policy Research Working Paper 2209*, Washington, DC

Williamson, E.O. (1981) 'The Modern Corporation: Origins, Evolution, Attributes', *Journal of Economic Literature*, **19**, 1537–1568

Wills, Jr, John E. (2002) *Eclipsed Entrepot of the Western Pacific, Taiwan and Central Vietnam, 1500–1800*, Aldershot: Ashgate

Woetzel, J., J. Devan, L. Jordan, S. Negri and D. Farrell (2008) 'Preparing for China's Urban Billion', Summary of findings, McKinsey Global Institute

Wong, L.K. (1978) 'Singapore: Its Growth as an Entrepot Port, 1819–1941', *Journal of Southeast Asian Studies*, **9** (1), 50–84

Wu, F. (2003) 'The (Post-)Socialist Entrepreneurial City as a State Project: Shanghai's Reglobalisation in Question', *Urban Studies*, **40** (9), 1673–1698

Wu, F. and L. Ma (2006) 'Transforming China's Globalizing Cities', *Habitat International*, **30** (2), 191–198

Wu, J., J.E. Gyourko and Y. Deng (2010) 'Evaluating Conditions in Major Chinese Housing Markets', *NBER Working Paper, w16189*, Cambridge

Xiamen Daxue Lishixi (ed.) (1982a) *Zheng Chenggong yanjiu lunwenxuan*, Fuzhou: Fujian Renmin Chubanshe

Xiamen Daxue Lishixi (ed.) (1982b) *Taiwan Zheng Chenggong yanjiu lunwenxuan*, Fuzhou: Fujian Renmin Chubanshe

Xiamen Daxue Lishixi (ed.) (1984) *Zheng Chenggong yanjiu lunwenxuan (xuji)*, Fuzhou: Fujian Renmin Chubanshe

Xiamen Daxue Lishixi (ed.) (1989) *Zheng Chenggong yanjiu guoji xueshu huiyi lunwenji*, Nanchang: Jiangxi Renmin Chubanshe

Xin, H. (2005) 'Headquarter Economy Strategies Booming in China's Metropolises', *People's Daily Online*

Xinhua (2010) 'China Unveils New Rules for Foreign Investment', 13 April

Yamaguchi, K. and T. Kato (eds) (1988) *Ryotaisenkan no*

Yokohama-Shokin-Ginko (Yokohama Specie Bank during the Inter-war Period), Tōkyō: Nihon Keieishi Kenkyujyo

Yamaguchi, T. (1991) *Nihon Kinsei Shogyoshi no Kenkyu* (Research on Commercial History in Early Modern Japan), Tōkyō: Tōkyō University Publishing

Yamamoto Kitsuna (1983) *Nagasaki Tōjin Yashiki*, Tōkyō: Kenkōsha

Yamawaki Teijirō (1983(1964)) *Nagasaki no Tōjin bōeki*, Tōkyō: Yoshikawa Kōbunkan

Yamori, N. (1997) 'Do Japanese Banks Lead or Follow International Business? An Empirical Investigation', *Journal of International Financial Markets, Institutions and Money*, **7** (4), 369–382

Yamori, N. (1998) 'A Note on the Location Choice of International Banks: The Case of Japanese Financial Institutions', *Journal of Banking & Finance*, **22** (1), 109–120

Yang Congchun (2005) 'Tax Revenue', *World Finance*, March, p. 106

Yang Yanjie (1984) '1650 zhi 1662 nian Zheng Chenggong haiwai maoyi de maoyie he lirun'e gusuan', in Xiamen Daxue Lishixi (ed.) *Zheng Chenggong yanjiu lunwenxuan (xuji)*, Fuzhou: Fujian renmin chubanshe, pp. 221–235

Yao, Souchou (2007) *Singapore: The State and the Culture of Excess*, Abingdon, UK and New York, NY: Routledge

Yeandle, M. and M. Mainelli (2009) 'Cooperation during Crisis: The Future of Financial Centres', published on *Washington Times Global*, available at http://www.washingtontimesglobal.com/ (accessed June 2009)

Yeoh, C., W. How and A.L. Leong (2009) '"Created" Enclaves for Enterprise: An Empirical Study of Singapore's Industrial Parks in Indonesia, Vietnam and China', *Entrepreneurship & Regional Development*, **17** (6), 479–499

Yeung, H. (1998) 'Capital, State and Space: Contesting the Borderless World', *Transactions of the Institute of British Geographers*, **23**, 291–309

Yeung, H.W.-C. (2001) 'Organising Regional Production Networks in Southeast Asia: Implications for Production Fragmentation, Trade, and Rules of Origin', *Journal of Economic Geography*, **1** (3), 299–321

Yeung, H.W.-C., J. Poon and M. Perry (2001) 'Towards a Regional Strategy: The Role of Regional Headquarters of Foreign Firms in Singapore', *Urban Studies*, **38** (1), 157–183

Yeung Y.-M. (2006) 'Three Chinese Cities and their Pathways to Globalization', *Town Planning Review*, **77** (3), 345–351

Yoshikuni, S. (2008) 'Asia as a Financial Centre: Opportunities and Obstacles', *Journal of Asset Management*, **9** (2), 87

Young, A. (1999) *Transport, Processing and Information: Value Added and the Circuitous Movement of Goods*, working paper, Chicago, IL: University of Chicago

Yu Ke (2003) 'Beijing Neng Cheng Wei Guo Ji Jin Rong Zhong Xin Ma?' (Can Beijing become an International Financial Centre?), *Jingji (Economic Monthly)*, **9**, 26–29

Yu, Z. (2005) 'The Making of an Innovative Region from a Centrally Planned Economy: Institutional Evolution in Zhongguancun Science Park in Beijing', *Environment and Planning*, **37** (6), 1113–1134

Zhang, M. and Y. Xu (2008) 'A Comprehensive Measurement of the Hot Money in China', *CASS Research Center for International Finance Working Paper, 0814*, Peking

Zhao, H. (2004) *Headquarter Economy: New View of Beijing Economy Development (1) and (2)*, Chinese City Economy

Zhao, H. (2010) *Zhongguo zong bu jing ji fa zhan bao gao 2010–2011* (The development report of China's headquarters economy 2010–2011), China: Social Sciences Academic Press

Zhao, S.X.B. (2003) 'Spatial Restructuring of Financial Centers in Mainland China and Hong Kong: A Geography of Finance Perspective', *Urban Affairs Review*, **38** (4), 535–571

Zhao, S.X.B. and L. Zhang (1995) 'Urban Performance and the Control of Urban Size in China', *Urban Studies*, **32** (4–5), 813–846

Zhao, S.X.B., J.M. Qiao and S.P. Tong (2002) 'China's WTO Accession, State Enterprise Reform, and Spatial Economic Restructuring', *Journal of International Development*, **14** (4), 413–433

Zhao, S.X.B., Li Zhang and D.T. Wang (2004) 'Determining Factors of the Development of a National Financial Center: The Case of China', *Geoforum*, **35** (4), 577–592

Zhao, W. and R. Arvanitis (2008) 'L'inégal développement industriel de la Chine: capacités d'innovation et coexistence de différents modes d'apprentissage technologique', *Région et Développement*, **28**, 61–85

Zhou, E.Y. and B. Stembridge (2008) 'Patented in China: The Present and Future State of Innovation in China', Thomson Reuters, http://scientific.thomsonreuters.com/press/pdf/tl/WIPTChina08.pdf (accessed February 2009)

Z/Yen Group (2010) *2007–2010: The Global Financial Center Index 1–8*, London: City of London Corporation

Index